M000290232

GROWING *in* FAVOR

GROWING *in* FAVOR

Daily Devotions

—— *for* ——

Walking in Blessing

PAUL & BILLIE KAYE TSIKA

© Copyright 2018 – Paul and Billie Kaye Tsika

All rights reserved. This book is protected by the copyright laws of the United States of America. This book may not be copied or reprinted for commercial gain or profit. The use of short quotations or occasional page copying for personal or group study is permitted and encouraged. Permission will be granted upon request. Unless otherwise identified, Scripture quotations are from THE HOLY BIBLE, NEW INTERNATIONAL VERSION®, NIV® Copyright © 1973, 1978, 1984, 2011 by Biblica, Inc.® Used by permission. All rights reserved worldwide. Scripture quotations marked NKJV are from the New King James Version®. Copyright © 1982 by Thomas Nelson. Used by permission. All rights reserved. Scripture quotations marked KJV are from the King James Version. Holy Bible, New Living Translation, copyright © 1996, 2004, 2015 by Tyndale House Foundation. Used by permission of Tyndale House Publishers, Inc., Carol Stream, Illinois 60188. All rights reserved. All emphasis within Scripture quotations is the author's own. Take note that the name satan and related names are not capitalized. We choose not to acknowledge him, even to the point of violating grammatical rules.

DESTINY IMAGE® PUBLISHERS, INC.

P.O. Box 310, Shippensburg, PA 17257-0310

"Promoting Inspired Lives."

This book and all other Destiny Image and Destiny Image Fiction books are available at Christian bookstores and distributors worldwide.

Cover design by Eileen Rockwell
Interior design by Terry Clifton

For more information on foreign distributors, call 717-532-3040.

Or reach us on the Internet: www.destinyimage.com

ISBN 13 TP: 978-0-7684-4570-1
ISBN 13 EBook: 978-0-7684-4571-8
ISBN LP: 978-0-7684-4572-5
ISBN HC: 978-0-7684-4573-2

For Worldwide Distribution, Printed in the U.S.A.
1 2 3 4 5 6 / 21 20 19 18

DEDICATION

In the late '70s, we met a couple in Baton Rouge, Louisiana, that became some of our oldest and dearest friends, Rick and Carolyn Cappo. Through some of the darkest days of our life and ministry, this couple never wavered in their loyalty or friendship. We are often reminded of their faithful love and support, which helped carry us through many difficult times.

Their daughter, Brandi, was a bridesmaid in our daughter's wedding, and Rick, who is a fantastic Cajun chef, cooked the meal at each of our children's wedding rehearsal dinners, even traveling to North Carolina for our youngest son's wedding.

Rick and Carolyn founded "C&C Milling and Cabinet" in Baton Rouge; C&C stands for Christ and Cappo. They also founded "Suckers," which is the best BBQ sauce and rub this side of the Mississippi. They have been very successful entrepreneurs, who had a heart to honor the Lord. On the back of all of their business cards was this scripture: *"But the Helper, the Holy Spirit, whom the Father will send in My name, He will teach you all things, and bring to your remembrance all things that I said to you"* (John 14:26).

So, we would like to dedicate this devotional, with much love and appreciation, to our dear precious friends, Rick and Carolyn Cappo.

ACKNOWLEDGMENTS

Destiny Image Publishers: This is the fifth time we've partnered with Destiny in publishing our books, and each time the experience gets sweeter. I want to thank in particular Brad Herman and Meelika Marzzarella for their support and guidance through this publishing process. Without their help and patience, you would be wondering and wandering in the devotional wilderness. Once again, thank you Brad, Meelika, John Martin, Terry Clifton, Eileen Rockwell and Destiny for a great product.

Dr. J. Tod Zeiger: Many years ago, Tod and I met at a Bible Conference and began ministering together. We became close friends as well as co-laborers. He has an excellent heart for the Lord along with a great gift for the family of God. His heart and giftedness continue to add tremendous value to me personally as well as our ministry. He's an insightful man of God, and we are blessed to call him a friend. We bless the Lord for him and our partnership.

Billie Kaye Rexroad Tsika: I could write a book about her love, patience, and forgiveness. Oh, we already did, *Get Married Stay Married*. Like all couples, we have our struggles, but I can honestly say that we are where we are in life because of her love for me. I can't even imagine where I would be without her. She helps me, encourages me, and faithfully points me to what honors God. So it would be impossible for me to write, preach, or minister without always acknowledging the one God put in my life to complete me. Thank you BKT for ALWAYS being there for me.

CONTENTS

OVERVIEW AND SUGGESTIONS FOR READING YOUR DAILY DEVOTION

As with our previous popular devotional, *Growing in Grace,* we encourage all believers to begin a daily devotion. We know of nothing that can help your day get off on the right footing like a consistent time with the Lord. Daily devotions encourage you to pray, focus on the Lord, and help you to do right all day, every day. Billie and I want you to be blessed, encouraged, and discover how to *dream about your destiny* in this simple yet profound five-day-a-week devotional. We offer the following six helpful suggestions, assuring you that you have your heavenly Father's favor.

We suggest you read:

1. **Prayerfully.** Before beginning your daily reading, ask the Holy Spirit to open your heart to what He is communicating with you today.

2. **Thankfully.** Have a grateful and thankful heart for the Word of God that is quick and powerful and sharper than any two-edged sword.

3. **Personally.** As you're reading, make certain you "take things personally." God is speaking to "your" heart.

4. **Practically.** The Word of God is practical and applicable to your daily walk so that you may be empowered to live each day victoriously.

5. **Thoughtfully.** God has given you a mind for a reason, so that you can think—so think about what you're reading. Fix your heart on the words of the devotion and don't let your mind wander.

6. **Reflectively.** Blank lines for journaling have been provided in the back of the book so that you may record your thoughts, ideas, and feelings as God speaks to you. Usually, the first thought that comes to your mind should be recorded. This way you can reflect from year to year the changing seasons of your life and how God is speaking to you. We highly encourage you to take time daily to journal.

Suggested prayer before reading:

Heavenly Father, as I continue to seek You daily through reading this devotional, I pray that You will open my heart and mind to Your glorious favor in my life. In Jesus' precious name I pray, amen.

START STRONG

*I am the new year. I am an unspoiled page in your book
of time. I am your next chance at the art of living.
I am your opportunity to practice what you have
learned during the last twelve months about life.
All that you sought the past year and failed to find
is hidden in me; I am waiting for you to search it
out again and with more determination.
All the good that you tried to do for others and didn't
achieve last year is mine to grant—providing you
have fewer selfish and conflicting desires.
In me lies the potential of all that you dreamed but didn't dare
to do, all that you hoped but didn't perform, all you prayed
for but did not yet experience. These dreams slumber lightly,
waiting to be awakened by the touch of an enduring purpose.
I am the new year.*

AUTHOR UNKNOWN[1]

YOU HAVE NOT BEEN THIS WAY BEFORE

Then you will know which way to go, since you have never been this way before. But keep a distance of about two thousand cubits between you and the ark; do not go near it (Joshua 3:4).

FOR MANY YEARS JOSHUA SERVED MOSES, HIS MENTOR, FRIEND, AND SPIRITUAL leader. He could not imagine life without him. There came a day when he heard the following words from the Lord: *"Moses my servant is dead. Now then, you and all these people, get ready to cross the Jordan River into the land I am about to give to them—to the Israelites"* (Joshua 1:2). From a human standpoint, Joshua must have been terrified to think he was now "the man" in charge of more than two million freed slaves.

To remove any doubt and fear from Joshua's heart, God infused him with courage: *"No one will be able to stand against you all the days of your life. As I was with Moses, so I will be with you; I will never leave you nor forsake you"* (Joshua 1:5). The new leader had a bold challenge: he must guide them to a place they had never been before.

Their inheritance was waiting, but they had to make a choice. They could stay on the wrong side of Jordan and live lives of regret, or they could choose to obey God and march into their destiny. If they wanted all that God had for them, they had to get up and leave the comfort of the familiar for uncharted territory. They had to move to a place they had never been before!

Last year is filed away into the book of time. It is gone, and there is no going back. Our biggest challenge is to be grateful for the past, but not preoccupied with it. We can also reflect on the joyful times as well as the painful ones. It is helpful to learn from the past, but now it is time to move forward with the knowledge that God is still in control of our future.

The following says it all about how to face a new year: *"No one can go back and start a new beginning, but anyone can start today and make a new ending."*[2]

5

FORGET RESOLUTIONS— TRY COMMITMENT

These people honor me with their lips, but their
hearts are far from me (Matthew 15:8).

YOU KNOW WHAT HAPPENS EVERY NEW YEAR, RIGHT? IT IS THE TIME WE MAKE our list of new year's resolutions. Whether we want to admit it or not, most people have at least a mental list of everything we want to accomplish in the coming year. I have read that, on average, only about 45 percent of people make new year's resolutions. Of that number, approximately 9 percent will ever achieve any success.

So, what's the point of even trying? Why bother when you already know that on average you will be successful only 9 percent of the time? This time why not try something different. Forget about making meaningless resolutions and try making a commitment that will lead to a lasting change in your life. If what you are doing is not working, I have a suggestion for you. Stop any meaningless activity that is taking you in the wrong direction, and try a new approach.

Resolutions without a strategy are nothing more than a temporary emotional fix. And, without a plan, any action is doomed to fail. For example, how many times have you heard someone say they were going to get in shape and lose weight? By the end of January, the "emotion" has worn off, and before long they are in worse shape than they were before. If we aren't careful, making a resolution becomes nothing more than paying "lip-service" to changes we hope to make.

On the other hand, making a commitment demands that we lay out a course of action to reach our desired goal. It is a determination to "stay the course" long after the emotion has died. Losing weight, or any other meaningful goal, will never happen sitting on the couch eating cake. Commitment requires a decisive plan of action, not empty promises.

As a child of the King, facing a new year causes me to contemplate changes I need to make on my spiritual journey. I have determined to turn any empty resolutions into spiritual commitments—to look at every aspect of my life and make sure my commitment to Jesus is not "words" with no action.

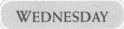
FOUR KEYS TO A GREAT YEAR

But grow in the grace and knowledge of our Lord and Savior Jesus Christ. To him be glory both now and forever! Amen (2 Peter 3:18).

IF YOU WERE TO ASK THE APOSTLE PETER HIS COUNSEL FOR MAKING THE COMing year your best year yet, I think I know what he would say. It's the same thing he wrote to the early disciples. It's one simple word—*grow!* Peter knew that spiritual growth was a necessity. The word "grow" means, "to increase; to become more fruitful; or, become greater." The ultimate goal is that we are transformed from one stage of glory to the next until we are fashioned into the image of Jesus Christ (see 2 Corinthians 3:18).

As you prepare for another new year, we offer four keys to having the best year of your spiritual life:

1. Fall in love with the Bible. We eat food for nourishment; likewise, God's Word is spiritual nourishment for our souls. A daily feasting on the Word is a vital element that helps us to grow in the knowledge of His will for our lives. At the end of the next twelve months, we will be the same person we are today if we don't determine to feed on God's Word (see Matthew 4:4; 1 Peter 2:2).

2. Find your way to the prayer closet. If we choose to ignore the privilege of having a conversation with God, we leave ourselves open to the attack of the evil one. A plant cannot grow without air and water, and we cannot expect to grow without prayer and faith (see Philippians 4:6).

3. Reject any sinful patterns. Many times, we get "stuck" in neutral, which in turn produces spiritual dryness. It could be because we have allowed some sinful pattern to take a foothold in our lives. Mark the new year with a confession of any known sin and cover it with a humble attitude. Freedom and deliverance are for anyone who seeks (see Micah 7:19).

4. Sow seeds to invest in others. I believe it is impossible to live for Christ and grow to spiritual maturity and not plant seeds of the "good news" with those around you. Determine this year to step out of your comfort zone and focus on the needs of those who are hungry for the life-giving truth of the Gospel of Christ (see Romans 1:16).

GO AHEAD AND DREAM BIG

Joseph had a dream, and when he told it to his brothers,
they hated him all the more (Genesis 37:5).

JOSEPH WAS A DREAMER. I AM CONVINCED THAT ANY PERSON WHO HAS EVER accomplished anything for good and God, started with a dream. Consider this young man Joseph, who was not afraid to share the things God put in his heart. He was a dreamer; and like all dreamers, he quickly learned two valuable lessons:

1. He discovered his dream was much bigger than himself. He knew that his dream was sowed in the seedbed of his spirit, and not in his flesh. He wasn't out to "prove himself" to his family, but to follow God's dream for his life. His dream soon became a magnet pulling him toward his destiny.

2. He also discovered not everybody was happy about his dream. You most probably know the familiar story of Joseph and how his siblings hated him because he dared to share the vision God gave him. He didn't wait for his brothers to confirm his dream, nor did he get hung up on the fact they had no faith in him whatsoever. He kept moving forward even though there were plenty of pitfalls along the way.

In finding your dream path, there are several things to remember:

First, God will never hold you accountable for someone else's dream. Your dream track is tailor-made for you and you only. Don't fall into the trap of thinking that everyone has to be onboard with your dream. Some people are like a fire hose—as soon as you catch fire they want to douse you with water!

Second, God always pays His way. As the old saying goes, "If it's His will, it's His bill." He will never instill you with a dream and not provide the resources to do it. Don't wait for someone to give you everything you need. Yes, God does use people, but He is not dependent on what others might do when it comes to providing resources.

Third, God does not call the qualified; He qualifies the called. He loves us so much that when He gives us a big dream, He also provides us the ability to accomplish it (see Ephesians 3:20). What about you? Will you dream big? What's holding you back from discovering your God-given dream?

DON'T TAKE SHORTCUTS

Noah did everything just as God commanded him (Genesis 6:22).

WHEN SPEAKING OF TAKING SHORTCUTS, I'M NOT REFERRING TO THE FACT that we need to learn from others. There is plenty we can learn from observing others, and there is nothing wrong with that. Learning how to avoid mistakes and doing the right things to avoid them is part of any learning process. What I'm referring to is the attitude, *"I don't have to pay the price to follow my dream."* That kind of thinking will always distract you from God's plan for your life.

Consider Noah. He did *"everything"* (not just a few things), *just as God commanded him."* He didn't try to cut a deal with God and shortcut the process of filling the ark. He never tried to convince God that he knew a better way to get the job done. Noah is a prime example of someone who refused to cut corners.

Consider Jesus. If you are ever tempted to take a shortcut, you are in good company. The devil tried every trick in the book to tempt Jesus to shortcut God's plan for the redemption of humanity. Jesus came to die on a cross not jump off the pinnacle of the temple. He came to give people the "bread of life" not fulfill His physical needs (see Matthew 4:1-11).

In following our dreams, we must always be on guard for the temptation of just doing enough to get by. Even a farmer knows to get a good harvest he cannot shortcut the process. He understands that planting and reaping are two different seasons.

Shortcuts will eventually produce shortcut thinking and shortcut living. And, when you combine those two attitudes, you fall into the pit of:

- Taking what's easy instead of what's best.
- Settling for what's acceptable instead of what's excellent.
- Demanding instant gratification over long-term goals.

Don't follow the example of Abraham and Sarah who decided God was never going to fulfill His promise of a son. What they produced was an Ishmael, and that turned out badly! Remember, shortcuts may take you somewhere you may not want to go (see Genesis 16:1-16).

THE UNLIMITED POWER OF PURPOSE

Many are the plans in a person's heart, but it is the Lord's purpose that prevails (Proverbs 19:21).

EVERYTHING GOD CREATED STARTED WITH A PURPOSE IN MIND. IT IS THE understanding of our purpose that makes life an adventure. The definition of *purpose* is "something set up as an object; or end to be attained: intention; resolution, or determination."[3] A perfect recipe for a life of frustration is when we give our time and effort to things that don't take us to our destiny.

God has designed every person with a purpose, and the greatest discovery in life is knowing the reason *why* you were born! He didn't create you and then sit down and try to figure out what you were going to do. There are no accidents with God. You are not sent into the world to wander around like the children of Israel in the desert. You were designed with an eternal destiny to fulfill, and anything short of that will lead you to live a life of despair.

If you fail to "aim" for your purpose in life, you will never be able to achieve your best. Don't spend the rest of your life always wondering if there is more that you are designed to do. I'm not suggesting that everyone who reads these lines are unsure of their purpose. But if you are confused and simply not sure, let me help you by asking three simple questions:

1. *What is your passion?* What speaks to your deepest thoughts and feelings? What sets you on fire? What motivates you to keep moving forward into another new year? Your passion will be wrapped around your burden. What moves you to action is considered a burden that cannot be ignored.

2. *Do you believe in your potential?* You cannot act in a manner inconsistent with the way you see yourself. Myles Munroe observed: *"What lies behind you is history and what lies before you is future, but these are both tiny matters compared to what lies within you."*[4]

3. *When should you start the process of finding your purpose?* How about right now? Don't wait any longer. Go ahead, ask for wisdom and insight. According to Scripture, the Lord won't deny you! (See James 1:5.)

525,600—WHAT WILL YOU DO WITH ALL THOSE MINUTES?

Be very careful, then, how you live—not as unwise but as wise, making the most of every opportunity, because the days are evil. Therefore, do not be foolish, but understand what the Lord's will is (Ephesians 5:15-17).

ON AVERAGE, EACH YEAR HAS THE SAME AMOUNT OF TIME. WHEN YOU BREAK it down in minutes, it comes to 525,600. Seems like a lot when you look at it that way, doesn't it? The truth is we all have the same amount no matter how you break it down. Whether it is days, weeks, or months, we have the same amount as any world-class athlete or the head of a Fortune 500 company. The question then is not "quantity" but "quality." What will we do with the time we have?

There are a lot of things we can do with time: *we can waste it; try to save it; we can make it our friend; or, it can become our worst enemy.* One thing we can't do is make more of it! The phrase *making the most* means to "redeem." Why does time need to be rescued and made whole? If we don't "redeem it," we run the risk of squandering it on things that have no eternal consequences.

Apostle Paul does not leave us in the dark as to the motivation for redeeming the time. It is because the days are indeed evil. I think you would agree that we live in a wicked time. In another letter, Paul told young Timothy that in the latter days perilous times will come and he outlines a list of grave sins that would be prevalent during those dark days (see 2 Timothy 3:1-9).

How can we redeem the time? We can start by dedicating ourselves to use every minute, hour, or day, not going after the latest tech invention or the shiny gadgets of the world, but finding a better use of our time. Doing something to change our mindset and produce what is Christ-centered, not self-centered is a better alternative. Using the minutes we have been given to honor and praise Him is the right place to start. There are many godly ways to redeem the time—find one and watch what happens!

How to Kill a Perfectly Good Year

Whatever your hand finds to do, do it with all your might, for in the realm of the dead, where you are going, there is neither working nor planning nor knowledge nor wisdom (Ecclesiastes 9:10).

Satirist Douglas Adams once declared, "I love deadlines. I love the whooshing noise they make as they go by."[5] Missing a deadline, or failing to complete a project, as painful as it might be, is not the issue. They are just symptoms of a larger problem. The underlying "root" is a habit that kills the entrepreneurial spirit and the drive to make your year the greatest ever. It is the all-time, number one, worst habit of *procrastination!*

Procrastinate is a verb that means "to put off intentionally and habitually: to put off intentionally the doing of something that should be done"[6] Can you think of something you have been putting off? Are you lying awake at night wondering if that list of items that seemed so important six months ago will ever be completed?

> Procrastination is not a problem of time management or of planning. Procrastinators are not different in their ability to estimate time, although they are more optimistic than others. Telling someone who procrastinates to buy a weekly planner is like telling someone with chronic depression to just cheer up!"[7]

Do you have something unpleasant that you have been putting off? Take some time over the next few days to apply a simple three-step strategy that will jump-start you toward a successful year.

1. Determine to change your attitude and perception and take the first step.
2. Don't create a to-do list with more than three items at a time. (You can only eat an elephant one bite at a time.)
3. Do reward yourself each time you finish a project, no matter how small.

Breaking the cycle of procrastination is a choice and act of the will to never allow this bad habit to control your life. A new year is a perfect time to break all habit patterns that are holding you back, and begin a new cycle of success.

STICKS AND STONES

*The mouths of the righteous utter wisdom, and their
tongues speak what is just* (Psalm 37:30).

A FRIEND OF MINE ONCE TOLD ME HE WAS CONFRONTED BY SOMEONE WHO had sharp and unkind words to say about a particular matter. As he was preparing his response, he said he could hear the words of his second-grade teacher ringing in his ear. One day when one classmate said something hurtful to another classmate at recess, she said, *"Remember children, sticks and stones may break your bones, but words will never hurt you!"* Of course, she was trying to remind the children that even though words can be very damaging, nothing could be as bad as being bludgeoned by a stick or a stone!

After working with people for many years, I know a thing or two about hurtful and unkind words; I have concluded that what his teacher said is not the whole truth. Sticks and stones may leave a bruise, but those will heal in time. Words spoken the wrong way can have a devastating impact that can last a lifetime. Poor communication skills are the culprit almost every time.

Communicating with others is more than exchanging information between you and someone else. It is about making what you want to say, what you actually say, and what other people hear, the key to avoiding unnecessary hurt and confusion. The basis of effective communication is lining up our actions to match the words that pour out of our mouth. It is better to say nothing until you are confident that your actions will back up what you say. As the old saying goes, *"You never have to apologize or explain what you don't say!"* Paul tells us the right attitude in Ephesians 4:32, *"Be kind and compassionate to one another, forgiving each other, just as in Christ God forgave you."*

Jesus Christ is the greatest communicator who ever walked on planet Earth. He demonstrated by His words and actions key principles in effective communication. He not only knew how to speak with poise and grace, but He was also a good listener. He used His words not to hurt or vilify, but to encourage and lift up. No one wants to get hit over the head with a stick, nor do they want to be punched in the heart with an unkind word! (See Proverbs 12:25; 15:24; 16:24.)

FRIDAY

DON'T BLAME EVE

The man said, "The woman you put here with me—she gave me some fruit from the tree, and I ate it." Then the Lord God said to the woman, "What is this you have done?" The woman said, "The serpent deceived me, and I ate" (Genesis 3:12-13).

BLAMING SOMEONE ELSE FOR YOUR FAILURES IS NOT A NEW PHENOMENON. The "blame game" has been around for thousands of years. Our first parents—Adam and Eve—lived in an atmosphere of perfect oneness with God. Everything they needed for success was provided. But instead of focusing on their assignment to tend and keep the garden, they fell for the snare of the evil one (see Genesis 2).

You probably know the story of the snake, temptation, and one bite of fruit that led to their failure. Adam and Eve invented the blame game. Together they started something that continues to this very day. Eve took a bite of the forbidden fruit and said, "I better get someone else in on my failure." No doubt she was the first one to play the, "If you love me"—you will eat the fruit too. God showed up and started asking questions. Instead of owning up and taking personal responsibility, what did they do? They started spinning the wheel to see who they could blame!

- Eve blamed the snake. "The devil made me do it" syndrome was also invented at the same time.
- Adam blamed Eve, and by de facto blamed God for giving her to him in the first place.
- The snake shrugged his shoulders and said, "Don't blame me—all I did was make a few suggestions. It's not like I held a gun to their head!"

They came full circle with blame and ended up dumping it all at Heaven's doorstep! Taking personal responsibility for your actions is the key. If you're playing the blame game, stop for a moment and look in the mirror and ask yourself this question, "Do I have enough discipline to finish what I start; and if it doesn't work out, am I willing to get up and start again, without blaming anyone else?" The road to a successful year begins with, *"I refuse to blame others for my failures!"*

THE CURE FOR STINKING THINKING

*Finally, brothers and sisters, whatever is true, whatever
is noble, whatever is right, whatever is pure, whatever is
lovely, whatever is admirable—if anything is excellent or
praiseworthy—think about such things* (Philippians 4:8).

YOU HAVE TO MAKE A CHOICE ABOUT YOUR THOUGHT PATTERN. I HAVE NEVER met anyone who began each day with the attitude of, "I will start my day by allowing my mind to dredge up the most painful, negative things to think about!" No, it seems the negative thoughts just show up on their own. Stinking thinking has its own language; if allowed to continue, a false view of yourself will develop. It will even rise to the level of convincing you that when others say positive things about you, you will find a way to make it negative.

The words we speak are reflections of what we think. Words are powerful magnets drawing circumstances, both positive and negative, toward you at the speed of sound. If you want to see the power of words, go back to the beginning of creation, and there you will see what the power of words can do (see Genesis 1).

Popular speaker Chris Widener stated:

> The saying is that you can achieve what you believe. Ask yourself what kinds of beliefs you hold. Are you an optimist or a pessimist? If you don't believe then you can achieve, then you won't. Your pessimism will prove you right every time. You will find that you subconsciously undermine yourself. Develop your optimism. Look for ways to believe that you can achieve success.[8]

If you want to develop the habit of directing your thoughts toward positive self-talk, here are a few thoughts to help you get started: *First,* decide you're going to change. Reject the idea that negative thoughts will dictate the direction of your life.

Second, ask the Holy Spirit to give you a thought life filled with peace and a right relationship with Jesus. *Third,* capture each negative thought and replace it with what Paul describes in Philippians 4:8.

The Bible promises that when we align our thoughts with God's Word, His peace that transcends all understanding will keep our hearts and minds through Christ Jesus (see Philippians 4:7-9).

GOD HAS A PLAN

*"For I know the plans I have for you," declares the Lord, "plans
to prosper you and not to harm you, plans to give you hope and
a future. Then you will call on me and come and pray to me,
and I will listen to you. You will seek me and find me when
you seek me with all your heart"* (Jeremiah 29:11-13).

THE "CONTEXT" OF ANY SCRIPTURE IS IMPORTANT. MORE THAN ONE BATTLE
has started over lifting a verse out of its larger meaning. Jeremiah is writing to a group of people who are being held captive. He had a positive message
for them, in spite of their adverse circumstances. They were not forgotten! Obvi-
ously, they were in a different place from what they thought they would be. They
didn't ask to be taken captive nor did they ask for cruel treatment. Instead of
"writing them off," God spoke through the man of God to let them know He
still had a plan for their lives.

Although God will eventually restore them, He didn't want to give a false
impression. Their removal from the situation was not going to happen overnight.
If that sounds a bit cruel, it's not. God is merely telling them (and us) that no
matter what situation you find yourself in, God's plans will prevail, and His judgment will be executed.

We sometimes act as though God's plans for our lives never involve times of
struggle and stress. We somehow think if we are following God's will we will
never face any situation that tries our faith. My dear friend, He has never promised to make us comfortable; He will challenge us at each level of the maturing
process. It was Job who said, *"But he knows the way that I take; when he has tested
me, I will come forth as gold"* (Job 23:10).

You may think God has abandoned you. You may feel He has forgotten your
zip code and phone number. Just because the circumstances don't look favorable,
doesn't mean His plan has been negated or replaced. His Word is a word of hope, not
despair. If you are like me, there are times when I wish He would let me look over
His shoulder and get a glimpse of the plans! But, if not, I will trust Him to the end.

Here's what we *can* know: His plans are not evil. He desires to give us a *"future
and a hope."* Those are words to live by!

BURN OUT OR BURN ON

*Never be lacking in zeal, but keep your spiritual
fervor, serving the Lord. Be joyful in hope, patient in
affliction, faithful in prayer* (Romans 12:11-12).

ARE YOU FACING SOME FORM OF BURNOUT? ARE YOU AT THE POINT OF WALK-
ing away? The Message translation of Paul's statement to the Romans brings
the issue into focus: *"Don't burn out; keep yourselves fueled and aflame. Be alert
servants of the Master, cheerfully expectant. Don't quit in hard times; pray all the
harder."*

According to author Kent Crockett:

> Burn-out occurs when we give out more than we take in. We go from
> giving out to giving up. Cars that aren't refueled will run out of gas.
> Wells that are not replenished will run dry. Batteries that are not
> recharged will have no power. We are not any different. A Christian
> that is not refueled, replenished, and recharged will burn out.[9]

No one is immune from burnout. We especially don't want to admit we are
dealing with some form of it because we are afraid of being accused of not being
spiritual. Many times, it is much safer to "fake it," because we have learned the
language of passion even if the *fire* of passion is burning low. One of the fastest
ways to burn out is to think that we have to control everything. It's not that we
believe that we are God, it's just that we act like we can handle every situation we
face. David says in Psalm 100:3, *"Know that the Lord is God. It is he who made us,
and we are his; we are his people, the sheep of his pasture."*

The root of all burnout is playing God. You and I were created by Him and
for Him. We need to realize that God never meant for us to manage every detail
of our lives. To stop burnout and to live a life of *"burn on,"* we must learn to sit
at His feet and seek His face. We must also seek His heart, not just His hand;
and allow God's grace to overwhelm and strengthen us. Wrap your mind around
God's unconditional love and watch what happens (see Romans 8:35; 1 John
4:16).

TOMORROW

Moses said to Pharaoh, "I leave to you the honor of setting the time for me to pray for you and your officials and your people that you and your houses may be rid of the frogs, except for those that remain in the Nile." "Tomorrow," Pharaoh said. Moses replied, "It will be as you say, so that you may know there is no one like the Lord our God" (Exodus 8:9-10).

THE SINGLE MOST DANGEROUS WORD IN THE HUMAN LANGUAGE IS FOUND IN Exodus 8. Consider the story of Pharaoh and the plague of frogs. Pharaoh refused to set God's people free, so Moses was sent by the Lord to tell him to let them go or face the consequences. Pharaoh was the most powerful ruler on the planet, and he was not about to this sheepherder, and his sidekick tell him what to do. The second plague was about to be unleashed, and it was terrifying. It started raining frogs, frogs, and more frogs.

Moses gave Pharaoh a choice. He could allow Moses to remedy the situation, or he could try to handle it himself. What would you do? I know what I would do. The answer is simple; *"Moses do what you have to do but get rid of the frogs!"* Pharaoh, possibly thinking he had the power to save his kingdom from the plague, said, *"Tomorrow!"* Wait…What? It was as though he was saying, *"Go away Moses, I've got this all figured out."* I guess Pharaoh decided he could tolerate this horrible situation one more day.

The word "tomorrow" can sound so hopeful, can't it? The word "tomorrow" is used to describe problems we think about today, and hope somehow they will change tomorrow. There is nothing wrong with having hope for tomorrow. We think just because we talked about something today it will change all by itself.

Do you know what happened when Moses was finally allowed to pray? God eliminated the frogs! What you have struggled with for years God's power can kill in a minute. No matter how big the frog (insert problem here) God's power can deal with it. Maybe it's time to clean house and allow God to do for you what He did for Pharaoh. Why would you wait one more day? Friend, God has a forty gallon can of Frog-be-gone, and He's not afraid to use it on your behalf!

LIVING IN THE FOG

*Surely, Lord, you bless the righteous; you surround them
with your favor as with a shield* (Psalm 5:12).

I HAVE GREAT NEWS! IF YOU ARE A CHILD OF THE KING, YOU ARE WALKING IN the *fog* right now. You may be scratching your head and wondering, *What in the world is the fog?* I don't mean you are walking in some dense, dark, smoky cloud unsure of your next step. I'm talking about the Favor Of God! The literal translation of the word "favor" is from a Hebrew word meaning "cause for rejoicing, exultation, exuberant joy, and gladness of heart."

You are God's favorite, His prized possession, and nothing can take that away from you. You have royal blood flowing through your veins, not based on something you did, but based on the shed blood of Jesus Christ. Therefore, favor is a gift, and not something you can earn or buy. God does not owe you favor, but chooses to give you favor. We must also remember God's blessings and favor are not just to help you, but are provided to help you help others find the same joy and peace you have seen.

I urge you to trace for yourself the excellent benefits of favor found in Scripture. Here are just a few things you will find:

- God's favor will bring increase and promotion (see Genesis 39:21).
- God's favor will bring restoration of everything the enemy has stolen from you (see Exodus 3:21).
- God's favor will give you honor in the midst of your adversaries (see Exodus 11:3).
- God's favor will bring recognition, even when you seem the least likely to receive it (see 1 Samuel 16:22).
- God's favor will give you victories in battle in which you won't have to fight (see Psalm 44:3).

Don't ever be afraid to pray for God's favor over your job, your family, and everything that concerns you. No matter how big the challenge, remember that God's favor is around and with you, even when you don't feel it. His favor will protect you and keep you safe and shielded from the effects of evil. If something terrible should happen, God can take even that and use it for your good and His glory (see Romans 8:28).

ACT LIKE A SOLDIER

*Join with me in suffering, like a good soldier of Christ Jesus. No
one serving as a soldier gets entangled in civilian affairs, but rather
tries to please his commanding officer* (2 Timothy 2:3-4).

PAUL LOVED TO USE WORD PICTURES TO DESCRIBE THE CHRISTIAN LIFE. ONE
metaphor he often used is a Christian is much like a professional soldier. I
can imagine that kind of description would not sit well with many in the faith.
There is a kind of "feel good religion" that wants to believe the life of a believer
is a playground, not a battleground. We are in a war whether we want to admit it
or not. Just because someone refuses to believe something does not make it any
less real; ignoring reality doesn't change things, it only makes it worse when the
truth slaps us in the face.

As a soldier, there are some things to endure. Another Bible translation of
verse 3 says, *"You therefore must endure hardship as a good soldier of Jesus Christ"*
(2 Timothy 2:3 KJV). According to *Wuest's Word Studies,* the meaning of *"endure
hardship"* is "to endure hardship together with someone else." He goes on to
explain: "Paul is exhorting Timothy to endure hardships with him."[10] No matter the Scripture translation, the meaning is the same—as a dedicated Christian,
I must possess spiritual endurance and a willingness to fight like a soldier. I must
have the patience and perseverance to stay the course even when the battle is hot
and others are falling by the wayside.

As a soldier, there are some things to stay away from. The root meaning of
"entangled" is a picture of vines weaving themselves around a plant or a tree. Paul
is not saying as Christians we must avoid the world around us. He is not saying
we should refuse to work and provide for our family. What he is saying is that we
are not supposed to be so "tied up" by the affairs of the world that we cannot fulfill our calling.

As a good soldier, there is someone he is to *"please."* A Christian is *"to please
his commanding officer"*—and His name is Jesus. How? By magnifying Him and
remembering our sole purpose is to bring glory and honor to His name, not
ours. Good soldiers know their duty is to the Commanding Officer—Jesus—
and nothing comes before that.

FOLLOW THE RULES
LIKE AN ATHLETE

*Similarly, anyone who competes as an athlete does
not receive the victor's crown except by competing
according to the rules* (2 Timothy 2:5).

ANOTHER FAVORITE METAPHOR OF PAUL'S TO DESCRIBE A CHRISTIAN IS THAT of an athlete. You can see throughout his writings his use of athletic contests as examples and illustrations of the Christian life (see Hebrews 12:1; Philippians 2:16; 1 Corinthian 9:24-26). Paul was very familiar with sports. The culture of his day was enthusiastic about the Olympic games, and for Paul, it became a source of inspiration.

An athlete who trains and works to achieve the pinnacle of success (a crown) must do so according to the requirements of the particular contest entered. The Olympic game officials were and are most careful about enforcing the rules. Each person who competes must be a citizen (trueborn) of the country, possess a good reputation, and follow specific training standards. If the judges discover that a participant broke the rules, he or she is disqualified. It is not uncommon for an athlete to have won first place only to be discovered to have broken the rules. In such cases, the athlete immediately loses the "crown" then—the medal now.

If you look at the life of Paul from the world's point of view, he sure looked more like a loser than a winner. The last thing you would say is that he deserved any crown at all. After all, he was in prison and would soon die as a common criminal. In spite of all he endured, he was anticipating a winner's crown. He said, *"Now there is in store for me the crown of righteousness, which the Lord, the righteous Judge, will award to me on that day—and not only to me, but also to all who have longed for his appearing"* (2 Timothy 4:8).

Paul was trying to tell Timothy that the most important thing in the world is to obey the Word of God. My friend, it doesn't matter what others do or say, you and I are not running the race to gain fame or glory. We are running to please Him who has chosen us from the foundation of the world!

WORK LIKE A FARMER

The hardworking farmer should be the first to
receive a share of the crops (2 Timothy 2:6).

HERE AGAIN, PAUL IS USING ONE OF HIS MANY METAPHORS TO DESCRIBE THE believer. He now compares a Christian to a farmer. What is it about the life of a Christian that lends itself to such a comparison?

First, a farmer must be willing to *work hard*. He knows if he does not work the field in a timely manner, it will produce nothing but dirt and weeds. I think Solomon had this picture in mind when he wrote, *"I went past the field of a sluggard, past the vineyard of someone who has no sense; thorns had come up everywhere, the ground was covered with weeds, and the stone wall was in ruins. I applied my heart to what I observed and learned a lesson from what I saw: A little sleep, a little slumber, a little folding of the hands to rest—and poverty will come on you like a thief and scarcity like an armed man"* (Proverbs 24:30-34). A Christian who is lazy will never produce a spiritual harvest.

Second, a farmer must have *patience*. The Bible says, *"Be patient, then, brothers and sisters, until the Lord's coming. See how the farmer waits for the land to yield its valuable crop, patiently waiting for the autumn and spring rains"* (James 5:7). Can you imagine a farmer going out and digging up his seed every other day to check on its growth? If he did, he would never have a harvest. Likewise, just as the farmer waits patiently for his crop, we must wait on God to finish what He started in our lives (see Philippians 1:6).

Third, a farmer *deserves a portion* of the harvest: *"For Scripture says, 'Do not muzzle an ox while it is treading out the grain,' and 'The worker deserves his wages'"* (1 Timothy 5:18). A wise farmer would never get up early or stay up late just to have something to do. The sole focus of his attention is a reward at the end of the process. Each of us has a portion of the field to work. Be like a wise farmer and enjoy the fruits of your labor!

DON'T JUST SIT THERE— DO SOMETHING!

Now there were four men with leprosy at the entrance of the city gate. They said to each other, "Why stay here until we die? If we say, 'We'll go into the city'—the famine is there, and we will die. And if we stay here, we will die. So, let's go over to the camp of the Arameans and surrender. If they spare us, we live; if they kill us, then we die" (2 Kings 7:3-4).

AUTHOR AND PROFESSOR JOHN A. SHEDD COINED A PHRASE THAT HAS BEEN used to inspire and motivate people from all walks of life. It was written in his book, *Salt from My Attic.* He wrote, "A ship in the harbor is safe, but that is not what ships are built for."[11] Shedd leaves no doubt as to the meaning. There comes a time when you must decide to leave the safety of the harbor—your comfort zone—and move into the open waters. If you take a ship away from its mooring, it can be risky; but to get to where you want to go, certain risk is always involved.

The story from Second Kings is a perfect example of leaving the safety of the harbor. There are four men who knew that to change their circumstances they had to get up and take action. Their choices were few: they could go into the city and die, or stay where they were and die. They did not see much of a choice. Either decision they made looked like bad news.

But, there was a third choice that turned out to be the right one. They decided to move to the enemy's camp and plead for mercy. Their attitude was, "If they show mercy we will live, and if they don't we will die, so let's at least give it a shot." They had no idea God had already prepared the way for a miracle. When they got to the camp, the enemy was gone. After enjoying the spoils, they reported the good news to the palace! (See 2 Kings 7:5-10.)

Here's the point: there are times when our desperation for change may take us into unfamiliar territory. Faith to move is not a blind leap in the dark. NO, it's a step into the light of God's purpose. Walking in the revelation you have received is all God requires. I think it is normal to want to have all the details up-front before making a decision. The only question I need to ask is, "What's the next step?" Don't waste your opportunities for victory waiting on God to give you the fine print.

MICROWAVES, CROCKPOTS, AND THE WILL OF GOD

Yet the Lord longs to be gracious to you; therefore he will rise up to show you compassion. For the Lord is a God of justice. Blessed are all who wait for him! (Isaiah 30:18)

ISAIAH SAYS IN THIS VERSE THAT IF YOU WANT TO BE BLESSED, JUST WAIT ON God. Well, who doesn't want to blessed? But here's the rub—we have to take on a mindset that goes against our nature. Waiting on God is not our strong suit. Do you think the Lord doesn't know we live in a microwave generation that demands things be done now, not later? Of course, He does!

I think most Christians desire to know and walk in the will of God. But the problem is we want God to do it now, not next week—now. It seems we have a microwave than a crockpot mindset when it comes to our destiny. Sorry friend, it just doesn't happen that way.

Microwaves are great for heating food fast. It's claim to fame is that it is built for convenience and superfast heating. Crockpots, on the other hand, work slowly. A crockpot operates on the premise that if you want it fast, don't use me. A crockpot will tell you: "Give me a roast, a little water, and in eight hours I'll give you a piece of meat so good you will think you have died and gone to Heaven!"

I could point to many examples about the difference in mindsets, but let's consider the apostle Paul. If we aren't careful, we might think that he was an overnight success. We read of his instant conversion on the road to Damascus and think his ministry was put in Heaven's microwave and boom, it was done. But in fact, Paul was simmering for at least fourteen years before his ministry was ready to be shared with the world. In the Kingdom of God, there is no such thing as instant maturity. If we want God's purpose in our life, there must be a willingness to allow Him to set the timetable of our destiny.

If we are willing to wait on God, it will produce something so rich and inviting that others will want what we have. The next time you find yourself in hot water and it seems it is taking forever for things to happen, remember—just because something is fast and convenient doesn't make it better. Trust God in the process; it is worth the wait!

LOVE IS THE THEME

Of the themes that men have known,
One supremely stands alone;
Through the ages it has shown,
'Tis His wonderful, wonderful love.
Love is the theme, love is supreme;
Sweeter it grows, glory bestows;
Bright as the sun ever it glows!
Love is the theme, eternal theme!
ALBERT C. FISHER (1886-1946)[12]

A RADICAL CONCEPT

Whoever does not love does not know God,
because God is love (1 John 4:8).

WHEN JOHN SAID, *"GOD IS LOVE,"* HE DECLARED AN ETERNAL TRUTH SO radical and new that it was hard for many (including new Christians) to grasp. They were taught that gods were to be feared, not loved. They were told that gods could get angry and take revenge. But, they were certainly not to love them.

John is not talking about a love that is impersonal or distant. If that were the case, he would have said, *"Love is God."* But he didn't say that, he said, *"God is love."* The Gospel of Jesus Christ is the only message that declares sinful humans can have an intimate relationship with the God of the universe. Islam doesn't say that; Buddhism doesn't say that; and none of the other religions of the world do either.

While Jesus was here on the earth, He demonstrated a love that the world had never seen before. By His words and actions, He showed them, and us, a new and better way. He loved the unlovely and loved others who even refused to love Him back. It didn't matter to Jesus whether a person was poor or rich, He loved them all the same. Jesus did not come to earth to die on a cross to start another religion. He did not rise from the dead so we would have to follow a strict set of rules and regulations to gain eternal life. No! He came to offer forgiveness, healing, and hope to a lost and dying world.

My friend, if we claim to know Jesus Christ as our Lord and Savior and harbor hate toward others, we are not walking in God's love. Hate and bitterness cannot live in the same heart with the love of God. If we don't show God's love to others, where are they going to go to find it? The only place a dog-eat-dog culture can discover what real love is all about is from people who have experienced His love. My heart's desire is that when people examine my life, they will say, *"See how he loved Jesus!"*

WITHOUT LOVE, IT'S JUST NOISE

*If I speak in the tongues of men or of angels, but do not have
love, I am only a resounding gong or a clanging cymbal. If I
have the gift of prophecy and can fathom all mysteries and all
knowledge, and if I have a faith that can move mountains,
but do not have love, I am nothing. If I give all I possess to the
poor and give over my body to hardship that I may boast, but
do not have love, I gain nothing* (1 Corinthians 13:1-3).

PASTOR KEITH KRELL SHARED THE FOLLOWING ILLUSTRATION TO POINT OUT
the way many people feel when it comes to actually loving those around us:

> A *Peanuts* cartoon shows Lucy standing with her arms folded and a
> stern expression on her face. Charlie Brown pleads, "Lucy, you must
> be more loving. This world really needs love. You have to let yourself
> love to make this world a better place." Lucy angrily whirls around
> and knocks Charlie Brown to the ground. She screams at him, "Look,
> Blockhead, the world I love. It's people I can't stand."[13]

Paul did not write about love to give the Corinthian Christians something to
make them feel all warm and cozy inside. They were acting like spoiled children
opening presents on Christmas day. Their primary focus was on who had the best
gift of the Spirit, while ignoring the fact they were treating each other with contempt. It is no coincidence that the love chapter (1 Corinthians 13) is between the
two chapters that focus on the gifts of the Spirit (see chapters 12–14). It didn't
matter if they exercised one or all of the gifts if they didn't demonstrate the love
of the Father. They were displaying gifts without the cushion of love. Therefore,
they were just making a bunch of noise. Do you know how annoying a clanging
cymbal can be?

The origin of sacrificial love is in the heart of the Father. It is His nature to
love unconditionally and to impart love to His children. The Holy Spirit can only
produce a sacrificial love that goes into action on behalf of someone else. The
world can never provide that kind of love. Godly love will always be backed up
with action. From Heaven's point of view, we can practice the gifts all day long,
but without a loving spirit, we *gain nothing!*

IT'S OUT OF THIS WORLD

*Love is patient, love is kind. It does not envy, it does
not boast, it is not proud* (1 Corinthians 13:4).

PAUL DID NOT LET UP ON HIS ADMONISHMENT TO THE IMMATURE BELIEVERS in Corinth. To show what *"Love is,"* he used word pictures to paint a portrait of the kind of love that flows from the heart of the Father through us to others. Every time I read his words, I am reminded how far short I come in displaying God's love to those around me.

Agape love is not found in the world system. The system of the world is based on "feelings and emotions." It is a "scratch my back, and I'll scratch your back philosophy" that permeates every walk of life. In the Greek language, there are several words used to describe love. But, standing above the rest is *agape* love. According to Greek scholar Kenneth Wuest, agape is "the noblest word for love in the Greek language."[14] The New Testament writers used this word to describe God's covenant love for His people (see John 3:16; 13:34-35; Romans 5:8).

Agape is divine love. It is vastly different from the kind of love we offer to each other. So often our love for others is coupled with an expectation of what can they do for us in return. God doesn't operate that way. He made a decision before the foundation of the world to love us, and that decision was not based on anything we could do to earn it. The psalmist declares, *"But from everlasting to everlasting the Lord's love is with those who fear him, and his righteousness with their children's children"* (Psalm 103:17).

Agape is the highest form of love in the universe. Those who demonstrate agape love are willing to do something that is entirely foreign to the natural mind. When Jesus says in Matthew 5:44 to *"love your enemies and pray for those who persecute you,"* He is telling us to do something that is not possible without *agape.* It is easy to love those we think deserve it, but how tough is it to love those who want to cause us harm? The only possible way is to let the love of God flow through us by the indwelling Holy Spirit.

LOVE IS PATIENT

*Love is patient, love is kind. It does not envy, it does
not boast, it is not proud* (1 Corinthians 13:4).

THE WORD "PATIENT" OR "LONG-SUFFERING" IS A COMMON WORD USED IN
the New Testament to describe our dealing with difficult people, not just
difficult circumstances. The literal meaning is "long-tempered." In Paul's day,
if you showed patience or a long-tempered attitude toward someone who had
harmed or even offended you, it was considered a weakness. Their philosophy
was if someone hurt you or harmed you, hurt them back. They took an "eye for
an eye" to a whole new level.

Bible teacher Rick Renner states:

> This word "long-suffering" is like a candle that has a very long wick.
> Because its wick is long, it is prepared to burn a long time. This is a
> picture of a person whose feelings for someone else are so passionate
> that he doesn't easily give up but instead, keeps on going and going.[15]

From the beginning of creation, God has set the bar for being patient or long-
tempered with us. It is His patience that gives us time to be saved. Peter declared
in Second Peter 3:9: *"The Lord is not slow in keeping his promise, as some understand slowness. Instead he is patient* [long-tempered] *with you, not wanting anyone
to perish, but everyone to come to repentance."* The examples are abundant in Scripture of God's patience and long-suffering with people who refused His overtures
of love. So, if God can demonstrate that kind of love toward us, how is it that we
can't show the same to each other?

The next time you are ready to throw someone overboard because they refuse
to listen or turn their life around, try taking the "wick" approach. Make up your
mind that you are going all the way and not give up. Ask God for a fresh infu-
sion of agape love and turn the situation around. It's a matter of choice. When it
comes to relationships, choose to be like a candle that refuses to burn out!

LOVE IS KIND

*Love is patient, love is kind. It does not envy, it does
not boast, it is not proud* (1 Corinthians 13:4).

IT IS NO ACCIDENT THAT "KINDNESS" AS LISTED IN THE "LOVE CHAPTER" (1 Corinthians 13), is also among the fruit of the Spirit in Galatians 5:22-23: *"But the fruit of the Spirit is love, joy, peace, forbearance, kindness, goodness, faithfulness, gentleness and self-control. Against such things there is no law."* The fruit of kindness is not something we can work up—it is something worked in by the indwelling Holy Spirit. Ephesians 5 is showing the "inner working" and First Corinthians 13 is the "outward demonstration." There is no law that can make people show kindness to one another. It has to be an "inside job"!

The basis of the word "kind" is "useful; profitable; well-fit for use (for what is really needed); kindness that is also serviceable."[16] No doubt Paul has this in mind when addressing the young believers in Corinth. He urged them to show kindness toward others, inside and outside the body of believers. He knew if the church was ever going to make an impact, they must act and react different from the world.

How is it possible to show kindness? As with all the attributes of love (agape), Jesus Christ is the supreme example. According to Titus 3:3-5, when we needed kindness and love, Jesus Christ stepped down from Heaven and demonstrated the love of the Father: *"At one time we too were foolish, disobedient, deceived and enslaved by all kinds of passions and pleasures. We lived in malice and envy, being hated and hating one another. But when the kindness and love of God our Savior appeared, he saved us, not because of righteous things we had done, but because of his mercy...."*

If you are having relationship issues with a fellow believer, why not try a little kindness? As the old saying goes, "A little kindness can go a long way in resolving unpleasant circumstances." Instead of throwing someone overboard by being quick to condemn and criticize, why not show kindness by helping them find a path of restoration and redemption. The best relationship advice ever given has to be Ephesians 4:32: *"Be kind and compassionate to one another, forgiving each other, just as in Christ God forgave you."*

LOVE DOES NOT ENVY

*Love is patient, love is kind. It does not envy, it does
not boast, it is not proud* (1 Corinthians 13:4).

PROVERBS 27:4 SAYS, *"ANGER IS CRUEL AND FURY OVERWHELMING, BUT
who can stand before jealousy?"* Depending on which Bible translation you use,
the words "envy" and "jealousy" are interchangeable. They both come from the
same root word, *zeloo* meaning "an onomatopoetic word, imitating the sound of
boiling water—properly, to bubble over because so hot (boiling); (figuratively) to
burn with zeal."[17]

Paul is now using the negative to show what agape love *is not*. You cannot have a
heart filled with the love of God and envy and jealousy at the same time. These young
believers in Corinth were more concerned about what their brothers and sisters were
doing, even to the point they allowed the green-eyed monster of envy to consume
them. Wanting to have your way is not new. This attitude may have begun in the
Garden of Eden, but it continues to this very day (see Genesis 3 and Philippians 1).

It is a sad day when we are more concerned about what others have that we can't
even appreciate and enjoy the things God has given us. If it weren't so sad, it would be
amusing to watch people find all kinds of reasons to be envious of their brothers and
sisters in Christ. In some cases, it's because they may drive a better car or live in a bigger house. People can become almost enraged with jealousy just by watching someone
move up the ladder of success while they feel it should have been them instead.

My flesh rebels anytime I try to take a back seat and let others receive the
praise that I think should have been mine. Scripture warns of this attitude: *"But
if you harbor bitter envy and selfish ambition in your hearts, do not boast about it or
deny the truth. Such 'wisdom' does not come down from heaven but is earthly, unspir-
itual, demonic. For where you have envy and selfish ambition, there you find disorder
and every evil practice"* (James 3:14-16).

God's love is always looking out for the needs of others. It is only when we
allow the Holy Spirit to fill us can we overcome feelings of envy.

LOVE DOES NOT BOAST

Love is patient, love is kind. It does not envy, it does
not boast, it is not proud (1 Corinthians 13:4).

YOU HAVE HEARD THE OLD EXPRESSION, "NOBODY LIKES A BRAGGART," RIGHT? Well, that is exactly what Paul is talking about when he says that love does not boast. Paul is describing someone who is a show-off, a person who needs attention. A boastful person is very good at self-promotion even if the facts don't back up the chatter. In today's culture, we might say that someone who is always bragging is living with the mantra, "It's all about me, myself, and I!"

Bragging and jealousy make a two-headed monster. Jealousy always wants what someone else has and bragging is making others jealous of what we have. Paul wrote to these young Christians to warn them about becoming spiritual show-offs. It did not matter to them how their bragging affected others or if their fellow believers were offended. The number one issue was they had to be the stars of the show!

I remember a pastor friend of mine telling me about the time he met with a high-profile minister to discuss reaching out to help pastors in a certain country. He said he was so excited that this "big name" minister wanted to discuss something of such importance with him. In recalling the essence of the meeting, he said, "The only thing this guy wanted to talk about was himself. I sat for over three hours listening to all his accomplishments. He talked incessantly about how powerful he was and how many names of important people he had in his contact list. He never asked me one personal question. Finally, I couldn't take it anymore and left the meeting. What a disappointment!"

Jeremiah offers this nugget of wisdom about bragging, *"This is what the Lord says: 'Let not the wise boast of their wisdom or the strong boast of their strength or the rich boast of their riches, but let the one who boasts boast about this: that they have the understanding to know me, that I am the Lord, who exercises kindness, justice and righteousness on earth, for in these I delight,' declares the Lord"* (Jeremiah 9:23-24). Pretty simple really. If you want to brag on someone, brag on the Lord. When you operate in agape, you never have to puff yourself up. Lift Him up, and He will do the rest.

LOVE IS NOT PROUD

Love is patient, love is kind. It does not envy, it does not boast, it is not proud (1 Corinthians 13:4).

IF YOU THINK IT IS DIFFICULT TO ENGAGE WITH A PERSON WHO IS CONTINUALLY bragging about themselves, try working with a leader (or a coworker) who is arrogant. Again, Paul uses a negative word to point out what agape is *not*. The definition of "pride": properly, excessive shining, i.e. self-exaltation (self-absorption), which carries its own self-destructive vanity.[18]

It is understandable that Paul would issue warning after warning to these new converts about the danger of pride (see 1 Corinthians 4:6,19; 5:2). He used the terms *puffed up, arrogant, and proud* to describe an attitude of heart that was the root of their problems. Being puffed up is another way of saying they were inflated with hot air of their importance!

The Bible is filled with warnings about the danger of pride. It is one of seven things the Bible says God hates (see Proverbs 6:16-19).

A brief sample of what pride can do:

- It deceives you: Jeremiah 49:16
- It hardens your spirit: Daniel 5:20
- It brings shame: Proverbs 11:2
- It creates strife among people: Proverbs 13:10
- It brings judgment: Proverbs 16:5
- It aids in your destruction: Proverbs 16:18

The lesson for us is a lot easier to understand than it is to apply. If we want to demonstrate the love of the Father, we must put people first. We are called to serve and not be served. When God's love is at the center of all we do, we will never belittle others because they have not achieved a level of success that we have. Agape lifts up people, it doesn't tear them down. Our attitude must be one of humility, not haughtiness, as expressed by Peter, *"In the same way, you who are younger, submit yourselves to your elders. All of you, clothe yourselves with humility toward one another, because, 'God opposes the proud but shows favor to the humble.' Humble yourselves, therefore, under God's mighty hand, that he may lift you up in due time"* (1 Peter 5:5-6).

LOVE DOES NOT DISHONOR OTHERS

It does not dishonor others, it is not self-seeking, it is not easily angered, it keeps no record of wrongs (1 Corinthians 13:5).

WHETHER YOU TRANSLATE THE WORD "DISHONOR" AS RUDE, UNSEEMLY, OR unbecomingly, the meaning is the same; Paul is describing a person who has bad manners, with no thought to the feelings of others, or you might call this kind of person tacky. Merriam-Webster says that "tacky" is "not having or exhibiting good taste."[19] In today's society—and in the Church—it seems that more and more displays of tackiness have become the rule and not the exception. I looked it up—being tacky is *not* a fruit of the Spirit!

Through the years, I have been around a few people who pride themselves on "straight talk." You know, the kind of person who says, *"I'm a straight shooter, and you'll never have to wonder what I'm thinking."* They seem to get some measure of satisfaction by letting the bullets fly, regardless of the damage caused. Going off like a double-barreled shotgun may be fine for the people pulling the trigger; but if they stop and consider the harm created, they have to ask themselves if it is really worth it to unload on people.

Paul says, *"Then we will no longer be infants, tossed back and forth by the waves, and blown here and there by every wind of teaching and by the cunning and craftiness of people in their deceitful scheming. Instead, speaking the truth in love, we will grow to become in every respect the mature body of him who is the head, that is, Christ"* (Ephesians 4:14-15).

Paul is referring to building people up, not tearing them down. He is telling us to apply God's love to everything we say and do. Being kind and gracious rather than being rude and tacky is a far better way to deal with those around us. How many times have the rudeness and tackiness of some Christians turned off those who would have otherwise given their hearts to Christ? We are never wrong to let our words and deeds be tempered with a heavy dose of agape. As I used to tell my teenagers, "Just because it floats into your brain, doesn't mean it has to come out of your mouth!"

LOVE IS NOT SELF-SEEKING

It does not dishonor others, it is not self-seeking, it is not easily angered, it keeps no record of wrongs (1 Corinthians 13:5).

A TOURIST WAS WALKING THROUGH AN OLD COUNTRY CHURCHYARD IN ENG-land when he discovered a plain slab of stone bearing this epitaph: "Here lies a miser who lived for himself and cared for nothing but gathering wealth. Now where he is or how he fares, nobody knows and nobody cares." The same tourist later visited St. Paul's Cathedral in London and observed a plain but massive statue beneath which was inscribed: "Sacred to the memory of General Charles George Gordon, who at all times and everywhere gave his strength to the weak, his substance to the poor, his sympathy to the suffering, and his heart to God." What a difference between those two records![20]

The type of people Paul had in mind are those who will do anything to get their way. He is speaking of those who need to be the focus of attention. The Church of Jesus has been infected with a type of spiritual manipulation that is in opposition to agape love. This attitude will even try to control and influence by twisting Scripture to suit their purposes. There have been many church wars fought over lifting Scripture out of context to suit the whims of self-serving leaders.

The childish behavior of the Corinthian believers is a prime example of the opposite of God's love. They thought that because they exercised the gifts of the Spirit, it somehow made them more spiritual than others. Paul would have none of it. He says, *"So it is with you. Since you are eager for gifts of the Spirit, try to excel in those that build up the church"* (1 Corinthians 14:12). Agape will never use manipulation to get its way. Love will always try to build up and never tear down!

In your relationships with one another, have the same mindset as Christ Jesus: Who, being in very nature God, did not consider equality with God something to be used to his own advantage; rather, he made himself nothing by taking the very nature of a servant, being made in human likeness. And being found in appearance as a man, he humbled himself by becoming obedient to death—even death on a cross! (Philippians 2:5-8)

LOVE IS NOT EASILY ANGERED

It does not dishonor others, it is not self-seeking, it is not easily angered, it keeps no record of wrongs (1 Corinthians 13:5).

THE PHRASE *"NOT EASILY ANGERED,"* IS PAUL'S WAY OF SAYING, "LOVE IS not overly sensitive or easily offended." In today's culture, we find almost anything and everything is offensive to someone or some group. Today's atmosphere is supercharged with angry words from every segment of society. We have become so "touchy" that to have a conversation with opposing views is libel to set someone ablaze with anger.

Have you ever heard someone try to explain his or her anger? It usually goes something like this, "I couldn't help myself, they just made me angry!" First of all, we *can* help ourselves; and second, no one can *make* us angry. That is an excuse, not an explanation. The only thing someone can do is reveal the anger that is already inside us. Just like a tube of toothpaste, when squeezed, guess what comes out? That's right, toothpaste. What comes out of us when pressed is what is already inside.

In Luke 15, we read the story of the elder brother. I call him the prodigal who stayed at home. When he heard his wayward brother had returned from the far country and his father was throwing a party, he was angry. He refused to join in the celebration. I maintain he wasn't angry because his brother came home. He was angry because he never received the proper recognition from his dad. It's the familiar, "But what about me syndrome?" The words of his father provoked him, and he missed an excellent opportunity to express love instead of anger.

When someone uses words to provoke or offend you, instead of retaliating, why not use it as an opportunity to show God's love? Don't take the bait and end up doing or saying something you will regret. Apostle James says:

> *"My dear brothers and sisters, take note of this: Everyone should be quick to listen, slow to speak and slow to become angry, because human anger does not produce the righteousness that God desires. Therefore, get rid of all moral filth and the evil that is so prevalent and humbly accept the word planted in you, which can save you"* (James 1:19-21).

LOVE KEEPS NO RECORD OF WRONGS

It does not dishonor others, it is not self-seeking, it is not easily angered, it keeps no record of wrongs (1 Corinthians 13:5).

THE PHRASE *"KEEPS NO RECORD"* IS A BOOKKEEPING TERM. ACCOUNTANTS worth their salt know how important it is to keep a meticulous record of all financial transactions. Accountants must make a permanent record in case there is ever any question about a specific account—their (and their clients') very life blood depends on it. A sloppy bookkeeper will not stay in business very long.

Sadly, many Christians have become excellent bookkeepers. They keep a record of all wrongs, offenses, disappointments, and hurts. Real or imagined, they keep a permanent ledger so they can occasionally go back and review the list to be reminded of what someone said or did. Living with an offended spirit will sap your spiritual strength and put out the flame of love. Many years ago, I heard someone say that staying offended is like drinking poison and hoping the other person dies!

Aren't you glad God doesn't treat us the way we treat others? He has chosen not to parade our sins before us (and the world) but rather to forgive and heal. Psalm 103:3 says God, *"forgives all your sins and heals all your diseases."* Even though He has every right to punish us according to our sin, He chooses not to. Instead of treating us like common outcasts, He treats us as sons and daughters of the King. Psalm 103:10 tells us that God, *"does not treat us as our sins deserve or repay us according to our iniquities."*

God has separated our sins from us as far as the East is from the West: *"For as high as the heavens are above the earth, so great is his love for those who fear him; as far as the east is from the west, so far has he removed our transgressions from us"* (Psalm 103:11-12).

Apostle Paul declared that God has given up the bookkeeping business: *"Blessed is the one whose sin the Lord will never count against them"* (Romans 4:8). Remember, if we are keeping records, it's a sure sign that God's love is absent. Maybe it is time to burn the books!

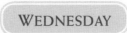

LOVE DOES NOT DELIGHT IN EVIL, IT REJOICES WITH TRUTH

Love does not delight in evil but rejoices with the truth (1 Corinthians 13:6).

LOVE AND EVIL ARE OPPOSITES THAT DO NOT ATTRACT. THE MEANING OF THE word "rejoice" is "joy" or "feeling exuberant." Paul says that love is not happy when something evil happens to others.

Proverbs 24:17 cautions us, *"Do not gloat when your enemy falls; when they stumble, do not let your heart rejoice."* How do you react when hearing a bit of bad news about someone? Do you immediately think the best or worst of that person? If we are honest, it is more "juicy" to hear bad news about someone than good news. Lapping up gossip about a brother or sister who has had a moral breakdown has become part of the culture of the modern church. You expect this type of behavior from society in general, but it is to our shame that we have allowed it to spread among the brothers and sisters. Spreading evil and taking satisfaction upon hearing a believer has fallen is *not* the attitude of love. God's love does not gloat over the sins of others, it rejoices in the truth that sets us all free. When a moral breakdown occurs, it is an occasion for sorrow, not throwing a party.

The culture around us says there is no such thing as objective truth. It is all about the individual perspective, and what makes you feel good. The twisted logic of a lost society is that evil is good, and good is evil. Isaiah warned us about this attitude thousands of years ago: *"Woe to those who call evil good and good evil, who put darkness for light and light for darkness, who put bitter for sweet and sweet for bitter"* (Isaiah 5:20).

John tells us what Jesus said to those who believed in Him, *"If you hold to my teaching, you are really my disciples. Then you will know the truth, and the truth will set you free"* (John 8:31-32). The issue is clear. How can we rejoice with the truth if we don't know what truth is? When the truth of God's Word is ignored, it is virtually impossible to demonstrate God's love! It is time to return to God's Word and let the truth of God's Word be our light in a dark world.

LOVE PROTECTS

It always protects, always trusts, always hopes,
always perseveres (1 Corinthians 13:7).

WHEN PAUL USES THE WORD "PROTECTS" (OR "BEARS" NKJV), HE WAS painting a word picture that carries the idea: "to place under roof, to cover-over (with a roof); to cover closely (so as to keep water out), generally to bear up under."[21]

Having a roof over your house is an absolute necessity. If you have ever driven through an area hit by a tornado or a hurricane you will notice blue tarps spread on tops of houses. It seems roofs are the first to be damaged in a storm. Without the protection of a roof, we are subject to every possible disaster you can name. Believe me, if a storm should rip off your roof, you don't need some well-meaning neighbor to come over and bring you the latest brochure about the importance of having a roof. No, what you need is an insurance agent with a check and the number of the fastest roof repair company in town!

As believers, we should be so filled with agape love that when a storm hits a brother or sister, we will be there to protect and cover them. I'm not suggesting we sweep things under the rug or glorify sin. Love does not try to justify or let sinful behavior go unchecked. It is quite the opposite. Love is willing to discipline and rebuke if necessary, but will never do anything to fan the flame of gossip.

- Proverbs 10:12: *Hatred stirs up conflict, but love covers over all wrongs.*
- Proverbs 17:17: *A friend loves at all times, and a brother is born for a time of adversity.*
- John 15:12-13: *My command is this: Love each other as I have loved you. Greater love has no one than this: to lay down one's life for one's friends.*

I pray there will never come a day when a tornado of despair or a hurricane of condemnation rips the roof off your world. If it does, I pray a "friend" will come by your side and point you back to the love of the Father. Isn't that the attitude the apostle Peter was trying to convey in First Peter 4:8? *"Above all, love each other deeply, because love covers over a multitude of sins."*

LOVE ALWAYS TRUSTS

It always protects, always trusts, always hopes,
always perseveres (1 Corinthians 13:7).

THE LEGAL CODE IN THE UNITED STATES INCLUDES A STATEMENT THAT SETS us apart from many other countries. If someone is accused of a crime, that person is "innocent until proven guilty." It is sad that the Christian world does not adhere to the same policy. How many times have we heard of a fellow believer who stumbled and the rush to judgment was overwhelming? Why is it we are so quick to condemn? Why is it we don't practice what the Bible teaches when we see someone fall? A favorite aerobic exercise among Christian is jumping to conclusions!

Job's friends are perfect examples of how *not* to help a believer in distress. As they watched Job suffer, they seemed to have all the answers. Surely his suffering must be because of something he did. They were not willing to consider that maybe there was a redemptive purpose in Job's pain. Their first reaction was to believe the worst about Job, not the best. If Job was looking for comfort from his friends, he was going to be very disappointed (see Job 4:7-8; 8:20).

In First Corinthians 13:7, Paul is not saying that to *"always trust"* is to be gullible. Love carries with it an expectation to believe the best about a person, not the worst. Agape is willing to withhold judgment until all facts are revealed. When and if a dreadful situation arises, the desire of love is to watch over and cover that person, and do everything possible to bring healing and restoration. I submit that Galatians 6:1 is a good place to start: *"Brothers and sisters, if someone is caught in a sin, you who live by the Spirit should restore that person gently. But watch yourselves, or you also may be tempted."*

Why not follow the example of Jesus who gave us a demonstration of love in dealing with the woman taken in adultery? He set her free: *"Jesus declared 'Go now and leave your life of sin'"* (John 8:11). Jesus forgave her sin and pointed her to the future. He did not put chains around her neck to tie her to the past. God's love never gives up!

LOVE ALWAYS HOPES

It always protects, always trusts, always hopes,
always perseveres (1 Corinthians 13:7).

THE DEFINITION OF "HOPE" IS: "TO TRUST IN; WAIT FOR; LOOK FOR; OR DESIRE something or someone, or to expect something beneficial in the future."[22] I don't know of anyone who has not faced difficult circumstances. Some have had tougher things to deal with than others, but the fact remains we will face situations that try our faith. It may be a rebellious child, a spouse who has fallen into sin, or a close friend who shipwrecked their faith. You may even look toward Heaven and declare, "Lord, I have no more faith in this situation, You have to help me." What then? When faith runs dry, what can you do? You hang on to *hope!*

Peter failed miserably by denying the Lord, and I am sure he thought there was no way that he could ever be used again. He may have thought his ministry was finished, but that is not what happened. After the resurrection, Jesus showed up during a seashore breakfast meeting and began the restoration process (see John 21). You can see from his questions to Peter that Jesus was not ready to give up on him. Jesus knew Peter could be used to shake nations with the Gospel message. It's as if Jesus looked straight into his eyes and said, *"Son, I know you messed up, but I am going to restore and use you."* Jesus wasn't interested in digging up the past, but moving Peter forward into his future.

To *always hope* does not suggest that sin and failure be ignored. What it does, however, is never take someone's failure as their last act. God's love believes, no matter the circumstances, that restoration is possible.

We are so thankful that God did not give up on us the multitude of times we failed Him. We are forever blessed each time we asked for forgiveness and healing He showed up with mercy and grace. He will do the same for anyone who calls on His name. We urge you never to give up hope that God can turn any situation around. Just look through the Bible, see how He took ordinary people (many who failed) and turned them into spiritual dynamos for the Kingdom. *Agape is in the faith and hope business.*

LOVE ALWAYS PERSEVERES

It always protects, always trusts, always hopes,
always perseveres (1 Corinthians 13:7).

THE WORDS "PERSEVERE" AND "ENDURE" HAVE THE SAME MEANING: "To remain firm under; to sustain; to undergo; to support without breaking or yielding; as, metals endure a certain degree of heat without melting."[23]

You will notice Paul did not say in First Corinthians 13:7 that love will "sometimes" endure. No, he said it *"always"* endures! Love will never succumb to the temptation to believe the fight is lost. No, love will never stop trying and will go to the very end for people, even when that love is rejected and trampled on.

You may be dealing with a rebellious child who refuses every act of kindness and love you express. No matter how hard you have tried, nothing seems to work. Instead of giving in to the temptation to quit, remember how God treated you when you were in rebellion. He didn't give up on you, and you should never give up on that child, or anyone else for that matter.

If we could pull back the curtain and see how many lives have been changed because of His enduring love, we would be shocked and thrilled all at the same time. Never doubt that enduring love will stand its ground—even in the face of whatever forces the enemy may gather. Enduring love will always run toward the crisis, never away from it.

I challenge you to ponder the words of Psalm 136. For many generations, this psalm of praise has been sung at the end of the Passover meal. Many scholars believe this psalm is the one that Jesus and His disciples sang in Matthew 26:30, *"When they had sung a hymn, they went out to the Mount of Olives."* I might suggest reading and meditating on the words of this Scripture every morning as you face another day.

Psalm 136:1-4

> *Give thanks to the Lord, for he is good. His love endures forever. Give*
> *thanks to the God of gods. His love endures forever. Give thanks to the*
> *Lord of lords: His love endures forever. to him who alone does great*
> *wonders, His love endures forever.*

THE GREATEST OF THESE

*And now these three remain: faith, hope and love. But
the greatest of these is love* (1 Corinthians 13:13).

WHILE THE BELIEVERS IN CORINTH WERE SQUABBLING AMONG THEMSELVES about who had the greatest gift, Paul injected a touch of spiritual reality. As important as the gifts of the Spirit were to the life of the church, he wanted them to know there is one supreme virtue standing above the rest. Paul named the three most significant virtues as *faith, hope, and love.* Then he adds that *love* is supreme over the rest. My friend, you can't have faith and hope without the love of God.

The great American revivalist Jonathan Edwards made the following observation:

> All the fruits of the Spirit which we are to lay weight upon as eviden-
> tial of grace, are summed up in charity, or Christian love; because this
> is the sum of all grace. And the only way, therefore, in which any can
> know their good estate, is by discerning the exercises of this divine
> charity in their hearts; for without charity, let men have what gifts
> you please, they are nothing.[24]

One day while Jesus was teaching His disciples, the Pharisees posed a question. They wanted to know what He considered to be the greatest commandment in the Law. Please understand they were not asking because they wanted to follow Him; they were trying to trap Him into saying something they could condemn.

> *Hearing that Jesus had silenced the Sadducees, the Pharisees got together.
> One of them, an expert in the law, tested him with this question:
> "Teacher, which is the greatest commandment in the Law?" Jesus replied:
> "'Love the Lord your God with all your heart and with all your soul and
> with all your mind.' This is the first and greatest commandment. And
> the second is like it: 'Love your neighbor as yourself.' All the Law and
> the Prophets hang on these two commandments"* (Matthew 22:34-40).

The love of God is at the very core of all we do because love is at the very core of who we are. As Christians, if we do not demonstrate the love of the Father, then we are not much different from all other religions of the world.

LOVE IN ACTION

This is how God showed his love among us: He sent his one and only Son into the world that we might live through him. This is love: not that we loved God, but that he loved us and sent his Son as an atoning sacrifice for our sins (1 John 4:9-10).

WORDS OF LOVE DON'T MEAN MUCH IF THEY ARE NOT FOLLOWED UP WITH action. A friend of mine said that a church he pastored started an outreach called Love in Action. When my friend inquired about the name of the ministry, he was told that for too long the community only "heard" about God's love, it was now time to "demonstrate" it by meeting the needs of the community.

Talking about love without showing action to back it up is why so many people are turned off when the subject of God's love is discussed. Skepticism is birthed in the gap when our words and actions don't match up. Sorry, but talking a good game doesn't mean you were actually on the field playing the game. The modern church has perfected the art of talk with no action. Gathering on Sunday to hear sermons about "taking love to the streets" will never get the job done. Saying we are going to feed the hungry will never fill their bellies! Talk is cheap; I guess that's why there's so much of it!

God wanted to prove to humankind that His words of love were not empty, so He backed them up with action. John wrote about the greatest demonstration of God's love: *"This is love: not that we loved God, but that he loved us and sent his Son as an atoning sacrifice for our sins"* (1 John 4:10). Paul said it this way in Romans 5:8: *"But God demonstrates his own love for us in this: While we were still sinners, Christ died for us."* Think about that a minute. God did not send an angel to declare the good news or give us a new set of religious rules to follow. He sent His only Son into the world to die for our sins.

Trying to explain this great love to someone who has never experienced it is like trying to teach a first grader the finer points of the theory of relativity. It just doesn't compute. One verse many of us learned from our childhood says it all: *"For God so loved the world that he gave his one and only Son, that whoever believes in him shall not perish but have eternal life"* (John 3:16).

BIRTHMARKS

*Everyone who believes that Jesus is the Christ is born of God,
and everyone who loves the father loves his child as well. This is
how we know that we love the children of God: by loving God
and carrying out his commands. In fact, this is love for God: to
keep his commands. And his commands are not burdensome, for
everyone born of God overcomes the world. This is the victory
that has overcome the world, even our faith* (1 John 5:1-4).

WHEN A PERSON RECEIVES JESUS CHRIST AS LORD AND SAVIOR, THAT PERson then becomes part of the family of God. The person's life is totally changed (see 2 Corinthians 5:17). When a person has experienced a radical new birth, you should be able to see specific "family" characteristics that set the person apart. How many times have you looked at someone's child and thought he or she looked, talked, and acted just like the parents? You automatically sense "that child belongs to them!"

John points out there are certain family characteristics or "birthmarks" that should be recognizable for every child of God:

1. A believer will love Father God: *"and everyone who loves the father."* There is only one way to really know someone and that is to spend time with the person. You can read all the books you can find about a certain individual, but nothing will ever replace having a face-to-face discussion with the person. A new Christian will probably not understand all God did when He sent His Son to provide a sacrifice for sin. The natural progression is the more we get to know Him on an intimate level, the more we love Him.

2. A believer will love other brothers and sisters in Christ: *"loves his child as well."* I am not talking about the "natural" family you were born into, but the family of God. If another person is a child of the King, then it doesn't matter their skin color or cultural upbringing, they are our brothers and sisters, and we have the capacity to love them.

3. A believer can live an overcoming life: *"for everyone born of God overcomes the world."* If you see a defeated Christian, it could be because the person is not using the weapons available to live an overcoming life. Whether we like it or not, we are in a spiritual battle, and in this war, there will be causalities. But it doesn't have to be this way if we utilize what God has given us to overcome the evil one!

HEROES

Could it be…that the hero is one who is willing to set out, take the first step, shoulder something? Perhaps the hero is one who puts his foot upon a path not knowing what he may expect from life but in some way feeling in his bones that life expects something of him.

—P. L. Travers in *The World of the Hero* [25]

WHAT MAKES A HERO?

We who are strong ought to bear with the failings of the weak and not to please ourselves. Each of us should please our neighbors for their good, to build them up (Romans 15:1-2).

EVERYONE LOVES A HERO. OUR CULTURE IS PRIMARILY BASED ON HERO WORship at its highest form. We have sports heroes, comic book heroes, and movie heroes of all shapes and sizes. But for me, I love heroes who are real flesh and blood folks who struggle like I do. What makes them stand out is at some point they reach another level of courage. When God created us, He had a purpose in mind, or we would not be here. It is just not enough to live out our days hiding in the shadows or hoping we will never be called on to take a stand for righteousness. We are to be voices to our generation, not just echoes of the past.

The dictionary defines a hero as "a person admired for achievements and noble qualities: one who shows great courage: the central figure in an event, period, or movement."[26] Romans 15:1-2 describes certain marks of a hero. I will grant you it is not what our modern culture thinks a hero looks like, it is just the opposite.

From Heaven's viewpoint:

- A real hero will find a need and meet it.
- A real hero will lift up those who are weak.
- A real hero will build up others for their good, not just for our benefit.

Without a doubt, there are many things I will never do. I will never hit a grand slam to win a World Series or a throw a game-winning touchdown to win the Super Bowl. Those things are reserved for those bigger and stronger (and younger). But I can open my eyes to the needs of others. I can ask the Holy Spirit to give me the courage to stand in the gap, even if I have to risk my well-being in the process.

In the following pages, we will meet just a few of God's heroes. Men and women of character who displayed extraordinary sacrifice for the cause of Jesus Christ. Some you will encounter are more recognizable than others, but all exhibit the similar characteristics of sacrifice and service for the Kingdom of God.

ABRAHAM: HE DIDN'T SETTLE

Terah took his son Abram, his grandson Lot son of Haran,
and his daughter-in-law Sarai, the wife of his son Abram, and
together they set out from Ur of the Chaldeans to go to Canaan.
But when they came to Harran, they settled there. Terah lived
205 years, and he died in Harran (Genesis 11:31-32).

THE VERY FIRST SCENE IN THIS DIVINELY INSPIRED DRAMA CALLED THE LIFE of Abraham is when God spoke to Terah (Abraham's dad) and told him to take his family and move to a foreign land. The destination was Canaan. In those days, moving any substantial distance was no easy task. When the word came that Canaan was their destination and it was 1,100 miles from their hometown of Ur, you can imagine the emotions they felt.

They made it as far as a city named Harran and settled down. But, that was still 600 miles short of their destination. Why did they stop short? Maybe they were just plain tired of the hardships of traveling. Maybe Terah thought this was just as good a place as any to raise his family. Or, perhaps Terah thought God wouldn't notice they never made it to the Land of Promise.

It was only after Terah died that God spoke to Abraham and told him to leave Harran (Genesis 12:1) and take his household to the Land of Promise. Here is the key that unlocked his future… *"So Abram went, as the Lord had told him"* (Genesis 12:4). Abraham didn't become a hero of faith by leaping tall buildings in a single bound. He became a model of faith by simply trusting God's word enough to risk it all.

None of what we know about Abraham would have mattered if he hadn't taken the first step in obedience. He came close to short-circuiting his destiny by settling down in a place that was not the final point of his journey with God. When God wants to take you to Canaan, don't stop short—pursue His promise at all cost. Don't get distracted by hardships or disappointments along the way. Never settle for Harran—the good—when God is taking you to the Land of Promise—the best.

Do you want to be a hero? It starts by trusting God and not settling for second best.

GIDEON: AN UNLIKELY HERO

The angel of the Lord came and sat down under the oak in Ophrah that belonged to Joash the Abiezrite, where his son Gideon was threshing wheat in a winepress to keep it from the Midianites. When the angel of the Lord appeared to Gideon, he said, "The Lord is with you, mighty warrior" (Judges 6:11-12).

IF ALL THE CHARACTERS IN THE OLD TESTAMENT WERE LINED UP AND YOU asked me to pick someone who would become a hero, I'm not so sure Gideon would make the cut. He was full of doubt and lacked any shred of self-confidence.

In the context of the story, the nation of Israel was being oppressed by the Midianites. Something had to be done to break the cycle before it was too late. Enter Gideon. This "unlikely hero" is found threshing wheat in a winepress. This was unusual, as threshing wheat typically took place in the open so the wind could blow away the chaff. Instead of rallying the troops for battle, he's ducking in a winepress to hide from the enemy. So much for standing strong in times of peril!

The word of the Lord to him was as surprising as it was life changing, *"The Lord is with you, mighty warrior."* Yes, Gideon, you heard the Word correctly, the Lord just called you a mighty warrior. In spite of his objections and skepticism (Judges 6:13), the Lord was speaking to his future, not his past or present circumstances. Voicing objections to the call of God is not new. We tend to view ourselves in light of our weaknesses and failures, while God sees us in a different light. The key to this story is not how brave Gideon was or how many of the enemy he destroyed. The focus of attention is not on Gideon, but on how God took an unlikely candidate to accomplish great things.

The Lord is famous for using people the world would never consider heroes (see 1 Corinthians 1:27-29). The next time God calls you to achieve the extraordinary, remember the story of Gideon. You know the old saying, *"He never calls the qualified, but He does qualify the called!"*

Do you want to be a hero? Start believing what God says about your future—not what the devil says about your past!

ANDREW: JUST AN ORDINARY GUY

Andrew, Simon Peter's brother, was one of the two who heard what John had said and who had followed Jesus. The first thing Andrew did was to find his brother Simon and tell him, "We have found the Messiah" (that is, the Christ) (John 1:40-41).

YOU WON'T FIND HIS NAME LISTED IN THE "HEROES HALL OF FAME" IN Hebrews 11. Most of the time he is referred to only as *"Andrew, Simon Peter's brother."* You might wonder how in the world Andrew qualifies as a hero in the Bible. Sure, he was chosen by the Lord Jesus to be one of His followers (Matthew 4:19), but that is only part of his story. When you dig deeper, you discover he was kind of like the Forrest Gump of the Bible. He somehow found a way to be at the right place at the right time at the major events in the ministry of Jesus (see John 1:35-42; Matthew 4:18).

After Andrew found Jesus, he went home and told his brother the good news. This was not an easy thing to do. His brother was none other than Simon Peter, the rough and tough fisherman. The Bible says, *"He brought him to Jesus."* The next time we see Andrew, he is in the middle of a food crisis (see John 6). He introduces a boy with a small lunch to Jesus, and the Lord used it to feed the multitudes. Later on, Andrew is seen introducing men who were hungry to know more about Christ (see John 12:20-22).

Finally, fast forward to the day of Pentecost, and you can imagine Andrew's joy as he watched his brother stand and preach the Gospel message where at least three thousand people were born into the Kingdom of God.

The bottom line—every time you see Andrew, he is introducing someone to Jesus. Seems to me when people fall in love with Jesus, they want to tell others about it. Andrew gives me hope. I may not be able to preach like Peter or worship like David, but one thing I can do is introduce others to my wonderful Savior!

Do you want to be a hero? Start introducing people to Jesus. You never know what might happen!

PAUL: THE VILLAIN WHO BECAME A HERO

And that is just what I did in Jerusalem. On the authority of the chief priests I put many of the Lord's people in prison, and when they were put to death, I cast my vote against them. Many a time I went from one synagogue to another to have them punished, and I tried to force them to blaspheme. I was so obsessed with persecuting them that I even hunted them down in foreign cities (Acts 26:10-11).

I AM SURE THE EARLY CHURCH MUST HAVE FELT OVERWHELMED BY THE FLOOD of persecution leveled against her by the religious establishment. But they learned a truth we must all recognize. Nothing is impossible with God, and it is never too late for someone to change.

Is it possible to go from a zero to a hero? Consider the case of the early church's most vile persecutor, Saul of Tarsus. This young Pharisee was so zealous for his faith that if you didn't agree with him, he would try to have you thrown in prison and even executed (Acts 7:58; 8:1). How was it possible for him to turn around so quickly and so completely? He is a prime example of the grace and power of God.

As Paul was headed to Damascus to flush out more of this community of blasphemers, he had a life-changing experience with Christ (see Acts 9). After his conversion, he began to preach the very Gospel he tried to stamp out! The most dangerous threat to the Church would become her most influential writer and missionary. The conversion of Saul was once thought to be an impossibility, now it had become a reality.

Is there something we can learn from Paul's story? Yes, and it is this: never give up on anyone. I don't care if the situation looks hopeless with no end in sight. I am confident the early church prayed for this man Saul to be converted. Like so many of us they hoped God would do something, but when He did, they couldn't wrap their minds around such a great miracle. The old man Saul was gone, and the new man Paul was born into the Kingdom of God!

Do you want to be a hero? Start praying for someone's life to change; who knows, they may end up changing the world!

BARNABAS: SON OF ENCOURAGEMENT

Joseph, a Levite from Cyprus, whom the apostles called Barnabas (which means "son of encouragement"), sold a field he owned and brought the money and put it at the apostles' feet (Acts 4:36-37).

NICKNAMES CAN BE COOL OR CRUEL DEPENDING ON HOW THEY ARE USED. For me, one of the best nicknames ever is the one given to a man by the name of Joseph from Cyprus. The apostles were so taken by this man's kindness and generosity that they gave him a unique name, Barnabas, which means *"son of encouragement."*

The best example of how this "encourager" made an impact on the early church was when he took a young convert by the hand and introduced him to the church at Jerusalem. This convert was well known to the church, not as a friend, but as an enemy. Saul (later Paul) had behaved like a wild beast trying to stamp out this new and fast-growing movement called Christianity (Acts 9:1-2; Galatians 1:13-14). As he traveled to Damascus to hunt down Christians, the Lord revealed Himself to Saul. When word reached Jerusalem about his conversion, you would have thought there would have been shouts of joy, right? Wrong! They were afraid and refused to believe Paul was a convert. They wanted nothing to do with this guy.

Enter Barnabas, the son of encouragement: *"But Barnabas took him and brought him to the apostles. He told them how Saul on his journey had seen the Lord and that the Lord had spoken to him, and how in Damascus he had preached fearlessly in the name of Jesus (Acts 9:27).* Barnabas took him by the hand and said, "Come with me, it's going to be all right." From that moment on, the course of history was changed!

This was not the only time when Barnabas reached out his hand of encouragement (Acts 15:36-40). The history books may not list Barnabas as a world-shaker, but without his hand of encouragement to Paul, we probably wouldn't have three-fourths of the New Testament! He was just an ordinary man who believed everyone should have a second chance in life. We may never preach to thousands on a foreign field or plant a church, but there is one thing we can all do—find someone to encourage.

Do you want to be a hero? Find someone who needs encouragement and offer the person a second chance.

SIMON OF CYRENE: JUST A FACE IN THE CROWD

A certain man from Cyrene, Simon, the father of Alexander
and Rufus, was passing by on his way in from the country,
and they forced him to carry the cross (Mark 15:21).

SIMON DIDN'T ASK TO BE A HERO. THERE ARE CERTAIN TIMES IN LIFE WHEN stepping into circumstances beyond our control forces us to step out of our comfort zone. I doubt Simon ever thought that his experience in Jerusalem would put him at the center of the world's greatest event. Most Bible scholars agree he had traveled hundreds of miles from Africa (modern-day Libya) and like thousands of others, was in Jerusalem to observe Passover. This was probably a once in a lifetime experience, and he was not going to miss it.

His introduction to Jesus wasn't sitting on a hillside hearing the Master teach, or in the Temple watching Jesus challenge the religious establishment. No, the circumstances were brutal and hard to imagine. After a night of torture, Jesus, beaten and bloody, could only physically carry the cross so far (see John 19). Simon was pressed into service. Why was he chosen? Nobody knows for sure; he was just another face in the crowd. I doubt that Simon had any idea that this was the day his life would change forever.

Think about the fact Simon had come to Jerusalem to celebrate Passover and ended up walking with the true Passover Lamb! We will never know the details about his experience with Jesus this side of Heaven. However, I do believe there are indications that it transformed his life. In Mark's version of events, he called him *"Simon, the father of Alexander and Rufus."* This indicates that these two sons of Simon are known to the people to whom Mark is writing. They had become part of the family of God, which indicates that Simon was indeed a Christian (Romans 16:13; Acts 13:1).

What Simon did literally is what we are called to do figuratively: *"Then he said to them all: "Whoever wants to be my disciple must deny themselves and take up their cross daily and follow me"* (Luke 9:23). Crosses were for dying, and the implication for us is to die to ourselves and allow His life and light to shine through us.

Do you want to be a hero? Take up your cross of self-denial and live for Jesus!

SILAS: A TEAM PLAYER

Then the apostles and elders, with the whole church, decided to choose some of their own men and send them to Antioch with Paul and Barnabas. They chose Judas (called Barsabbas) and Silas, men who were leaders among the believers (Acts 15:22).

SOME FOLKS WILL NEVER BE CONTENT WITH JUST BEING A TEAM MEMBER. They view the idea of assisting or helping others succeed as some sort of leadership failure. That kind of attitude is the opposite of Silas (also called Silvanus; 2 Corinthians 1:19) who served faithfully in the early church. As Alex Haley once said, "Anytime you see a turtle up on top of a fencepost, you know he had some help."[27]

Even though Silas was described as one of the leading men of the church in Jerusalem, he is perhaps best known as part of the missionary team headed by Paul. Silas shared some of the most exciting (and painful) experiences of his ministry as he traveled with Paul sharing the Gospel message. It seemed wherever the team landed, one of two things happened—a revival or a riot, and in some cases, both at the same time (see Acts 16). Silas kept going in spite of imprisonment, shipwreck, and persecution. As far as we know, he never complained or threatened to quit the team. The apostle Paul was the one who always seemed to be on top of the fence post, but it was men like Silas who helped him get there!

Paul offered a lot of encouragement about the importance of being a team player. I think it was because he saw a practical demonstration of the team attitude in Silas. To the church at Philippi, he wrote: *"Do nothing out of selfish ambition or vain conceit. Rather, in humility value others above yourselves, not looking to your own interests but each of you to the interests of the others"* (Philippians 2:3-4). He was talking about a "what's in it for me" attitude that will destroy any chance of winning as a team. Silas made his life purpose to serve the Lord by helping others. By doing so, his impact is still being felt today.

Do you want to be a hero? Learn from Silas, and become the best team player you can be.

APOLLOS: WILLING TO LEARN

*Meanwhile a Jew named Apollos, a native of Alexandria, came
to Ephesus. He was a learned man, with a thorough knowledge
of the Scriptures. He had been instructed in the way of the
Lord, and he spoke with great fervor and taught about Jesus
accurately, though he knew only the baptism of John. He began
to speak boldly in the synagogue. When Priscilla and Aquila
heard him, they invited him to their home and explained to
him the way of God more adequately* (Acts 18:24-26).

ONE OF MY FAVORITE HEROES OF THE NEW TESTAMENT WAS A ZEALOUS
young preacher by the name of Apollos. If he was alive today, there is no
doubt he would be preaching the Gospel on every television and radio station
around the globe. He was the ultimate go-getter! But he had a slight problem.
This well-educated and articulate young man was missing critical elements of the
Gospel truth. If someone did not share with him with the complete message of
the Gospel, his ministry would crash and burn before it ever got off the ground.

Enter Priscilla and Aquila. One day while listening to Apollos preach, this
couple realized something was missing. They did what we need in the church
today—they refused to criticize him in public or in private. Instead, they invited
him to their home for a chicken dinner, followed by a time of instruction. He
needed mentoring, and this couple was willing to invest time and energy into his
life. Apollos continued to be a valuable asset to the Kingdom of God because he
was ready to listen and learn from those who had more experience (see 1 Corinthians 1:12; 3:4; 4:6; 16:12).

Even heroes need to be willing to learn what they don't know. Having an
"I know it all" attitude is a fast track to failure in ministry, business, and relationships. What would our churches and businesses look like if we were open
to learning things we don't know and were willing to turn around and share
that knowledge with others? What if we chose to stop the destructive practice
of openly trashing our brothers and sisters and instead decided to invest positive things into their lives. Just because someone doesn't have the knowledge
and experience we have, it doesn't make them incapable of moving to next level
of success.

Do you want to be a hero? Be a mentor to those who are willing to learn what they don't know!

STEPHEN: TRUTH TO POWER

While they were stoning him, Stephen prayed, "Lord Jesus, receive my spirit." Then he fell on his knees and cried out, "Lord, do not hold this sin against them." When he had said this, he fell asleep (Acts 7:59-60).

STEPHEN MIGHT HAVE BEEN THE FIRST IN A LONG LINE OF "UNSUNG" HEROES who filled the pages of Bible history. We don't know much about him. He flashes across the pages of the Bible like a roman candle—brief, brilliant, and gone (Acts 6–7). His name gives away a lot about him: Stephen means "victor's crown," and that pretty much sums up his life. He is merely remembered as a part of the initial group of (servants) deacons and the first Christian martyr of the Church.

How was it possible for this simple deacon to have the courage to speak to the religious establishment with such boldness and power? Acts 6 gives us insight into the qualifications for those first servants of the church, *"Brothers and sisters, choose seven men from among you who are known to be full of the Spirit and wisdom…"* (Acts 6:3). Stephen was filled with the *Holy Spirit and wisdom,* which gave him the supernatural ability to stand before the religious crowd and speak truth to power. In doing so, he paid the ultimate price (see Acts 7:54-60).

If we are going to make a difference in a world filled with opposition to the things of God, we have to call on God every day for a fresh filling of the Holy Spirit and wisdom. We cannot lean on our understanding and limited strength. As a child of God, the Holy Spirit is already resident in our life, and He must have preeminence in all we think or do. We must have men and women (like Stephen) who are not afraid to speak the truth of the Gospel.

I'm not saying we will suffer physical harm, but I am suggesting we must always be ready to give witness to the marvelous things God has done in our lives. *"But in your hearts revere Christ as Lord. Always be prepared to give an answer to everyone who asks you to give the reason for the hope that you have. But do this with gentleness and respect"* (1 Peter 3:15).

Do you want to be a hero? Ask God for daily wisdom and a fresh filling of the Holy Spirit.

DEBORAH: "GOD'S BEE"

*Now Deborah, a prophet, the wife of Lappidoth,
was leading Israel at that time* (Judges 4:4).

THE HEBREW DEFINITION OF THE NAME DEBORAH IS "BEE." SHE WAS THE first and only woman to serve as a judge and leader of the Jews. Serving as a judge equaled the highest office in all of Israel. Just as bees swarm behind a leader, the people of God followed the guidance of this great wartime leader.

It was during the dark days of a national crisis that God chose this unlikely hero to rally the people and turn the nation back to God. Even her general, Barak, refused to lead the army against the oppressive Canaanites unless she went with him (see Judges 4:4-8). The Lord delivered the people, and it was Deborah who was credited with the victory.

We need to learn the lesson of Deborah lest we think her story is confined to the dusty pages of the Old Testament. The same God who used this most unexpected candidate to deliver His people is the same God who can turn your defeat into victory. More often than not, God will use those who would never be considered the strongest or the wisest. You may not read their names in history books, but I guarantee you that Heaven knows who they are.

You may be facing battles and wondering how God could ever use you. You may think you have to become strong and mighty, and then God will be able to use you. Remember, just as God worked through Deborah to give the Israelites the strength to throw off the oppression of the enemy, He promises to provide us victory in the battles we face. It is never by our wisdom or strength that we live an overcoming life—but by His Spirit (see Zechariah 4:6).

Paul said it best in Second Corinthians 12:9-10: *"But he said to me, 'My grace is sufficient for you, for my power is made perfect in weakness.' Therefore, I will boast all the more gladly about my weaknesses, so that Christ's power may rest on me. That is why, for Christ's sake, I delight in weaknesses, in insults, in hardships, in persecutions, in difficulties. For when I am weak, then I am strong."*

Do you want to be a hero? Don't go into battle without God's strength and wisdom to guide you.

LYDIA: ENTREPRENEUR EXTRAORDINAIRE

*One of those listening was a woman from the city of Thyatira named
Lydia, a dealer in purple cloth. She was a worshiper of God. The
Lord opened her heart to respond to Paul's message. When she and
the members of her household were baptized, she invited us to her
home. "If you consider me a believer in the Lord," she said, "come
and stay at my house." And she persuaded us* (Acts 16:14-15).

WE DON'T KNOW MUCH ABOUT LYDIA, EXCEPT SHE WAS A *"DEALER IN
purple cloth."* She was a businesswoman who made and sold expensive
purple fabric, and she was also a worshiper of God. Being a Gentile, she was
limited in her opportunities to hear about the true God; but down by a river-
bank, she listened to the truth of the Gospel message. God opened her heart,
and suddenly Lydia had a new business consultant—the Holy Spirit.

I find it fascinating how Lydia responded to her salvation experience. After
her conversion, the first thing she did was introduce her entire family to the Gospel and then opened her home to the evangelistic team. I see no evidence where
Lydia hesitated or used her business as an excuse for not getting involved or offering assistance the missionary team. Later on, Paul and Silas were thrown into
prison for casting a demon out of a slave girl (see Acts 16:16-34) and after being
beaten and abused, they were released and found their way back to the home of
Lydia (Acts 16:40).

Her story is not found in the Bible because she was a prophet or a preacher, it
is because she was willing to be used by God. Because of her generosity, her home
became the foundation of one of the most significant churches in the New Testament, the church at Philippi. Out of that humble beginning, the message of
Christ would eventually be heard around the world!

You may think that because you don't occupy a pulpit or have a national television ministry God can't use you. Nothing could be further from the truth.
God is looking for more Lydias to become entrepreneur extraordinaires by using
their business success to finance the Kingdom of God. May God give us men and
women who are willing to turn their businesses over to God and let Him determine how the resources can benefit the Gospel message.

Do you want to be a hero? Be available, because God wants to use what you have.

DAVID: A MAN AFTER GOD'S OWN HEART

After removing Saul, he made David their king. God testified concerning him: "I have found David son of Jesse, a man after my own heart; he will do everything I want him to do" (Acts 13:22).

A LOT OF THINGS COULD BE SAID ABOUT DAVID. MUCH HAS BEEN MADE OF his life because he had to deal with a multitude of problems, including some pretty horrible sins. But with all of his faults and troubles, he was still a *man after God's own heart!*

David was a man who lived his life on a spiritual roller coaster. One day he was on the mountaintop ready to conquer the world, and the next day he was walking in the deepest, darkest valley. One reason we can identify with David that is at some point we have been there. One day we are on the mountaintop, and the next day we don't even want to get out of bed. God never intended for us to live a roller coaster existence.

First Kings 15:5 says this about David: *"For David had done what was right in the eyes of the Lord and had not failed to keep any of the Lord's commands all the days of his life—except in the case of Uriah the Hittite."* Notice the little add-on phrase at the end—*"except in the case of Uriah the Hittite."* It is great when that the Lord brags about David, but then He throws in the exception, didn't He? Yes, David blew it. But the good news is God did not cancel out all of the good things that David did; He forgave him and judged his sin in the context of his entire life.

If you want to know what God really thought about David, look no further than Acts 13:22. If God had written him off, I doubt He would have said that he was *"a man after my own heart."* God did not wink at David's sin or forget about it. Once David came to terms with his sin (see Psalms 37 and 51), God forgave and restored him. The Lord is not waiting for us to mess up so He can condemn us. If we are willing to confess our sin, He will do the same for us as He did for David!

Do you want to be a hero? Don't allow your mess-ups, mistakes, or moral breakdowns to keep you from repenting and starting fresh with God.

RAHAB: THE BAD GIRL WHO MADE GOOD

Then Joshua son of Nun secretly sent two spies from
Shittim. "Go, look over the land," he said, "especially
Jericho." So, they went and entered the house of a prostitute
named Rahab and stayed there (Joshua 2:1).

ONE OF THE STRANGEST ENCOUNTERS IN THE BIBLE OCCURRED IN THE SEC-ond chapter of Joshua. The Israelites were heading for the Land of Promise, and the next city on God's "hit list" for them was the city of Jericho. It was an imposing sight, and for such a young army it must have looked impossible. Joshua did the smart thing; he sent two spies into the city to find out useful information. Landing at the house of Rahab the prostitute was divinely inspired. No doubt her reputation was widely known, and city officials would never think enemy spies would be hiding in such a place of ill repute.

She not only hid the spies, but she also lied about their presence to protect them (Joshua 2:2-3). In the following conversation with the two spies, she revealed her true feelings. She then secured a promise of deliverance for herself and her family (see Joshua 9-14). The story ends with the entire city being destroyed and every-one in it, except Rahab and her family.

Here's the real story: God uses imperfect people! Rahab is an example of the kind of person God will use to accomplish His purposes. When God looked at Rahab, He saw something inside her that others couldn't see—a person with flaws and rough edges that could be refined for His use. No, she wasn't perfect, and neither are we. Where did we ever get the idea that God will only use people who live a near-perfect Christian life?

The story of Rahab gives hope for all. It tells me that no matter my past or my present circumstances, if I am willing, God will use me for His glory. So be encouraged today. God will use everyone who makes themselves available and allows Him to do His refining work. He wants to make meaning of our less-than-perfect lives. God had a plan for Rahab, and He has one for you.

Do you want to be a hero? Don't allow others to define who you are in Christ.

ESTHER: THE RIGHT PLACE AT THE RIGHT TIME

For if you remain silent at this time, relief and deliverance for the Jews will arise from another place, but you and your father's family will perish. And who knows but that you have come to your royal position for such a time as this? (Esther 4:14)

GOD NEVER DOES ANYTHING WITHOUT A PURPOSE IN MIND. ALTHOUGH HIS name is never mentioned in the Book of Esther, you can see the hand of God is moving behind the scenes to guide this unfolding drama.

Enter Esther: She was ripped from her family and sent to the palace of a foreign king. Although her beauty opened the door to become the new queen, it was God who gave her favor to occupy such a position of influence. The fact she was a Jew was known only to one man, her uncle, Mordecai. The fate of the Jewish people hung by a thread, and it will take courage to expose the enemy's plot.

As the story unfolds, a wicked man named Haman comes up with a scheme to have the Jews put to death (see Esther 3:8). Mordecai implores Esther to intervene on behalf of the Jews and ask the king to prevent this demonic plan from being realized. Mordecai reminds her, *"And who knows but that you have come to your royal position for such a time as this.* A tragedy was averted because one woman had the courage to function in her place of assignment. Esther could have kept silent. She could have used the excuse that by revealing her identity she would lose her position and her life. She chose to risk it all to save her people.

Has it occurred to you that God has put you on earth at this very moment to accomplish a specific purpose? Don't despise your circumstances, but rather pray for God's assignment to be revealed; who knows what God has in store for you. Instead of complaining, ask for revelation which will lead you to a life of fulfillment. A good start would be asking God to give you influence with those you come in contact with who may not know Christ as their Savior.

Do you want to be a hero? Don't complain, just bloom where you are planted.

Week Twelve

JETHRO: NO JOKING MATTER

Moses' father-in-law replied, "What you are doing is not good. You and these people who come to you will only wear yourselves out. The work is too heavy for you; you cannot handle it alone. Listen now to me and I will give you some advice, and may God be with you…" (Exodus 18:17-19).

I DON'T LIKE IN-LAW JOKES. MOST OF THE ONES I'VE HEARD TEND TO PICTURE our extended family in an unfavorable light. God gave Moses a father-in-law who was no joking matter. You can just imagine how long the days were as Moses tried to judge an entire nation by himself. Jethro watched Moses spend countless hours doing a job that was too much for one man. The wisdom of Jethro was straightforward and to the point. He told Moses he needed to utilize his time and energy more wisely by delegating the work out to trusted men.

Some might say that Jethro was sticking his nose where it didn't belong. Based on the response of Moses, that was not how Jethro's counsel was received. Moses demonstrated a willing heart and a teachable spirit. The most crucial thing Jethro did was show Moses a blind spot that needed correction. He did not want to see the great law-giver go down in flames when it could have been avoided.

We all have blind spots, and that is why we need at least two types of people in our lives: *First*, we need a seasoned veteran like the apostle Paul. Someone who can point out where all the land-mines are and warn us when we are about to blow ourselves up with a hasty decision.

Second, we need someone like Jethro. It may not be a family member, but someone we trust who will come alongside and gently point out areas of weakness that need correction. The writer of Hebrews says, *"No discipline seems pleasant at the time, but painful. Later on, however, it produces a harvest of righteousness and peace for those who have been trained by it"* (Hebrews 12:11). Having people around us who love us enough to tell us the truth is a rare commodity, but an absolute necessity.

Do you want to be a hero? Listen to your Jethro. He may keep you from burning out!

AQUILA AND PRISCILLA: A PATTERN TO FOLLOW

Greet Priscilla and Aquila, my co-workers in Christ Jesus. They risked their lives for me. Not only I but all the churches of the Gentiles are grateful to them. Greet also the church that meets at their house... (Romans 16:3-5).

YES, WE HAVE MET THEM BEFORE. THE CONTRIBUTIONS OF THIS COUPLE TO the Kingdom were so vital they deserved another look. Not only were they responsible for mentoring a young preacher by the name of Apollos (see Acts 18:24-28), but they set a pattern of service that we would be wise to follow.

Aquila and Priscilla were tentmakers by trade, working and living in one of the most corrupt cities in the Roman empire. In any reference to this couple, you will not find them complaining about the fact they were not given the task of preaching or planting churches. It is evident they viewed their assignment as God-given, therefore why create a problem.

In our Scripture, Paul says, *"Greet also the church that meets at their house."* In First Corinthians 16:19 Paul writes, *"Aquila and Priscilla greet you warmly in the Lord, and so does the church that meets at their house."* During those early days of formation, many local churches were meeting in private homes. It was more out of necessity than choice, because violent persecution was breaking out against Christians. This couple was so committed to the work of Christ they were willing to open their home for worship, knowing full well it could cost them their lives.

Toward the end of his ministry, Paul writes in Second Timothy 4:19, *"Greet Priscilla and Aquila and the household of Onesiphorus."* Bible scholars believe this greeting was written some fourteen years after Paul first met this faithful couple. In spite of obstacles, they were still going strong for the cause of Christ. I cannot find one negative word about them in any of Paul's writings. There is no doubt this pair belongs in the long list of Christian heroes who set an example of what ministry ought to be. May it be said of us that we are just as strong and faithful at the end as we were at the beginning.

Do you want to be a hero? Stay consistent and faithful like Aquila and Priscilla.

TIMOTHY: WARNING—
DANGER AHEAD

*Timothy, my son, I am giving you this command in keeping
with the prophecies once made about you, so that by recalling
them you may fight the battle well, holding on to faith and a
good conscience, which some have rejected and so have suffered
shipwreck with regard to the faith* (1 Timothy 1:18-19).

ON JULY 16, 1945, THE USS INDIANAPOLIS SET OUT ON A SECRET MISSION.
She was carrying the first atomic bomb that would later be dropped on the
Japanese city of Hiroshima. On her return trip to the Island of Guam, she was
ripped apart by Japanese torpedoes and in less than twelve minutes sank to the
bottom of the Pacific Ocean. Of the 1,196 souls onboard, 300 sailors went down
with the ship, and for the remaining 900 who went into the water that night, the
horrible ordeal was just beginning. After enduring four days of shark attacks and
dehydration, a Navy reconnaissance plane spotted the men floating in the ocean
and nearby ships rushed to the scene. Only 300 of the original 900 who went
into the water were rescued, constituting the largest loss of life in naval history.[28]

Paul's letter to Timothy was not only a note of encouragement but also a
warning about the danger that lies ahead. He cautioned him not to fall victim
to spiritual shipwreck, as others had done. He names two in particular, *"Among
them are Hymenaeus and Alexander, whom I have handed over to Satan to be
taught not to blaspheme"* (1 Timothy 1:20).

Falling victim to spiritual shipwreck usually starts with a faulty belief system that opens the door to sinful behavior. These two men threw overboard the
very things that establish a solid foundation and a commitment to Jesus Christ,
"faith and a good conscience" (1 Timothy 1:19). Paul reminded Timothy to never
give up the fight of faith. He must hold on to belief in the truth of the Gospel,
which establishes right conduct.

The danger of "spiritual torpedoes" is still very real. The tragedy of the
USS Indianapolis could have been averted. You see, a cable was sent warning
the captain of impending danger. History records that the message was never
delivered. The ship sailed without protection, and as a result, hundreds died.

The message from Paul has been sent to us, and we have been warned of danger ahead—so please take heed!

Do you want to be a hero? Stay alert, there is potential danger everywhere.

JACOB: THE FIX WAS IN

So Jacob was left alone, and a man wrestled with him till daybreak. When the man saw that he could not overpower him, he touched the socket of Jacob's hip so that his hip was wrenched as he wrestled with the man (Genesis 32:24-25).

JACOB HAD ISSUES, LOTS OF ISSUES. IT WAS TIME TO RETURN HOME AND SOMEhow, someway make peace with his brother. He was in a full-blown crisis. He knew if he didn't make things right, his entire family could be wiped from the face of the earth. Instead of running away, again, he spent a sleepless night wrestling with God. If you have ever spent one of those nights, you know what it is like waking up in the morning and feeling like you just went fifteen rounds with Mike Tyson!

Some have suggested this was a fixed fight. After all, do we think a mere human could out-wrestle God? But that's not the issue. The real question is, "What did Jacob do when he was faced with a life-altering circumstance?" He wrestled with God until he received what he needed. He persevered and didn't give up or give in. It was only when daylight came that he realized he had been wrestling with God, and he lived to tell about it!

Jacob's encounter with God affected him in many ways that are too numerous to count. For the rest of his life, he walked with a limp. His limp was a constant reminder that his encounter with God cost him physically. Jacob was also given a new name, Israel (Genesis 32:28). And, his family crisis ended with forgiveness and a fresh start with his brother, Esau.

The transformation of Jacob only happened when he was willing to stay in the fight until the blessing of assurance came. The Lord has some strange tools to bring us to our senses. He will allow pressure and the fire of crisis to get our attention to accomplish His purposes. In my life, it is in those times of trial when I find myself getting closer to Him and opening my heart and my spiritual ears to hear His voice. The secret for Jacob is the same for you. Don't let go until you receive the blessing, the transformation, and the victory!

Do you want to be a hero? Keep struggling until the answer comes.

JOHN THE BAPTIST: POLITICALLY INCORRECT

*For Herod himself had given orders to have John arrested,
and he had him bound and put in prison. He did this
because of Herodias, his brother Philip's wife, whom he had
married. For John had been saying to Herod, "It is not lawful
for you to have your brother's wife" (Mark 6:17-18).*

I F YOU WERE TO ASK JESUS WHO WAS THE MOST SIGNIFICANT PERSON EVER born, what do you think He would say? Would He say Abraham, or perhaps Moses, or some other notable saint? No, Jesus stated that John was the greatest of them all (Matthew 11:11). That was some endorsement!

This forerunner of Jesus (Matthew 11:10) was not afraid to speak truth to the religious establishment or to be politically incorrect. It is obvious he never read *How to Win Friends and Influence People.* He was a man with convictions, and he would not change his views based on circumstances or popular culture.

His life ended not fighting for freedom on some battlefield, but in the palace of a king. His crime was to speak truth to the political power of his day, and it cost him his head. The king was living in open sin with his brother's wife, and John dared to speak against it. In today's society, he would be called many things, not the least of which would be "closed-minded" or "intolerant." You probably know how this story ends. Herodias got her way. She thought the only way to shut him up was to kill him (Mark 6:21-27).

We are living in strange times. What used to be sin is now called a mistake. What once was clear-cut is now being muddied by the slime of political correctness. Jesus said, *"I am the way and the truth and the life. No one comes to the Father except through me"* (John 14:6). Standing up for truth is never popular. Some would argue that Jesus was narrow-minded like His cousin, John. If your goal is to be liked and admired by the world's system, standing for God's truth will never gain you popularity. Holding firm to God's Word will extract a price. If you are not sure about that, just ask John or Jesus or any of the other men and women of God who have paid the ultimate sacrifice for truth.

Do you want to be a hero? Stand for truth, even if the stars fall from Heaven, STAND!

HE'S ALIVE!

Low in the grave he lay, Jesus my Savior,
waiting the coming day, Jesus my Lord!
Up from the grave he arose;
with a mighty triumph o'er his foes;
he arose a victor from the dark domain,
and he lives forever, with his saints to reign.
He arose! He arose! Hallelujah! Christ arose!

ROBERT LOWRY (1826-1899)[29]

BETRAYAL

Now Judas, who betrayed him, knew the place, because Jesus had often met there with his disciples (John 18:2).

HISTORY HAS PRODUCED MANY NAMES THAT ARE SYNONYMOUS WITH EVIL: Stalin, Hitler, Osama bin Laden, Mao Tse-tung, just to name a few. But the most hated and despised name in human history has to be the name Judas. The Bible calls him the betrayer, a devil, a thief, and the son of perdition. Jesus said it would have been better for that man to have never been born.

No one would have ever predicted that one of Christ's inner circle would betray Him. After all, wasn't Judas the one who the other disciples placed in a position of trust and respect? This man who would betray Jesus was at every major event in the ministry of Jesus. He had the privilege of watching the Son of God perform miracles, touch Heaven with His prayers, and yet none of these things moved Judas. This wolf in sheep's clothing seemed so close to the Lord, but as it turned out, he was just a devil in disguise!

The betrayal of Jesus is the most heinous deed ever committed (see John 18:5). This evil man was willing to trade his honor and integrity for thirty pieces of silver. You may be thinking, *I would never do that, I will serve Jesus no matter the cost!* We must be careful not to become so full of pride as to allow sin to take us down the same road that Judas traveled. It is possible, even for Christians, to become so disillusioned with how God works out His purpose that we fall into the same trap. This horrible deed should serve as a warning that there are those who seem close to the Lord Jesus, but by their actions prove they don't love Him. Our words don't mean very much if our actions don't match up.

The forces of hell are on the move while Heaven holds its breath. The devil's messenger has done his deed. Now all that's left to do is make sure the crucifixion takes place. On the surface, it looks like all is lost. But the one thing the forces of evil did not count on—God always has the last word!

THE REST OF THE STORY

Wanting to satisfy the crowd, Pilate released Barabbas to them. He had Jesus flogged, and handed him over to be crucified (Mark 15:15).

PILATE HAD A PROBLEM. HE WAS CAUGHT IN THE MIDDLE OF A RELIGIOUS FIRE-storm. The Bible points out that it was customary for the governor of Rome to set a prisoner free during a feast (Mark 15:6-9). Two men were brought before the crowd. On the one hand was Jesus, and on the other stood Barabbas. Both men were facing execution, but not for the same crime. Jesus had committed no crime except to challenge the religious establishment; Barabbas was involved in a riot and was guilty of murder (Mark 15:7). One was innocent and the other guilty. It looked like a no-brainer for Pilate, so he left it up to the crowd (or as I like to call them, the mob) to decide the fate of these two men.

Keep in mind Pilate was a politician, not theologian, but he knew enough to know Jesus was an innocent man who deserved freedom, not death. But the religious crowd had another opinion and demanded another outcome—Jesus had to die (Matthew 27:22-23). Pilate must have been shocked when after offering the Jews a choice between the two men, they chose Barabbas instead of setting free an innocent man. Pilate knew the truth, but he was more interested in currying favor with the religious establishment than standing for what was right. The crowd made their choice: *"Crucify him!"* (Mark 15:14).

Paul Harvey used to close his daily radio broadcast saying, "Now, for the rest of the story." The rest of the story here is: *nothing is accidental with God.* Don't get distracted by the actions of Pilate or the screaming mob. And we should not look down on Barabbas and puff out our chests that we would never act like this man. Let me remind you that we are all just as sinful as Barabbas. His sin is no worse than our sin. The fact is—we all need the Savior!

First Peter 2:24-25 says, *"'He himself bore our sins' in his body on the cross, so that we might die to sins and live for righteousness; 'by his wounds you have been healed.' For 'you were like sheep going astray,' but now you have returned to the Shepherd and Overseer of your souls."*

ONE OF US

*Who, being in very nature God did not consider equality with
God something to be used to his own advantage; rather, he
made himself nothing by taking the very nature of a servant,
being made in human likeness. And being found in appearance
as a man, he humbled himself by becoming obedient to
death—even death on a cross!* (Philippians 2:6-8)

WHEN JESUS CAME INTO THE WORLD, HE LAID ASIDE HIS HEAVENLY GARment of glory and became one of us. Jesus never used divine privileges for Himself. He always turned His attention to others. When satan tempted Him in the wilderness, He refused to demonstrate the power that was at His disposal. He met the enemy as a man using the power of the sword of the Spirit; the Word of God!

In every way, Jesus identified with humanity. From the moment of His birth until His death on the cross, every aspect of His ministry demonstrated His humility. He was born in a borrowed stable and buried in a borrowed tomb. Jesus Christ who was Lord of the universe became a servant of all to make way for sinful humanity to know abundant life.

Paul said Jesus took the final step of condescension as He *"humbled himself by becoming obedient to death—even death on a cross!"* In Psalm 22:6, the psalmist described what Jesus must have felt as He hung on the cross: *"But I am a worm and not a man, scorned by everyone, despised by the people."* In our modern culture, we tend to think of the cross as something that sits on top of a church, or as an adornment on a bracelet. We have missed the point by a thousand miles. In His day when someone was sentenced to die on the cross, it was the most gruesome and horrible death imaginable. It was considered the final act of shame for a wasted life!

But thank God Paul had more to say. He did not leave Jesus hanging on the cross. The very next statement is Paul's offering of his doxology of praise:

*"Therefore God exalted him to the highest place and gave him the name
that is above every name, that at the name of Jesus every knee should
bow, in heaven and on earth and under the earth, and every tongue*

acknowledge that Jesus Christ is Lord, to the glory of God the Father" (Philippians 2:9-11).

All I can say is, HALLELUJAH! WHAT A SAVIOR!

AT THE CROSS

Carrying his own cross, he went out to the place of the
Skull (which in Aramaic is called Golgotha). There they
crucified him, and with him two others—one on each
side and Jesus in the middle (John 19:17-18).

THE CROSS OF JESUS CHRIST IS THE FOCAL POINT OF THE CHRISTIAN FAITH. In spite of all that satan and his demons attempted to do, when Jesus died on the cross, it spelled victory over death, hell, and the grave—and it sealed the destiny of evil! Phillips Brooks, speaking about that day said: "We may say that on the first Good Friday afternoon was completed that great act by which light conquered darkness and goodness conquered sin. That is the wonder of our Saviour's crucifixion."[30]

Without the work of the cross there would be no empty tomb, and without an empty tomb, there would be no salvation or hope for sinners. Paul said, *"And if Christ has not been raised, your faith is futile; you are still in your sins. Then those also who have fallen asleep in Christ are lost. If only for this life we have hope in Christ, we are of all people most to be pitied"* (1 Corinthians 15:17-19). The Father's love for lost humans was revealed by offering His Son as the perfect sacrifice. Whatever you may be facing today, I want you to know it has been covered by the work of the cross. Are you suffering from unconfessed sin, guilt, depression, or hate? Whatever it may be, there is hope and healing at the cross of Christ.

As I write this today, one of my favorite hymns is ringing in my heart. I don't care how many times I've heard or have sung this precious hymn, it still moves me to rejoice in the cross of Christ. Let the words sink deeply into your heart:

Alas! And did my Savior bleed, and did my Sov'reign die?
Would He devote that sacred head for such a worm as I?
Was it for crimes that I had done He groaned upon the tree?
Amazing pity! Grace unknown! And love beyond degree!
At the cross, at the cross where I first saw the light, and
the burden of my heart rolled away, it was there by faith I
received my sight, and now I am happy all the day![31]

LAST WORDS

When they came to the place called the Skull, they crucified
him there, along with the criminals—one on his right,
the other on his left. Jesus said, "Father, forgive them, for
they do not know what they are doing." And they divided
up his clothes by casting lots (Luke 23:33-34).

NOT EVERYONE HAS AN OPPORTUNITY TO GIVE A FINAL STATEMENT OR SPEAK a last word at the moment of death. I would like to think that when my time comes, I will be surrounded by family and friends, laying on some silk sheets—but there is no guarantee any of that will happen. Fortunately for us, history has preserved some of the more famous last words of believers as well as non-believers.

For example, the apostle Paul said, *"For I am already being poured out like a drink offering, and the time for my departure is near. I have fought the good fight, I have finished the race, I have kept the faith"* (2 Timothy 4:6-7). And then there was the great evangelist, D. L. Moody, who on his deathbed said, *"Is this dying? Why this is bliss. There is no valley. I have been within the gates. I see Earth receding, and heaven is opening. God is calling me."³²*

Then there was Aaron Burr. He served as Vice President of the United States under Thomas Jefferson, and it is likely he would have become no more than a historical footnote had he not murdered Alexander Hamilton in a duel. It was common knowledge that Burr proclaimed himself to be an atheist, and as such lived his life devoid of biblical standards. As Burr lay dying, his friend, the Reverend P.J. Van Pelt, made an effort to get him to state that there was a God. Burr's last words were: *"On that subject I am coy."³³*

In the following pages, we will examine the most famous last words ever spoken. Seven times Jesus spoke from the cross, and each statement is pregnant with meaning. While the forces of hell were celebrating His death, the Father was doing His greatest work, the work of redemption. From the world's point of view, the death of Christ on the cross was a crushing defeat, but from Heaven's perspective, a pathway to the throne of God was opened by the shed blood of Jesus (see Ephesians 1:7).

"FATHER, FORGIVE THEM"

Jesus said, "Father, forgive them, for they do not know what they are doing." And they divided up his clothes by casting lots (Luke 23:34).

As Jesus was dying on the cross, He spoke seven times. Each statement is filled with significance. It was not unusual to hear dying men cry out in pain and agony, but to hear someone pray a prayer of forgiveness for the very ones who were causing the pain was quite shocking.

The Roman culture of the day was not one of forgiveness, but of revenge. The mindset was, *"eye for eye, tooth for tooth"* (see Exodus 21:24). Jesus demonstrated something they had never seen or heard before. He was at His darkest hour, betrayed by His disciples, and hounded by a pack of demonic dogs who cheered His suffering. He could have prayed, "Father rescue Me," but He didn't. He could have prayed, "Father, rain fire from Heaven and destroy them." But He didn't. He simply prayed a prayer of forgiveness.

The phrase, *"Father, forgive them,"* is seen in the Greek language as repetition. He repeated the prayer over and over again. As they drove spikes into His hands and feet, He prayed, "Father, forgive them." When they lifted the wooden beam, and dropped it into a hole in the ground, our Savior prayed, "Father, forgive them." As He hung between two thieves, crucified as a common criminal, He repeatedly prayed, *"Father, forgive them."*

Don't misunderstand His prayer. He was not excusing sin or justifying the actions of those around the cross. Jesus was taking on all debt of sin, even those who were responsible for putting Him to death. He was, the Lamb slain from the foundation of the world (see John 1:29); therefore, He could in essence say, *"Father, forgive them, and put their sins on My account!"*

One of the most challenging and difficult things for us to do is forgive others who have hurt or mistreated us. Our first reaction is to hurt back and harbor an unforgiving spirit against them. You may be hurting and feeling betrayed today. When you to get to the place of understanding that God does care and His purpose will be revealed, then you too can look into the Father's face and declare, "Father, forgive them, for they don't know what they're doing."

"WITH ME IN PARADISE"

*One of the criminals who hung there hurled insults at him:
"Aren't you the Messiah? Save yourself and us!" But the other
criminal rebuked him. "Don't you fear God," he said, "since
you are under the same sentence? We are punished justly, for
we are getting what our deeds deserve. But this man has done
nothing wrong." Then he said, "Jesus, remember me when you
come into your kingdom." Jesus answered him, "Truly I tell you,
today you will be with me in paradise"* (Luke 23:39-43).

JESUS SPEAKS FOR THE SECOND TIME. IN HIS FIRST STATEMENT, HE STOOD IN the gap for all sinners as He prayed a prayer forgiveness. And now He speaks a word of salvation to one man who was dying next to Him.

We tend to overlook that three men were crucified. Two thieves, one on either side of an innocent Man. Both thieves appealed to Jesus. On one side an appeal was made to be saved by force, *"Aren't you the Messiah? Save yourself and us!"* On the other side an appeal was to be saved by faith, *"Then he said, 'Jesus, remember me when you come into your kingdom.'"*

Both thieves could hear the crowd as they railed at Jesus. One of the dying men chose to join with the crowd and hurl insults (see Luke 23:35-37). He hoped against hope that this "Messiah" could do something to save them. He was not interested in salvation but an escape. Maybe he thought by goading Jesus he could push Him into action. All he got was a rebuke from his partner in crime (Luke 23:40).

The salvation of the dying thief has been a source of conversation for centuries. I have heard people say they were going to wait, like the thief on the cross, until the last minute to give their heart to Jesus. My question and comment to them, "How do you know you will have the opportunity to wait until the last minute? Your life could end without warning, and without an opportunity to speak."

This much I know. When the dying thief admitted his sin and asked Jesus to remember him, he received the gift of eternal life. Was he saved? I do believe he was, but don't take my word for it. Jesus can speak for Himself. *"Jesus answered him, 'Truly I tell you, today you will be with me in paradise.'"*

"HERE IS YOUR SON... HERE IS YOUR MOTHER"

Near the cross of Jesus stood his mother, his mother's sister, Mary the wife of Clopas, and Mary Magdalene. When Jesus saw his mother there, and the disciple whom he loved standing nearby, he said to her, "Woman, here is your son," and to the disciple, "Here is your mother." From that time on, this disciple took her into his home (John 19:25-27).

THE FIRST THREE STATEMENTS JESUS MADE FROM THE CROSS SHOWED CONcern for others. In the first, He prayed for those who were responsible for His death. In the second, He lifted a dying thief from the pit of hell to be with Him in paradise. Now Jesus shows compassion to a handful of faithful followers, which included His mother.

Think about it for a moment. Jesus was demonstrating the love of the Father, even in His dying moments. Maybe He looked down to see Mary Magdalene and remembered the day she was delivered from seven demons (see Luke 8:2). But the focus is on His mother and the disciple standing next to her. Most, if not all, Bible scholars agree this disciple was John. Jesus is establishing a new relationship with His mother as He looked at both of them and said, *"Woman, here is your son," and to the disciple, "Here is your mother."*

I cannot grasp the pain Mary felt as she watched her Son die such a cruel death and in full view of everyone (see Acts 26:19-26). When Simeon prophesied to her in Luke 2:35, I doubt he understood the full meaning of his words: *"so that the thoughts of many hearts will be revealed. And a sword will pierce your own soul too."* The sword of fulfilled prophecy is now stabbing her heart, and like any mother, the grief is overwhelming.

Jesus is making sure His mother is taken care of and He entrusted John to ensure she would have a loving home. Jesus is no longer just a Son, now He is her Lord and Savior. Did Mary leave the scene of the crucifixion bitter and defeated? Did she turn her back on God? No, because the next mention of Mary is found in Acts 1:14, as she gathered with the other disciples to wait for the baptism of the Holy Spirit. She was a charter member of the very first church in Jerusalem!

"MY GOD, MY GOD, WHY HAVE YOU FORSAKEN ME?"

From noon until three in the afternoon darkness came over all the land. About three in the afternoon Jesus cried out in a loud voice, "Eli, Eli, lemasabachthani?" (which means "My God, my God, why have you forsaken me?") (Matthew 27:45-46).

I DON'T CLAIM TO HAVE ALL THE ANSWERS TO EVERY MYSTERY IN THE BIBLE, especially this one. For two thousand years, people have debated what Jesus meant when He uttered this fourth statement from the cross. I once heard a renowned Bible teacher say, "If you try to explain this cry of Jesus you may lose your mind; but if you try to explain it away, you will lose your soul!" Or, as Russell Bradley Jones observed, "None of the ready explanations of this extraordinary cry satisfy us."[34]

Instead of trying to give you the opinions of others, I will merely give you what this mystery means to me. From noon until three in the afternoon, darkness enveloped the land. At the pinnacle of darkness, Jesus cried out, *"My God, my God, why have you forsaken me?"* Jesus was willing to go into the darkness of hell to reclaim a poor lost sinner like me and you. When Jesus hung on the cross, He was bearing the burden of the sins of the world. He was dying in our place. Hebrews 13:11-12 tells us, *"The high priest carries the blood of animals into the Most Holy Place as a sin offering, but the bodies are burned outside the camp. And so Jesus also suffered outside the city gate to make the people holy through his own blood."*

It also means that Jesus was willing to be separated from the fellowship of His Father, for a brief time, so that we would never have to know the feeling of separation. In the Old Testament, on the Day of Atonement, it was the duty of the high priest to go behind the veil and offer blood on the Mercy Seat. He went in alone so no one could see what he was doing. It was a sacred act between the high priest and God.

On the cross, our High Priest—Jesus—was carrying out the great work of redemption, so God shut out prying eyes as the sacred work of redemption was being accomplished. Hebrews 2:17 says, *"For this reason he had to be made like them, fully human in every way, in order that he might become a merciful and faithful high priest in service to God, and that he might make atonement for the sins of the people."*

"I THIRST"

Later, knowing that everything had now been finished, and so that Scripture would be fulfilled, Jesus said, "I am thirsty" (John 19:28).

AS JOHN RECORDED THE FIFTH STATEMENT OF JESUS FROM THE CROSS, *"I AM thirsty,"* his complete statement reads, *"knowing that everything had now been finished, and so that Scripture would be fulfilled."* I can only interpret those words to mean Jesus was obedient to His assignment (see Luke 19:10). He had just endured three hours of darkness in which He offered Himself as a sacrifice for our sins. We will never know, on this side of Heaven, all that transpired between Father and Son. It was covered by darkness and shrouded in mystery. Suffice it to say the work of redemption was complete. And, in the process, every prophetic word spoken about His death was fulfilled (see Psalm 22:16; 31:5-11; 41:9; 35:11; Isaiah 53:7). Even the smallest detail was outlined by the psalmist:

> *You know how I am scorned, disgraced and shamed; all my enemies are before you. Scorn has broken my heart and has left me helpless; I looked for sympathy, but there was none, for comforters, but I found none. They put gall in my food and gave me vinegar for my thirst* (Psalm 69:19-21).

For Jesus to declare His thirst reflected His humanity, but it did not diminish His divinity. He was fully God and fully man. Make no mistake the suffering of Jesus was real, the pain horrific, and His thirst expected. Declaring His thirst is the only time He uttered a word about His physical needs.

His word of thirst is also a prophetic picture of sinful humanity. Jesus told the woman at the well that, *"Everyone who drinks this water will be thirsty again, but whoever drinks the water I give them will never thirst. Indeed, the water I give them will become in them a spring of water welling up to eternal life"* (John 4:13-14). He spoke of living water again in John 7:37-38, *"On the last and greatest day of the festival, Jesus stood and said in a loud voice, 'Let anyone who is thirsty come to me and drink. Whoever believes in me, as Scripture has said, rivers of living water will flow from within them.'"* My friend, the wells of the world will never satisfy anyone's thirsty soul. It is only to be found in Jesus Christ (see Jeremiah 2:13).

"IT IS FINISHED"

When he had received the drink, Jesus said, "It is finished." With that, he bowed his head and gave up his spirit (John 19:30).

THE ANCIENT GREEK LANGUAGE IS KNOWN FOR ITS BEAUTY AND SIMPLICITY. The phrase, "It is finished," is one ten-letter word in Greek; *tetelestai,* which means "complete." For over two thousand years, the enemies of the cross have tried to disguise this cry of victory from the lips of Jesus. A cover-up of cosmic proportions has taken place. Never in history has a spoken word had more potential for victory and more cause for celebration than this declaration of Christ.

Bible.org cites The Greek-English lexicon by Moulton and Milligan: "Receipts are often introduced by the phrase [sic] *tetelestai,* usually written in an abbreviated manner. The connection between receipts and what Christ accomplished would have been quite clear to John's Greek-speaking readership; it would be unmistakable that Jesus Christ had died to pay for their sins."[35]

The use of the word *tetelestai* or "finished," as it relates to debt is the perfect word to describe what Christ accomplished at Calvary. As that great old hymn says in its refrain, *"Jesus paid it all, all to him to him I owe; Sin had left a crimson stain, He wash'd it white as snow."*[36] The day you gave your heart to Jesus Christ was the day God stamped PAID on the debt that was owed. Good works could not erase the stain of sin, neither could any righteous deeds that we might perform satisfy the debt. It would take a perfect sacrifice.

By accepting Christ, we acknowledge our sin and receive forgiveness based on the shed blood of the spotless Lamb of God!

But God demonstrates his own love for us in this: While we were still sinners, Christ died for us (Romans 5:8).

God made him who had no sin to be sin for us, so that in him we might become the righteousness of God (2 Corinthians 5:21).

When they hurled their insults at him, he did not retaliate; when he suffered, he made no threats. Instead, he entrusted himself to him who judges justly. "He himself bore our sins" in his body on the cross, so that we might die to sins and live for righteousness; "by his wounds you have been healed." (1 Peter 2:23-24).

HE BREATHED HIS LAST BREATH

Jesus called out with a loud voice, "Father, into your hands I commit my spirit." When he had said this, he breathed his last (Luke 23:46).

THE LAST STATEMENT OF JESUS FROM THE CROSS HAS BEEN DISPUTED AND debated for many years. Was His death real, or fake? Some of us are old enough to remember when liberal theologians began to propagate the theory that Jesus did not actually die on the cross. One of the most popular was called the "swoon" theory. This so-called interpretation of the death of Jesus said when they placed Him in the tomb He was not really dead. He had merely "swooned" or "fainted" on the cross. It was the cool damp atmosphere of the tomb that revived Him. Really?

Of course, if He didn't die, then the resurrection appearances were nothing more than the exercises of a charlatan! This and all other lies about the death, burial, and resurrection of Jesus was satan's way of obscuring the real truth of what transpired when Jesus breathed His last breath. His death was real, not a fake; and His death was a victory, not a defeat! (see John 10:17-18).

What does it mean for us today?

Satan was defeated: *"The one who does what is sinful is of the devil, because the devil has been sinning from the beginning. The reason the Son of God appeared was to destroy the devil's work"* (1 John 3:8). From the beginning, satan had tried to stop God's plan of redemption. The crucifixion was his last attempt, and it failed.

The sting of death has been removed: *"Since the children have flesh and blood, he too shared in their humanity so that by his death he might break the power of him who holds the power of death—that is, the devil—and free those who all their lives were held in slavery by their fear of death"* (Hebrews 2:14-15).

We do not have to face the enemy alone: *"and teaching them to obey everything I have commanded you. And surely I am with you always, to the very end of the age"* (Matthew 28:20). His death assures us that no matter what the enemy may do, we have His power living within us. We are more than conquerors through Him who loves us and gave Himself for us! (see Romans 8:30).

AFTERMATH

And when Jesus had cried out again in a loud voice, he gave up his spirit. At that moment, the curtain of the temple was torn in two from top to bottom. The earth shook, the rocks split and the tombs broke open. The bodies of many holy people who had died were raised to life. They came out of the tombs after Jesus' resurrection and went into the holy city and appeared to many people (Matthew 27:50-53).

WHEN JESUS WILLINGLY LAID DOWN HIS LIFE, THE ATMOSPHERE WAS charged with miracles. God sent an electric shockwave of signs and wonders throughout His creation. Matthew recorded the aftermath, or should I say the eternal effects of the cross.

1. *The curtain of the temple was torn from top to bottom:* The curtain in the Temple was a barrier that separated sinful humankind from a holy God. When Jesus died, the barrier was torn, and the Holy of Holies was exposed for all to see. A pathway of access was open for sinful humanity to be forgiven and enjoy fellowship with the Father. Jesus paid the price so there would never again be a need for Old Testament sacrifices: *"Day after day every priest stands and performs his religious duties; again and again he offers the same sacrifices, which can never take away sins. But when this priest had offered for all time one sacrifice for sins, he sat down at the right hand of God"* (Hebrews 10:11-12).

2. *There was an earthquake:* The earthquake was a physical event, but it pictured a spiritual truth. When God gave the law to Moses, it was accompanied by an earthquake (see Exodus 19:16-19). Just as the quake on Mount Sinai established the "law of God" and put fear in the people, the earthquake on Calvary shouted to the universe the righteous law of God had been fulfilled (see Romans 10:4; 2 Corinthians 1:20; Hebrews 9:12). Once and for all the need for the shedding of blood was finished!

3. *The graves were opened, and many saints were resurrected:* Who were they? I have no clue, except what we are told in Scripture. Here is what I do know: Jesus won the victory over sin and death. The resurrection of the saints was another physical sign of spiritual truth. Just as the earth could no longer hold on to these precious ones, the power of death can no longer hold on to the children of God!

A SOLDIER'S CONFESSION

*When the centurion and those with him who were guarding Jesus
saw the earthquake and all that had happened, they were terrified,
and exclaimed, "Surely he was the Son of God!"* (Matthew 27:54)

WE DON'T KNOW THE CENTURION'S NAME OR WHATEVER BECAME OF HIM.
Being around men who were dying, whether on a distant battlefield or meting out punishment on behalf of the emperor, was nothing new. He and his band of soldiers were professionals doing their job. If you asked them how they felt, I'm sure they would tell you it was nothing personal. Three of four Gospel accounts recorded the centurion's confession (see Matthew 27:54; Mark 15:39; Luke 23:47).

I find it interesting that while the centurion was confessing the deity of Christ, His disciples were in hiding. These brave men who saw and heard the ministry of Jesus up close and personal were now cowering like frightened children. Scripture points out only a handful of women (including His mother) and one disciple (John) stayed close to cross. So much for loyalty.

What was it about this death that enlisted such a confession from the centurion? Was it the miracles that occurred as soon as Jesus commended His Spirit to the Father? Maybe so, but in Jesus, he saw something he had never seen before. Jesus displayed a character that was foreign to him. It was the display of the Divine, not the nature of a common criminal.

- Jesus prayed for His enemies to be forgiven.
- Jesus lifted a dying thief out of the pit of hell and took him to paradise.
- Jesus spoke words of compassion and concern to His mother.
- Jesus never asked His father to bring down judgment.

The centurion confessed something that all people must confess in order to be saved—the true identity of Jesus Christ. Confession is the central tenant of the Christian faith. Paul says in Romans 10:9-10: *"If you declare with your mouth, 'Jesus is Lord,' and believe in your heart that God raised him from the dead, you will be saved. For it is with your heart that you believe and are justified, and it is with your mouth that you profess your faith and are saved."* Have you confessed Him to be your Lord and Savior? If not, do it today!

COME AND SEE

*The angel said to the women, "Do not be afraid, for I
know that you are looking for Jesus, who was crucified.
He is not here; he has risen, just as he said. Come and
see the place where he lay"* (Matthew 28:5-6).

ON THAT FIRST EASTER MORNING, TWO WOMEN WENT TO THE TOMB OF Jesus. They approached with hearts heavy with sadness and disappointment. All they wanted was to see Jesus one last time and to anoint His body (see Luke 24:1). As they neared the entrance to the tomb, they were shocked to see the stone removed, and even more astounded to receive a message from an angel. His message was simple, *"Come and see the place where he lay."*

The angel's message is just as relevant today as it was two thousand years ago. The implication was *personal.* The angel was implying, *"You come and see."* Christianity is not built on a second-hand message. To be a follower of Christ is to have a personal relationship with Him. Just because your parents took you to church when you were a baby does not automatically make you a Christian. Nor does being born in a Christian home make you a Christian any more than being born in a garage makes you a car. It doesn't work that way; it's personal (see John 3:1-15).

The angel's message was not only *personal,* it was also *transformational.* The resurrection of Christ was the only event that could turn the disappointment of Mary, the doubt of Thomas, and the denial of Peter into a raging fire of hope and renewal! When people have a personal encounter with the risen Christ, it changes them forever. Paul says it best in Second Corinthians 5:17, *"Therefore, if anyone is in Christ, the new creation has come: The old has gone, the new is here!"* The difference between Christianity and other religious expressions is the resurrection of its leader. Whether it was Muhammad, Buddha, Confucius, or any other person who started a religious movement, they all have one thing in common—they died and are still dead!

The foundation of the Christian faith stands or falls on the resurrection of Christ. The message of the first century church is the same message the world needs to hear in the twenty-first century: *"Through him you believe in God, who raised him from the dead and glorified him, and so your faith and hope are in God"* (1 Peter 1:21).

HIDING BEHIND CLOSED DOORS

*On the evening of that first day of the week, when the disciples
were together, with the doors locked for fear of the Jewish leaders,
Jesus came and stood among them and said, "Peace be with you!"
After he said this, he showed them his hands and side. The disciples
were overjoyed when they saw the Lord* (John 20:19-20).

THIS NOT WHAT WE EXPECTED TO SEE—A FRIGHTENED CHURCH HIDING
behind closed doors! What part of the teachings of Jesus did they not understand? On more than one occasion He told them He would suffer and die, and
then be raised from the dead. For instance, in Matthew 16:21 we are told, *"From
that time on Jesus began to explain to his disciples that he must go to Jerusalem and
suffer many things at the hands of the elders, the chief priests and the teachers of the
law, and that he must be killed and on the third day be raised to life."*

Here was their problem; they had heard about the resurrection, but had not
seen the Lord for themselves. But, all of that changed when Jesus walked into the
room. His very presence did for them what no religious doctrine could ever do.

His presence dispelled their fear and bestowed peace. Fear and faith cannot coex-
ist in the same heart. Instead of shouting for joy over the fact of the resurrection,
they were hiding from the Jewish authorities. They saw what happened to Jesus
and they did not want the same fate. The presence of Jesus breaks the power of
fear (see Revelation 1:17-18). In an instant, His presence replaced the fear and gave
them peace. In John 14:27 Jesus says, *"Peace I leave with you; my peace I give you.
I do not give to you as the world gives. Do not let your hearts be troubled and do not
be afraid."*

Just look at the result of His presence, *"The disciples were overjoyed when they
saw the Lord."* My friend, if you are allowing fear to rob you of peace and joy, then
it is time to slow down long enough to get back into the presence of the Lord. As
the psalmist declares: *"You make known to me the path of life; you will fill me with
joy in your presence, with eternal pleasures at your right hand"* (Psalm 16:11).

MISSING IN ACTION

*Now Thomas (also known as Didymus), one of the Twelve, was not
with the disciples when Jesus came. So the other disciples told him,
"We have seen the Lord!" But he said to them, "Unless I see the nail
marks in his hands and put my finger where the nails were, and
put my hand into his side, I will not believe"* (John 20:24-25).

THOMAS IS A CASE STUDY IN DOUBT. I BELIEVE JOHN ADDED THIS ACCOUNT to his Gospel so that we may know what to do when doubt attacks our mind. We tend to think the disciples of Jesus were superheroes who never faced spiritual challenges. Nothing could be further from the truth. They were afflicted with the same issues we face—fear and doubt, just to name two of the many.

Doubt is the opposite of faith. Doubt will paralyze you from moving forward; faith will guide you even when the way is unclear. Doubt is proclaiming defeat; faith will triumph even when faced with overwhelming odds. Doubt will destroy hope; faith makes you come alive.

It has been suggested that Thomas was by nature a pessimistic individual (see John 14:5). He knew Jesus had been crucified and buried in a borrowed tomb. Maybe he thought, like others, it was all over. All of his hopes and dreams lie buried with Jesus, so what's the point of going on?

Thomas was the only one missing the first time Jesus met with the disciples. And, Thomas was the only one who doubted the second time they met. Do you see a pattern here? He wasn't where he should have been, and as a result, he missed out on one of the greatest experiences of history—hearing and seeing the resurrected Lord! Instead of rejoicing with the other disciples, all Thomas had to go on was what they were telling him. He refused to believe Jesus was alive and chose to live in the loneliness of doubt instead of the joy of faith.

The story of Thomas has a happy ending. His doubt was turned into certainty when he had a face-to-face encounter with Jesus. Are you plagued with doubt? Could it be because you have isolated yourself from other believers? The Christian life was never meant to be lived in a vacuum. When you and I are in fellowship with the Lord, there will be a desire to be in fellowship with other believers. How will your story end?

THE SIDE EFFECTS OF DOUBT

A week later his disciples were in the house again, and Thomas was with them. Though the doors were locked, Jesus came and stood among them and said, "Peace be with you!" Then he said to Thomas, "Put your finger here; see my hands. Reach out your hand and put it into my side. Stop doubting and believe." Thomas said to him, "My Lord and my God!" Then Jesus told him, "Because you have seen me, you have believed; blessed are those who have not seen and yet have believed" (John 20:26-29).

DON'T BE TOO HARD ON THOMAS FOR HAVING DOUBTS. I DON'T KNOW OF one person who at one time or the other hasn't had doubts. The issue is not whether we will have them, but what will we do about it.

Living with unresolved doubts has several side effects:

1. *There is a loss of happiness.* The first time, after the resurrection, Jesus met with the disciples, the atmosphere was filled with rejoicing (see John 20:19-20). The only one who missed out was Thomas. While the others were filled with joy, Thomas was filled with doubt. Doubt is a joy thief lurking in the shadows of your heart. If left unexposed to the light of the resurrected Christ, it will steal your happiness.

2. *There is the loss of helpfulness.* For a solid week, Thomas had no witness to give for Christ. Maybe that is the reason why so many so-called Christians do not give witness to Jesus today. Living with nagging doubt is like living with spiritual lockjaw. When certainty replaces doubt, we have no problem with our witness for Christ (see Psalm 66:16; 71:15-18; 119:46).

3. *There is a loss of holiness.* Thomas' doubt started dictating how Jesus must act: *"Unless I see the nail marks in his hands and put my finger where the nails were, and put my hand into his side, I will not believe."* Thomas was saying, "seeing is believing." Jesus said no, "believing is seeing." It is never wise to dictate to the Lord what He must do.

Thank God this event had a positive ending. Jesus was not afraid of Thomas' doubts but instead allowed Thomas to touch and see for himself that He was indeed the resurrected Christ. The best way to resolve uncertainty is to have a look at Calvary and remember what He did for you. The best cure for the side effects of doubt is a personal encounter with Jesus!

HOLY HEARTBURN

*Now that same day two of them were going to a village called
Emmaus, about seven miles from Jerusalem. They were
talking with each other about everything that had happened.
As they talked and discussed these things with each other,
Jesus himself came up and walked along with them; but
they were kept from recognizing him* (Luke 24:13-16).

THESE TWO DISCIPLES OF JESUS WERE TRAVELING BACK TO THEIR HOME. THE
scene pictured in Luke 24 is not what you would expect. Instead of men
filled with joy, the opposite was true. They were sad, not glad. When Jesus joined
the conversation, *"He asked them, 'What are you discussing together as you walk
along?' They stood still, their faces downcast"* (Luke 24:17).

They had the facts of the resurrection, but it did not produce the fire of the resurrection! They were there when Jesus was nailed to a cross. They saw the sights
and heard the sounds of the demonic madness that attended the crucifixion.
And, no doubt these two knew of earlier prophecies concerning the resurrection.
They even admitted knowing about the reports of an empty tomb. The good
news was spreading through Jerusalem like a raging forest fire.

I find it interesting that on the road to Emmaus the disciples expressed confusion (Luke 24:14-15), sadness (Luke 24:17), and doubt (Luke 24:19-21). But, after
being taught by Christ (Luke 24:25-27), they headed back to Jerusalem with
burning hearts and testimonies that Jesus was indeed alive (Luke 24:32-35).

These disciples remind me of many who claim to be Christians. Paul says in
Philippians 3:10, *"I want to know Christ—yes, to know the power of his resurrection
and participation in his sufferings, becoming like him in his death."* This should be the
desire of all who claim to be followers of Christ. It is great to know all the facts, but
facts alone will not produce the fire of commitment. Facts alone will not provide
testimony of God's grace and forgiveness. And, facts alone will not create courage
to witness to a lost and dying world. We need more than facts; we need *fire!*

These men were in desperate need of a baptism of holy fire. And that is exactly
what they received. Luke 24:32 says: *"They asked each other, 'Were not our hearts
burning within us while he talked with us on the road and opened the Scriptures
to us?'"*

NO RESURRECTION—NO GOSPEL

By this gospel you are saved, if you hold firmly to the word I preached to you. Otherwise, you have believed in vain. For what I received I passed on to you as of first importance: that Christ died for our sins according to the Scriptures, that he was buried, that he was raised on the third day according to the Scriptures (1 Corinthians 15:2-4).

IN PAUL'S DAY, SOME SAID THE RESURRECTION WAS OF LITTLE IMPORTANCE. They said to eat, drink, and be merry and the rest will take care of itself. To that kind of thinking, Paul said rubbish! The resurrection of Christ is the underpinning of the Christian faith. Leaving out the heart of the Gospel is like cutting out someone's heart. Without the heart, all that remains is a lifeless form.

Paul outlined the Gospel message:

1. *Christ died for our sins:* The death of Jesus was not the death of a martyr or a common criminal. He had committed no crime; hence, He was an innocent man, totally undeserving of death. He died for our sins and not for His own. Isaiah 53:5 tells us, *"But he was pierced for our transgressions, he was crushed for our iniquities; the punishment that brought us peace was on him, and by his wounds we are healed."* Jesus willingly gave His life for us. He took the punishment that was meant for us and died in our place.

2. *He was buried:* The Word teaches that when Jesus was buried, our sins were placed in the tomb with Him, and when He came out of the grave our sins were left behind (see Romans 6:6-7). The day you confessed Jesus Christ as Lord is the day He separated your sins as far as the East is from the West (see Psalm 103:12).

3. *He was raised on the third day according to the Scriptures:* If we only have the first two parts of the Gospel, we still do not have a complete message. Here is the heart of the matter: after three days Jesus walked out of the tomb and is *alive* forevermore! He is just as much alive today as He was two thousand years ago.

It is the full Gospel message, and it is the only message that transforms the human heart. If you say you are a Christian, you are professing the death, burial, and resurrection of Christ. Anything else is pure fantasy!

BREAKING POINT

BROKEN AND SPILLED OUT

One day a plain village woman
Driven by love for her Lord
Recklessly poured out a valuable essence
Disregarding the scorn
And once it was broken and spilled out
A fragrance filled all the room
Like a pris'ner released from his shackles
Like a spirit set free from the tomb
Broken and spilled out
Just for love of you Jesus
My most precious treasure
Lavished on Thee
Broken and spilled out
And poured at Your feet
In sweet abandon
Let me be spilled out
And used up for thee
STEVE GREEN[37]

IT'S JUST A TEST

Remember how the Lord your God led you all the way
in the wilderness these forty years, to humble and test you
in order to know what was in your heart, whether or not
you would keep his commands (Deuteronomy 8:2).

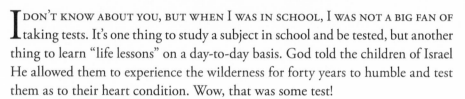

I DON'T KNOW ABOUT YOU, BUT WHEN I WAS IN SCHOOL, I WAS NOT A BIG FAN OF taking tests. It's one thing to study a subject in school and be tested, but another thing to learn "life lessons" on a day-to-day basis. God told the children of Israel He allowed them to experience the wilderness for forty years to humble and test them as to their heart condition. Wow, that was some test!

God wanted to know:

- Will you keep walking in faith when the answer to your crisis is nowhere in sight?
- Will you still trust Me when you don't have enough to eat?
- Will you stay positive when there is no water to drink?
- Will you believe Me when I tell you there is a Promised Land for you to occupy?
- Will you refuse to grumble and complain about the leaders I have anointed?
- Etc., etc.

It would be safe to say that every time they had an opportunity to make an "A," they made an "F." As my preacher friend used to say, "You don't ever flunk one of God's test; you just get to take it over again until you pass!" I believe they could have ended their journey to the Promised Land in two years instead of forty if they had just obeyed God. That is all He ever wanted them to do; just trust Him. And we are no different. Each day we are given opportunities to trust God to meet our needs. He wants to know if we will trust Him when nothing seems to be working.

For example, will we trust Him when we:

- Sow seed and no harvest is in sight?
- Are faithful to our assignment and no one else is?

- Invest time and money into someone's life and they walk away?
- Encourage others and never receive any in return?

I want to learn each lesson and pass the test the first time. I don't want to spend any more time in the wilderness than I have to. What test are you taking today?

ALL GOD'S CHILDREN EXPERIENCE CORRECTION

And have you completely forgotten this word of encouragement that addresses you as father addresses his son? It says, "My son, do not make light of the Lord's discipline, and do not lose heart when he rebukes you, because the Lord disciplines the one he loves, and he chastens everyone he accepts as his son" (Hebrews 12:5-6).

THE CHRISTIAN LIFE IS ABOUT BALANCE, NOT LIVING ON THE EDGE OF extremes. There will be seasons of sunshine, and there will be seasons of rain. When we focus on only one aspect (sunshine), the potential for confusion is always present, especially when God suddenly takes us to the "woodshed." I don't doubt that from a child's point of view correction equals pain (see Hebrews 12:11). But from the perspective of a loving parent, it is a necessary part of the growth process. Quite frankly, if you say you are a Christian and never experience God's correction, then you don't belong to God at all. You are "illegitimate" (see Hebrews 12:8).

God never does anything without a purpose. Just as a loving parent takes the time and effort to disciple a child, so God will do the same with His children. We may not like it or embrace it; but if we belong to the Lord, we can rest assured that He will not leave us in an unrepentant state for very long.

Jonah is a case in point. God had a specific assignment for him, and he failed to obey. Instead of winking at the situation, God took action and disciplined his backslidden preacher. I find it interesting that everything except Jonah obeyed God: the storm, the sailors, and the big fish all obeyed. Yes, everything obeyed except the prophet! When Jonah found himself at the bottom of the ocean, he then realized how serious God was about following His instructions (see Jonah 2:1-10). The Lord's discipline brought the preacher to the point of repentance and restoration. He could now be used to deliver the message of salvation to a lost nation.

According to Hebrews 12:11, the purpose of discipline is to train us so that we may partake of His holiness and yield the fruit of righteousness. I cannot find anywhere in the Bible or human history that God used anyone to bring glory to His name without first taking them through the correction process. Don't pull a Jonah and run from the process, it's not worth it.

PROMISES, PROMISES

*The Lord himself goes before you and will be with you;
he will never leave you nor forsake you. Do not be afraid;
do not be discouraged* (Deuteronomy 31:8).

A PROMISE IS ONLY AS GOOD AS THE ONE MAKING IT. I TRIED TO INSTILL IN MY children to never make a commitment you don't intend to keep. Your heavenly Father made you a promise—*"He will never leave you nor forsake you."* And, unlike some folks, He always makes good on His promises.

One point of confusion is trying to understand the difference between His *correcting* us and His *breaking* us. In the previous devotional, we saw that correction (Hebrews 12) is God, a loving parent, *training* us to live a life of peace and joy. Correction happens when we color outside the lines, and God takes steps to brings us back. On the other hand, *to break us is a process to take away the strength of self and release the life of God.* You have to understand that brokenness is not the judgment of an angry God. He loves us so much that He will even use adverse circumstances to bring out our best. The devil will use those same things to bring out our worse, never our best!

First Corinthians 10:13 states: *"No temptation has overtaken you except what is common to mankind. And God is faithful; he will not let you be tempted beyond what you can bear. But when you are tempted, he will also provide a way out so that you can endure it."* When you read the word "temptation" or "tempted," Paul is talking about "testing" or "tested" as in a trial, not a temptation to sin. Every engineer knows the limits or the stress points of a building or a bridge. A wise engineer will not allow too much pressure to be placed at any given point lest the building or bridge collapse. We have His promise that He will never go too far, or put on so much pressure that we shatter under stress (see Job 1:12).

He is not trying to destroy us, even though there are times when we may think so. One question that always comes up, "Will the process ever stop?" Yes, I believe it stops when to go any further would damage His purpose for our life. He will never take us into the deep water to drown us!

BROKEN GROUND

*This is what the Lord says to the people of Judah and
to Jerusalem: "Break up your unplowed ground and
do not sow among thorns"* (Jeremiah 4:3).

E VERY WISE FARMER WILL TELL YOU THAT SOIL MUST BE PREPARED FOR THINGS
to grow. Jeremiah uses an illustration from the "natural" world to point to a
spiritual truth. He states that "unplowed" or "fallow" ground is counter-productive to reap a harvest in the natural, and it is also counter-productive of them to
think they would receive a spiritual harvest if their hearts were hardened. In a
time when the people should have been seeking God's help and guidance, they
allowed their collective hearts to become hard and cold, much like a fallow field.
The prophet warns them to "break up" the ground before it is too late.

Easton's Bible Dictionary observes the following: "The cultivator of the soil
was careful to 'break up' his fallow ground, i.e., to clear the field of weeds, before
sowing seed in it. So, says the prophet, 'Break off your evil ways, repent of your
sins, cease to do evil, and then the good seed of the word will have room to grow
and bear fruit.'"[38]

Since our hearts are likened to the soil (see Mark 4:13-20), we need to stay vigilant and alert to keep our hearts pliable and receptive to God's word. The writer
of Hebrews gave a clear warning when he says, *"So, as the Holy Spirit says: 'Today,
if you hear his voice, do not harden your hearts as you did in the rebellion, during the
time of testing in the wilderness, where your ancestors tested and tried me, though for
forty years they saw what I did'"* (Hebrews 3:7-9).

The Lord has many tools at His disposal to break up the fallow ground of our
heart. Later in his prophecy, Jeremiah pictured the Word of God like a fire and
a hammer, *"Is not my word like fire,"* declares the Lord, *"and like a hammer that
breaks a rock in pieces?"* (Jeremiah 23:29). Make no mistake, the Lord loves us too
much to leave us with cold and hard hearts.

In the following devotions, we will see that brokenness is not something to
run from but a process to go through. It is never easy when God takes a hammer
and proceeds to breaks up the fallow ground of our hearts. But for growth to take
place, it is a necessity.

A BROKEN JAR

*While he was in Bethany, reclining at the table in the home
of Simon the Leper, a woman came with an alabaster jar of
very expensive perfume, made of pure nard. She broke the
jar and poured the perfume on his head* (Mark 14:3).

WE DO NOT HAVE A LOT OF INFORMATION ABOUT THE IDENTITY OF THIS woman. Instead of speculation, we would be better served to understand the spiritual truth behind her act of sacrifice. This is one of those moments when actions do speak louder than words.

First, by breaking the jar, she was saying, "I have no plans to use this again." As far as I know, she never spoke a word. She didn't have to. Her actions spoke volumes about her commitment to Jesus. You might say in today's terminology she was, "all in!" If you search the pages of the Bible and the history of the Christianity, you will not find anyone who has ever made an impact for the Kingdom of God without a total "sell out" to Christ. The sweet smell of the perfume was unknown until the jar was broken. A sign should be erected over the door to the Kingdom that reads, "Only broken men and women may apply."

Second, the smell of her sacrifice filled the room. Some Bible teachers have suggested that in her day a jar of perfume would have been worth the equivalent of a year's salary. No need to guess how she might have earned enough money to buy it. Suffice it to say her sacrifice cost her something, and she was willing to give it all to honor the Lord. A broken and sold-out believer does not have to say what he or she is doing. The believer's actions do all the talking necessary.

Third, any act of total commitment to Jesus will be criticized by someone: *"And they rebuked her harshly"* (Mark 14:5). Jesus defended her and at the same time called them out (Mark 14:7). So why did they rebuke her? Could it be they were embarrassed that this woman showed them a picture of real commitment? Don't be afraid to go *all in* for Christ thinking that some people might not like it. They probably won't, so just do it anyway!

A BROKEN ROOF

*Since they could not get him to Jesus because of the crowd,
they made an opening in the roof above Jesus by digging
through it and then lowered the mat the man was lying
on. When Jesus saw their faith, he said to the paralyzed
man, "Son, your sins are forgiven"* (Mark 2:4-5).

THE PEOPLE WERE FILLED WITH ANTICIPATION WHEN THE WORD SPREAD
that Jesus was in the house. Every inch of house was jam-packed, so much
so that no one could even stand in the doorway. In Luke's account, we are told
the power of the Lord was present on Jesus to heal (see Luke 5:17)—an indication of things to come.

Now imagine the scene. While Jesus was teaching, a loud ruckus could be
heard. Trying to discern where the noise was coming from, Jesus looked up and
saw the roof tiles being taken apart. And much to the astonishment of the crowd,
four men lowered a bed with a paralyzed man lying on it. What did Jesus do? Did
He tell the men they needed to wait their turn? Did He rebuke the sick man for
interrupting His sermon? Or did He apologize to the owner of the house for the
unwise actions of these men? No, none of the above. *Jesus saw their faith* and forgave the man's sins and healed him.

The healing would not have happened if these four men had not taken action.
How did Jesus see their faith? He saw the results of their faith. If someone says
they have faith, the logical response is, "Ok, let's see the actions to back up your
faith." I don't know anything about these four guys. But one thing I do know
is they were going to get their friend to Jesus and nothing was going to stand in
their way.

The roof was one barrier that had to be removed before anything could happen. To us, it might seem a bit extreme to tear a hole in a roof just to get a friend
healed. When you are desperate for God to move, you will do just about anything, even if you look foolish. What about you? What's standing your way?
What needs to be torn up to get you into a right relationship with Jesus? Think
about it, and then take action. You won't be sorry!

A BROKEN VISION (PART 1)

By the rivers of Babylon we sat and wept when we remembered
Zion. There on the poplars we hung our harps for there our
captors asked us for songs, our tormentors demanded songs of joy;
they said, "Sing us one of the songs of Zion!" (Psalm 137:1-3)

IN 587 B.C., THE JEWS WERE TAKEN CAPTIVE. IT WAS A PERIOD FILLED WITH gloom and despair. The psalmist gave a detailed description of a people who had lost their freedom. And, in turn, their hope and vision were drowning *"by the rivers of Babylon."* The river was a place of industry and commerce. The Jews had become a slave labor force and little by little, year by year, their vision of a bright future was breaking into pieces. It would be fair to say that the surrounding atmosphere was hostile and not conducive to the release of their potential.

To live our lives without vision is like a ship without a compass. Steaming full speed ahead is great, but if you don't know the direction of your destination, you could end up landing in a hostile environment at best or crashing on the rocks at worst.

Everything God created has been given an ideal environment to function and grow. What happens to a fish when it is taken out of the water? It may live for a few minutes, but before long it dies. Why? The fish's environment was violated. Fish were made to live in water. Removal from the proper environment can oftentimes produce negative results. If it works that way for plants and animals, what do you think that means for us?

Our potential for fulfillment and joy is directly tied to our environment. The people in this psalm were held hostage; and so I ask you, what is holding you hostage? What is holding you back from success?

- Is it a mind filled with doubt?
- Is it a habit that won't let go?
- Is it a relationship that you know is poisoning your spirit?
- Is it a decision you refuse to make?
- Or, is it a negative word spoken to you as a child?

There is an old Japanese proverb that says, "Vision without action is a daydream. Action without vision is a nightmare."[39] Don't let your vision become a daydream or a nightmare. Whatever is holding you hostage, it is time to take charge and do something about it!

A Broken Vision (Part 2)

By the rivers of Babylon we sat and wept when we remembered
Zion. There on the poplars we hung our harps for there our
captors asked us for songs, our tormentors demanded songs of joy;
they said, "Sing us one of the songs of Zion!" (Psalm 137:1-3)

A SHATTERED VISION AND A BROKEN HEART GO HAND IN HAND. AS THE psalmist continued to reveal what the captured Jews were going through, he gave us a picture of what it means to live with a broken vision.

- *A broken vision produces stagnation: "we sat and wept."* Living with passion produces a fire that becomes fuel in our hearts. It is the fuel that generates movement toward our dreams and goals. Because of their circumstances, the dreams and visions that once motivated them had deteriorated into the quicksand of inactivity. No doubt they were busy, but busyness does not always equal progress. Many believers are like the kamikaze pilot who flew 17 missions; he had lots of activity, but never hit his target!

- *A broken vision produces backward thinking: "when we remembered Zion."* There is nothing wrong with remembering the past. It becomes a problem when we spend more time back there than we do living in the present. The only thing the captured Jews could do was reflect on was what God did yesterday, not what He will do today. If we spend more time talking about things we did yesterday and never focusing on today, we might be in danger of losing heart. Too many people are frozen in the past because they are tied to some event—good or bad—that keeps them from moving forward.

- *A broken vision causes a loss of joy: "How can we sing the songs of the Lord while in a foreign land?"* (Psalm 137:4). I don't know if they were being mocked or not. But one thing I do know, anyone can praise God when things are going well. It takes believers who are living with passion for their vision to praise Him when things go wrong. When the bottom falls out, the enemy will chide you into believing that God doesn't care what you are going through. Don't fall victim to a broken heart. Throwing your dreams into the rivers of Babylon is a sad commentary on the power of the loving God!

A BROKEN SHIP

But the ship struck a sandbar and ran aground. The bow
stuck fast and would not move, and the stern was broken
to pieces by the pounding of the surf (Acts 27:41).

PAUL HAD MADE HIS CASE BEFORE KING AGRIPPA (SEE ACTS 26), AND AFTER-
ward exercised his right as a Roman citizen to defend himself before Caesar.
Here he is, along with other prisoners, being shipped off to Italy. The shipwreck
could have been avoided if those in charge had heeded Paul's warning. He told
them not to sail (see Acts 27:10), yet they ignored him; as a result, they almost
lost their lives.

God's plan is not a series of random events that have no connection. When
you and I are going through difficulties and hardships, it may look like God has
lost His mind. God's purpose for our lives can never be defined or determined
by a single event. From our point of view, it doesn't make sense. If we could view
every episode of our lives from Heaven's viewpoint, we would see how it all fits
together to make us into the image of Christ.

In Paul's case, it was a shipwreck. How can any redemptive purpose be seen
in such a tragedy? As Paul was still reeling from his conversion on the road to
Damascus, the Lord prophesied his ministry to Ananias saying, *"Go! This man is
my chosen instrument to proclaim my name to the Gentiles and their kings and to the
people of Israel"* (Acts 9:15). But that is not all God said. Paul was going to minister to "their kings," but the Lord didn't tell him how it was going to happen.
The "fine print" stated, *"I will show him how much he must suffer for My name."*

I doubt Paul ever envisioned how many times he would suffer as a result of his
testimony for Christ (see 2 Corinthians 11). Or that floating on a piece of wood
(Acts 27:44) would be part of his destiny plan to stand before a king! Never dis-
parage the vehicles God may choose to move you forward in your purpose. For
Paul, it was a prison ship (see Acts 27). For you and I it may be something entirely
out in left field. But don't ever think God is not in control of your life. *He is!*

A Broken Lunch

Taking the five loaves and the two fish and looking up to heaven, he gave thanks and broke them. Then he gave them to the disciples to distribute to the people (Luke 9:16).

THIS SITUATION HAD ALL THE EARMARKS OF A CATASTROPHE, AND SOMEthing had to be done, and quickly. The crowd was feeling the effects of a long day of teaching, combined with a hot and dusty environment. They were getting hungry, and it is not hard to figure out what could happen. The eversmart disciples of Jesus had the answer, *"Send the crowd away so they can go to the surrounding villages and countryside and find food and lodging, because we are in a remote place here"* (Luke 9:12). To which Jesus replied, *"You give them something to eat"* (Luke 9:13). They came back to Jesus and said, *"Sorry we only have five loaves and two fish, so there is nothing we can do"* (see Luke 9:13).

Once again the disciples missed the point. Instead of looking to Jesus, they looked at their meager supplies and failed another test. I wouldn't be too hard on them. We do the same thing. We get in a tight spot and immediately try to figure things out on our own. I believe all Jesus wanted them, and us, to do was to bring what they had to Him. I don't think He would have rebuked them if they said, *"Jesus, we don't know how to remedy this situation, so we will trust You."*

As long as the lunch was in *their* hands, it could only do what they could do. But, when the disciples placed it in *His* hand, it could do what He could do! When Jesus blessed and broke the small amount of food, He handed it back to the disciples. They not only fed the crowd, but had enough left over to enjoy later (see Luke 9:15).

There are spiritually hungry people all around us. They are starving for meaning and purpose in life. Spiritual malnutrition has taken hold, and they are looking at us with bloated stomachs and bulging eyes, hoping for a miracle. I can never feed them with my little, but I can give it to Jesus and allow Him to break, bless, and multiply it to slay their hunger. He doesn't want me to try to figure it out. He wants me to give Him all I have. You and I always have a choice. What will you do?

BROKEN IDOLS

Be careful not to make a treaty with those who live in the land where you are going, or they will be a snare among you. Break down their altars, smash their sacred stones and cut down their Asherah poles. Do not worship any other god, for the Lord, whose name is Jealous, is a jealous God (Exodus 34:12-14).

THERE WERE TIMES WHEN GOD SPOKE THROUGH MOSES TO REMIND THE people of His covenant with them. This was one of those times. There were blessings for those who obeyed Him, and great distress for those who did not. He told them in no uncertain terms what to do when they encountered foreign gods. They must be broken, smashed, and cut down. He did not politely ask them to dismantle or carefully lay aside the idols, but to demolish them completely!

When you think of an idol, what do you imagine? Do you picture a golden statue sitting on a hillside somewhere? Or inside a temple where mysterious men come to worship at the altar of some god or goddess? For the most part, our Western mindset does not allow for such foolishness. We may see such images on the television screen, but would never dream of worshipping an idol made with hands. A friend of mine gave the best definition of an idol I have ever heard. He said, "An idol is anything you love more than Jesus!" Now that is something we can wrap our heads around (see 1 John 2:15-17).

In our culture, idols may not sit in a man-made temple, but instead they may be parked in our driveway or located in a sports venue. *Whatever we love more than Jesus will become what we worship, no matter how innocent it looks.* It would seem we have moved the pagan idols from temples made with hands to the secret places of the heart. It is in those hidden areas where others cannot see that we erect the false gods of pride and self-indulgence.

We are living in idolatry if we exalt anything above our devotion to God, and it doesn't matter what we call them. Whatever challenges His right to our hearts becomes an enemy to Him; and that enemy, He will confront. God is jealous over us and will challenge us to repent of all hidden idols!

A BROKEN PROPHET

while he himself went a day's journey into the wilderness. He
came to a broom bush, sat down under it and prayed that
he might die. "I have had enough, Lord," he said. "Take my
life; I am no better than my ancestors" (1 Kings 19:4).

ELIJAH WAS SUFFERING FROM THE "I WANT TO QUIT" SYNDROME. IN HIS depressed state, he was ready to walk away from his calling. This was the same man who three days before had confronted the pagan priests of Baal and witnessed a demonstration of God's power (see 1 Kings 18:36-38). What changed? What made this man of God run for his life? What caused him to ask to die?

Whether we want to admit it or not, there are times when we want to give up. It doesn't matter if we are in full-time ministry or not, the call to serve is given to all who call on His name. So, what did God do with Elijah? Instead of berating him for his desire to quit, God gave him a prescription for renewal.

1. *It was time to refresh.* Elijah didn't need a sermon on how to confront the spirit of Jezebel. What he needed was simple. He needed sleep! And when he woke up an angel had prepared a meal for him (see 1 Kings 19:5-8). There are times when the most spiritual thing we can do is get a good night's sleep and eat a decent meal. Failure to rest leads to fatigue, and physical and mental fatigue leads us to make poor decisions.

2. *It was time to get real.* After Elijah's time of refreshment, he went to a cave and decided it was time to "school" God on how things really are (see 1 Kings 19:9-18). Elijah had the "superhero" complex, but it didn't take long for God to clear up any misunderstanding. The Lord is not afraid of our honesty, and we should not be afraid of His answers.

3. *It was time to redirect his vision.* A cure for the "I want to quit" syndrome is to refocus your vision away from yourself and back to things that matter. Elijah didn't stay in the cave for very long. He picked himself up and went back to work (see 1 Kings 19:15-18). Don't give up and quit. If you feel like you can't take it anymore, stop what you are doing and listen to the still small voice. God's trying to tell you something. Are you listening?

A BROKEN SPIRIT

*My sacrifice, O God, is a broken spirit; a broken and
contrite heart you, God, will not despise* (Psalm 51:17).

THE BIBLE DOES NOT GLOSS OVER SIN, NOR EXCUSE THE ACTIONS OF ITS MOST
celebrated leaders. A case in point is David. There are many lessons to learn
from David's experience, not the least of which is unconfessed sin exacts a hefty
price. He discovered that sin costs physically as well as spiritually. Combining
Psalm 32 with Psalm 51, we see the effects of unconfessed sin. Even though
David was still in his prime, when reading his words, he sounds like an old
man: *"When I kept silent, my bones wasted away through my groaning all day long.
For day and night your hand was heavy on me; my strength was sapped as in the
heat of summer"* (Psalm 32:3-4).

Sin affected his *eyesight: "For I know my transgressions, and my sin is always before
me"* (Psalm 51:3). Every time David looked at God's handiwork, the only thing he
saw was the reflection of his sin. When he closed his eyes at night, he saw a frame-
by-frame replay of his immoral behavior.

Sin affected his *mind: "Yet you desired faithfulness even in the womb; you taught me
wisdom in that secret place"* (Psalm 51:6). Sin robbed him of any rational thought that
what he had done with Bathsheba and her husband Uriah was sinful (see 2 Samuel
11). Get it straight; sin will lie to you and make you dumb to its consequences.

Sin affected his *hearing: "Let me hear joy and gladness; let the bones you have
crushed rejoice"* (Psalm 51:8). For many years, this sweet singer of Israel had written and composed music to be enjoyed by others. But now the joy and gladness of
God's voice were silent. The only sound he heard was the accusing whisper of the
enemy telling him all was lost.

I hasten to add that when David confessed his sin, God restored him and did
not disqualify him from future service. Yes, there was a price to pay, but David
found his way back into the fellowship of the Lord. You can fast forward to the
Book of Acts and read what God thought about David. He is referred to by the
Lord as *"a man after my own heart"* (see Acts 13:22).

Don't allow unconfessed sin to rob you of the joy and fellowship of the Lord.
It is not worth it at any price! (See 1 John 1:8-10.)

BROKEN FELLOWSHIP

Restore to me the joy of your salvation and grant me a willing spirit, to sustain me. Then I will teach transgressors your ways so that sinners will turn back to you (Psalm 51:12-13).

DAVID NOT ONLY COMMITTED A HORRIBLE SIN BUT SPENT TIME TRYING TO cover it up, hoping no one would find out. It worked, or so it seemed until the prophet Nathan visited him. The man of God exposed David, and in turn, David confessed what he had done (see 2 Samuel 12).

Every part of David's life was affected by his sin, but the one area affected the most was his fellowship with God. There is nothing more precious to a believer than knowing he or she is walking in harmony with the Lord. The loss of fellowship with our heavenly Father far outweighs any temporary pleasure we might derive from sin.

Broken fellowship with God will always lead to a loss of joy: *"Restore to me the joy of your salvation and grant me a willing spirit, to sustain me"* (Psalm 51:12). I wonder how often the servants of David asked why the king seemed so sad. Maybe they asked if this was the same man who used to spread such joy in the palace.

Broken fellowship with God will always produce a closed mouth and a stifled testimony: *"Then I will teach transgressors your ways, so that sinners will turn back to you"* (Psalm 51:13). What testimony did David have? How could he witness to the goodness and love of God when he was hiding his sin? Is it possible that unconfessed sin has closed the mouths of God's people?

David recognized one important truth. There is nothing we can do or sacrifice to take away the stain of sin (Psalm 51:16-17). He threw himself on the mercy of and God said in Psalm 51:7, *"Cleanse me with hyssop, and I will be clean; wash me, and I will be whiter than snow.* It is only through the shed blood of a sacrifice can we be forgiven and our fellowship with God restored. As the chorus of that old hymn says, *"Oh! Precious is the flow that makes me white as snow; No other fount I know, nothing but the blood of Jesus."*[40] Are you walking in fellowship with God? Have you allowed unconfessed sin to stop you from sharing a witness of God's love?

BROKEN WALLS

*By night I went out through the Valley Gate toward the
Jackal Well and the Dung Gate, examining the walls of
Jerusalem, which had been broken down, and its gates,
which had been destroyed by fire* (Nehemiah 2:13).

WHAT IS YOUR FIRST RESPONSE TO HEARING BAD NEWS? DO YOU CLOSE
your eyes and hope it goes away? Do you offer up a quick prayer and
forget about it? Or do you feel the burden of the situation, pray, and then take
action? If you are of the mindset of the latter option, then you are in the same
league as Nehemiah. While serving as cupbearer to King Artaxerxes, he received
troubling news from home: *"They said to me, 'Those who survived the exile and are
back in the province are in great trouble and disgrace. The wall of Jerusalem is broken down, and its gates have been burned with fire'* (Nehemiah 1:3).

Nehemiah decided he could not stand by while the walls of Jerusalem were
broken down. After a time of fasting and prayer, he strapped on his boots, put on
his hard hat, and took action. Why was he so concerned about the walls being
broken down? The physical wall around the city represented protection from
outside forces. God's people were always on high alert against the potential of
an attack. It was on the wall where watchmen would sound an alarm if danger
was approaching. If there were gaps or even small glitches in the wall, the enemy
would surely find a way to penetrate. Nehemiah's mission was to rebuild the walls
to restore peace, protection, and security for the people.

Around each of us, God has built a wall of protection. I'm not talking about a
physical wall, but something much stronger than that. I like to think of our spiritual covering as a building with four sides. On one side, the wall is God's *promise
of protection* (see Isaiah 54:17). The other side is the *power of answered prayer* (see
Psalm 4:1). The front of our wall is the *unlimited power of praise* (see Psalm 149).
And the back wall is the *indwelling presence of the Holy Spirit* (see Titus 3:6).

Have you inspected your spiritual building lately? It is up to each of us to care
for and examine our spiritual walls to make sure there are no gaps through which
the devil may attack. Just one small opening is all the enemy needs. Stay alert and
quickly repair any damage.

BROKEN PITCHERS

Gideon and the hundred men with him reached the edge of the camp at the beginning of the middle watch, just after they had changed the guard. They blew their trumpets and broke the jars [pitchers KJV] *that were in their hands* (Judges 7:19).

GOD WAS FAMOUS FOR GIVING UNUSUAL BATTLE PLANS (SEE JOSHUA 5-6; 2 Chronicles 20). In Judges 7, we have another plan that borders on the impossible. After thinning out his army of thirty-two thousand, Gideon is left with only three hundred brave warriors. What can an army of three hundred men do against an overwhelming force? Not much, unless they are acting on the orders from Heaven.

This band of brothers took on the mighty Midianites and won the day. The most important piece of their armament was not a new weapon, but a simple torch inside a clay pitcher. The plan was to fool the enemy into thinking there were more soldiers than there were. And it worked! Everything hinged on the fact that the pitchers had to be broken. Failure to follow orders would mean there would be no light, and without the light the plan would have failed.

The symbolism of this story is striking. Paul writes, *"But we have this treasure in jars of clay to show that this all-surpassing power is from God and not from us* (see 2 Corinthians 4:7). I can't say for sure if Paul was referring to Gideon or not. But Paul did know something about the breaking process. He is writing from personal experience (see 2 Corinthians 11:24-28).

We too must realize we are just jars of clay that contain the glory of God. It is only broken things that are usable. To talk about breaking, suffering, and adversity is not an attractive message for the modern church. The message of brokenness has been widely rejected and replaced by an atmosphere of success—at all cost. There is a price to pay for every level of maturity we attain. The Scripture is clear: without brokenness, there is no blessing.

Vance Havner was one of the most powerful preachers of his day. After walking through the valley death with his precious wife, he penned: "God uses broken things. It takes broken soil to produce a crop, broken clouds to give rain, broken grain to give bread, broken bread to give strength. It is the broken alabaster box that gives forth perfume. It is Peter, weeping bitterly, who returns to greater power than ever."[41]

BROKEN SHIELDS

*He carried off the treasures of the temple of the Lord and the treasures
of the royal palace. He took everything, including all the gold shields
Solomon had made. So King Rehoboam made bronze shields to
replace them and assigned these to the commanders of the guard
on duty at the entrance to the royal palace* (1 Kings 14:26-27).

WHEN SOLOMON BECAME KING, HE ASKED GOD FOR ONE THING, WISDOM to rule. God was so pleased He not only gave him wisdom but added wealth and power (see 1 Kings 3:9-13). The crown jewel of Solomon's kingdom was building the temple. It would be a fair statement to say that the reign of Solomon was a revival of the nation. There had never been a time in history when one man's rule exerted so much influence as in the days of Solomon (see 1 Kings 10:23-24).

During Solomon's reign, many traditions were established to show the manifest glory of the Lord. One of the most awe-inspiring was the making of three hundred shields of pure gold (see 1 Kings 10:17). You can imagine how visitors must have felt when they were greeted by three hundred golden shields lining the entrance to the King's residence. Each shield proclaimed a message: *the glory of God is in this place!*

However, in the latter years of Solomon's rule, the nation turned her back on God, and the glory faded. After his death, the kingdom split, with his son Rehoboam becoming king over Judah. Five years later they were invaded, and the nation was stripped of her golden shields. Instead of turning in repentance to God, the new king made replacement shields; instead of gold, they were made of bronze. The bronze shields were a cheap substitute and became a symbol of compromise. As far as we know, Rehoboam never tried to recapture the golden shields.

The lesson for us is obvious. When it comes to our relationship with God, we must never settle for bronze when we can have gold. The bronze of empty religion will never be an adequate substitute for the gold of a personal walk with God. It may be possible to fool others when our passion for the Lord begins to fade, but we can never fool God. Never settle for less when you can have the best!

A BROKEN SEED

*Very truly I tell you, unless a kernel of wheat falls to
the ground and dies, it remains only a single seed. But
if it dies, it produces many seeds* (John 12:24).

ONE TINY SEED IS A SELF-CONTAINED MIRACLE. YOU MAY THINK THAT EVERY-one knows the principle of seedtime and harvest; but unfortunately, not everyone is operating on the God-given principle. There are a lot of things you can do with a seed beside planting it in the ground. You can gather a basket full, crush them, and bake them in an oven. You can brag to all of your friends that you have collected different kinds of seed, and let them come over to your house to marvel at your collection. *However, until you plant a seed in the soil, it will never produce a harvest!*

Once a seed is planted in good ground, the process starts. From the outside looking in, it appears the tiny seed could never reproduce itself. What could one small seed ever accomplish? The seed goes into the dark soil, all alone, but a higher law takes over. Jesus said it is a natural principle: *"But if it dies, it produces many seeds."*

I believe He was using "natural" law to illustrate a "spiritual" truth. He was speaking of Himself, and the sacrifice He was going to make on our behalf. The harvest of souls started the day He hung on the cross. The spiritual seed—Jesus—was broken open in the moments of His death; He was the Seed going into the soil of sinful humanity. And we know that His death, burial, and resurrection was proof that the Seed did indeed produce a harvest of souls. Paul said, *"But Christ has indeed been raised from the dead, the firstfruits of those who have fallen asleep. For since death came through a man, the resurrection of the dead comes also through a man. For as in Adam all die, so in Christ all will be made alive. But each in turn: Christ, the firstfruits; then, when he comes, those who belong to him"* (1 Corinthians 15:20-23).

Jesus demonstrated the principle that only broken things can produce a harvest. That is still true today. God is not asking us to go and die on a cross, but He *is* asking us to submit our lives to Him so that He can break, bless, and multiply it to reach a lost and dying world!

BROKEN PILLARS

Samson said, "Let me die with the Philistines!" Then he pushed with all his might, and down came the temple on the rulers and all the people in it. Thus he killed many more when he died than while he lived (Judges 16:30).

THE STORY OF SAMSON HAD ALL THE ELEMENTS OF A TRAGIC PLAY. THE LORD called him to deliver Israel from her enemies, and at first, he was a national hero. He was set up to become the greatest of all the judges, yet Samson could not even deliver himself from his sinful desires. The power of his lust overshadowed his love for righteousness. The devil knew exactly where to attack; and when the attack came, Samson was unable to do anything about it. I think that one of the saddest verses in the Bible is the day of Samson's betrayal by Delilah and his capture by the Philistines: *"Then she called, 'Samson, the Philistines are upon you!' He awoke from his sleep and thought, 'I'll go out as before and shake myself free.' But he did not know that the Lord had left him"* (Judges 16:20).

This champion of the people was now blinded, bound, and grinding grain. One would think there would be no hope for redemption. In the final act in this drama, Samson is pulling down the pillars of the temple. If I didn't know the ending of this tragedy, I would never have surmised that he would have destroyed more at the end of his life than at the beginning. Just when the devil thinks he has won the battle, God will have the last word—He always does.

Here is a thought to ponder: Sin will always collect a payment. But as in the case of Samson, there can be restoration. Yes, he lost his sight and his freedom, but consider the idea that maybe it was in his weakened condition that he could finally see spiritually and depend on God's strength, not his own (see Judges 16:26-30).

You don't have to do what Samson did to learn the lesson that Samson learned. Our sins and failures may not come close to what Samson did, but God's restoration is accessible to all who will humble themselves and repent. Failure is not the final word. Just ask Samson—*"Thus he killed many more when he died than while he lived!"*

A BROKEN LIFE

*Then, leaving her water jar, the woman went back to the town
and said to the people, "Come, see a man who told me everything
I ever did. Could this be the Messiah?" They came out of the
town and made their way toward him* (John 4:28-30).

THERE WAS ONCE A WOMAN WHO WAS RESPONSIBLE FOR WINNING AN ENTIRE town to Jesus Christ. We don't know her name; she will just go down in history as, "The woman at the well." I'm afraid we spend more time talking about her past rather than her future. The fact that Jesus knew what she needed just at the right moment she needed it is often lost in the haze of her past sin.

There was a reason why she was coming alone, at the noon hour to draw water. I would guess it was because none of the other women wanted to be seen with her. To them, she was a "soiled" woman; but to Jesus, she was a woman who needed something she didn't have—*living water* (see John 4:7-13). It is no wonder she was shocked that this stranger wanted to talk to her. He moved past her objections and lovingly challenged her. He held up the mirror of truth and showed her a reflection of her life. He was tender but tough. His confrontation was intended to lead her to a place of salvation, not condemnation.

Her life was void of hope, as empty as the water pots she carried. Everything was lost until Jesus showed up, and suddenly in the flash of God's intervention, her world turned right side up. How can you tell this woman was changed? She had to tell someone! *"Many of the Samaritans from that town believed in him because of the woman's testimony, 'He told me everything I ever did'"* (see John 4:39). This outcast now became a flaming evangelist!

Many people are looking for answers, just like this woman. They will drink out of any well hoping against hope that their thirst for meaning will be quenched. Jeremiah said, *"My people have committed two sins: They have forsaken me, the spring of living water, and have dug their own cisterns, broken cisterns that cannot hold water"* (Jeremiah 2:13). Jesus Christ is in the business of repairing broken lives. If you are in need of a refreshing drink of living water, you can have as much as you want. Jesus will not turn you away!

UPSIDE DOWN LIVING

THE #1 THING YOU NEED TO KNOW

It goes with the territory. It often happens that when Jesus says "Let us go to the other side," a weird storm starts brewing. Don't let it bother you. Whenever you advance and occupy you should expect the enemy to demonstrate an element of resistance or disapproval on his way out. The writer of Hebrews calls it "enduring the contradiction."

—LANCE WALLNAU[42]

WHEN NOTHING MAKES SENSE

When John, who was in prison, heard about the deeds of the Messiah, he sent his disciples to ask him, "Are you the one who is to come, or should we expect someone else?" (Matthew 11:2-3)

THERE ARE TIMES IN THE LIFE OF A CHRISTIAN WHEN THINGS DON'T ADD UP. It is in those circumstances we see the difference between what we see on the outside and what we know on the inside.

John the Baptist is a good example of someone who was doing everything right, and yet things turned out upside down. He spoke truth to power, and it cost him his life (see Mark 6:18-25). Before his execution, he sent a strange message to Jesus: *"Are you the one who is to come, or should we expect someone else?"* I have to wonder why this man who was so sure that Jesus was the Lamb of God (see John 1:29) is now questioning his own testimony. John is facing something we all face—when life doesn't match up with what we thought to be true! It is those moments of "contradiction" when doubt shadows our mind.

John needed to remember that this was never about him. He needed to be reminded of what he said about Jesus prior to being thrown in prison. Did John mean it when he said about Jesus, *"He must increase and I must decrease."* (see John 3:30). What has changed? Why is John the Baptist now doubting the identity of Jesus? There can only be one reason; his circumstances went south and with it his confidence in his purpose for being.

When we were invited by God to join Him in this great adventure of living the Christian life, where did we get the idea things were going to be easy? I have heard preachers say, *"The safest place to be is in the center of God's will."* I understand what is meant by that statement, but I don't agree entirely with its premise. Being in the center of His will is the goal, but living without upsets and challenges is not in the plan. Jesus, John, Paul, and the others might have a differing opinion when it comes to the idea of being safe.

Don't let the contradictions of life throw you off balance. When nothing makes sense, don't give up, but press in closer to Him who has called you.

A STRANGE REPLY

Jesus replied, "Go back and report to John what you hear and see: The blind receive sight, the lame walk, those who have leprosy are cleansed, the deaf hear, the dead are raised, and the good news is proclaimed to the poor. Blessed is anyone who does not stumble on account of me" (Matthew 11:4-6).

JOHN THE BAPTIST WAS IN A VERY DARK PLACE, PHYSICALLY AND SPIRITUALLY. After all, his future was uncertain, and his prospects of rescue were slim. In his humanness, he sent an urgent message to Jesus: *"Are you the one who is to come, or should we expect someone else?"* What he was asking was actually, "Aren't You going to come and rescue me!" I decided a long time ago I would have probably asked the same thing. John needed help, and who better to ask than Jesus?

When John heard about the miracles taking place, he sent the message. Why is that? I would think it would make him glad, not sad, to hear that people were being healed. Could it be that John was pondering, *If all these miracles are happening, why not one more? Jesus, You have the power to change my circumstances.*

John did receive an answer, but it was not the one he was expecting. Jesus told him not to stumble over all the miracles of healing that were taking place (see John 11:4-6). What a strange reply. The answer doesn't seem to fit the context of the question unless you understand what Jesus was actually saying: John, you are in your place of assignment. If I interfere and stop the pain, then your purpose will be cut short. I'm not going to do that.

Countless numbers of Christians are offended at God right now because they thought walking with God would insulate them from pain and suffering. There is an expectation that God is going to come running with legions of angles and rescue us from whatever has the potential to harm us. He has made no such promise, but He *has* said, *"When you pass through the waters, I will be with you; and when you pass through the rivers, they will not sweep over you. When you walk through the fire, you will not be burned; the flames will not set you ablaze"* (Isaiah 43:2). Don't stumble over what God may or may not be doing with others. Rest in the truth that He is always in control of our lives!

DON'T BE IGNORANT

Anyone you forgive, I also forgive. And what I have forgiven—if there was anything to forgive—I have forgiven in the sight of Christ for your sake, in order that Satan might not outwit us. For we are not unaware of his schemes (2 Corinthians 2:10-11).

I don't mean to alarm you, but you have a determined enemy. His plans to stop your purpose and kill your assignment. He especially loves to strike when circumstances don't seem to make sense. He is the master of confusion and purveyor of lies. That is why Paul warned us to be on guard and not allow satan any opportunity to outwit us. The word "schemes" denote a plan that is thought out. The word is referring to the mind of the enemy, not just his strength. Every wise combat commander will tell you if they know how the enemy thinks, they can discern his plan and defeat him.

From Nehemiah, we get a glimpse of the strategy of the enemy.

1. *The enemy will try to create an atmosphere of darkness and confusion about your purpose.* As soon as Nehemiah started building the wall, the enemy pounced: *"and all of them conspired together to come and attack Jerusalem and create confusion"* (Nehemiah 4:8 NKJV). The enemy knows if he can cut you off from your future, you will always revert to your past. He will even use other people to dissuade you from moving forward.

2. *The enemy will try to convince you that you are too weak for what God has called you to do.* "For they all were trying to make us afraid, saying, 'Their hands will be weakened in the work, and it will not be done'" (Nehemiah 6:9 NKJV). When the enemy whispers in your ear you are too weak, just shout back, "I CAN DO ALL THINGS THROUGH CHRIST WHO STRENGTHENS ME!" That should shut him up.

3. *The enemy will try to stop progress completely.* "So, I sent messengers to them, saying, 'I am doing a great work, so that I cannot come down. Why should the work cease while I leave it and go down to you?'" (Nehemiah 6:3 NKJV). Don't be ignorant of satan's plan. Wise up and know when things are turned upside down and life doesn't make sense, that's when the enemy will attack. You don't have to fear, just stand in the strength and power of God!

UNSHAKABLE

*In the time of those kings, the God of heaven will set up a
kingdom that will never be destroyed, nor will it be left to
another people. It will crush all those kingdoms and bring them
to an end, but it will itself endure forever* (Daniel 2:44).

DANIEL MADE AN ASSERTION THAT FLIES IN THE FACE OF CURRENT EVENTS.
Day after day we are given the impression that God's Kingdom is on the
way out. If you believe the mainstream media, you surmise that Christianity (and
Christians) have no voice in modern society. What used to be subtle hints have
now become full-on frontal assaults.

Once we understand the meaning of the Kingdom of God, then we can fully
appreciate why Daniel made such a claim that *"the God of heaven will set up a
kingdom that will never be destroyed."* Author Peter Whyte observes, "The Kingdom of God is His rule, His authority, His government; to receive the Kingdom
of God is to accept God's government over our lives."43

Every living soul on planet Earth is living under one of two governments—
the rule of God or the rule of the evil one. There is no in-between, and there are
no exceptions. In Ephesians, Paul painted a before-and-after picture of a child of
God. Before we were saved, we lived under the rule or kingdom of satan: *"As for
you, you were dead in your transgressions and sins, in which you used to live when you
followed the ways of this world and of the ruler of the kingdom of the air, the spirit
who is now at work in those who are disobedient"* (Ephesians 2:1-2).

But, the after picture is much better: *"But because of his great love for us, God,
who is rich in mercy, made us alive with Christ even when we were dead in transgressions—it is by grace you have been saved"* (Ephesians 2:4-5).

The bottom line: As Christians, we don't have to live in fear that the forces of
satan will replace the Kingdom of God. Every generation has heralded the demise
of God's rule on the earth. The forces of darkness have lined up its pallbearers
to carry the Kingdom of God to the graveyard, only to discover the corpse rising
and outliving them all! Don't go by what you see around you, but what you know
to be true in God's Word!

WHOLE LOT OF SHAKIN' GOING ON

*At that time his voice shook the earth, but now he has
promised, "Once more I will shake not only the earth but also
the heavens." The words "once more" indicate the removing
of what can be shaken—that is, created things—so that what
cannot be shaken may remain* (Hebrews 12:26-27).

WHEN AREAS OF OUR LIVES ARE ABRUPTLY SHAKEN, WE TEND TO START pointing fingers at others. Surely there has to be someone to blame for the way things are going. The writer of Hebrews plainly states who is behind the shaking. It is not the devil, your boss, your children, or your spouse who is doing the shaking. Yes, God will use people to rub us in such a way that we want to blame them, but He is the prime mover behind it all. It is much easier to point the finger instead of realizing God has allowed these things to happen.

There will be times in our lives when things are going smoothly, then suddenly God shakes things up. I can testify from personal experience that when the shaking begins, my world becomes unstable. I also tend to get defensive and, if I'm not careful, I become offended at God.

Why would God do that? It's not because the Lord is angry, but because He loves us too much to allow specific areas of our lives to go unchecked. He will shake the areas of disobedience so we can see how toxic those things can be to our spiritual health. The Lord will shake our attitude when they become so cynical that it prevents us from seeing the goodness of the Lord. He will shake our relationships when they become barriers to our fulfillment of His purpose. He will even shake up our finances when we think that what we have in the bank is more important than our walk with Him.

Like peeling an onion, the Lord will peel back one layer at a time until He replaces what is shakable for what is unshakable. The purpose of shaking is to identify areas that are not built on solid ground. Don't play the blame game, just trust that God has your best interest at heart!

SHAKE AND BAKE

*Therefore, since we are receiving a kingdom that cannot be shaken,
let us be thankful, and so worship God acceptably with reverence
and awe, for our "God is a consuming fire"* (Hebrews 12:28-29).

SEVERAL YEARS AGO, THERE WAS A TELEVISION COMMERCIAL PROMOTING THE product Shake and Bake. The selling point was how easy it was to prepare a meal—just place the magic ingredients in a bag, add chicken, and shake until the chicken is coated. But for the perfect meal to be created, there was one final step—bake it in the oven. After the set time, a sumptuous meal was ready to be consumed. Unfortunately for us, life is not that simple.

God has His own "shake and bake" recipe. When the author of Hebrews says, *"for our 'God is a consuming fire,'"* he gave us a clue as to how the process works. We have to be careful what we wish for; we may just get something we were not expecting. If you have been asking God for a more intimate walk with Him, or for Him to show you any blind spots, I'm reminded of what a preacher said one day, *"Folks, when you ask God for more of Him, you better tie a knot on the end of the rope and hang on—things are about to get dicey."*

The preacher's statement was confusing at first and then I reread First Peter 1:6-7, *"In all this you greatly rejoice, though now for a little while you may have had to suffer grief in all kinds of trials. These have come so that the proven genuineness of your faith—of greater worth than gold, which perishes even though refined by fire—may result in praise, glory and honor when Jesus Christ is revealed."*

Yes, God has an oven. It is there in the heat of trials that He refines our character. There are many things we can learn from education or just the experiences of life. But as Christians, we can never rise any higher than our willingness to allow God to use the heat to shape and mold us into the image of Christ. If you find yourself in the oven and feel like God has left you to burn up, you can take heart. He knows just the right temperature and the right amount of time to produce a reflection of His character in you!

WHICH WAY TO THE TOP?

*The Lord will make you the head, not the tail. If you pay
attention to the commands of the Lord your God that I give
you this day and carefully follow them, you will always be
at the top, never at the bottom* (Deuteronomy 28:13).

THIS VERSE PAINTS A BEAUTIFUL PICTURE. WHO DOESN'T WANT TO BE LIVING at the top? The Lord promised that we will be the head, not the tail, always be at the top, never at the bottom. How can we beat a deal like that? The implication is pretty straightforward; if we give our lives to the Lord, we will be promoted to the head of the class. We won't have to go through any maturing process or experience any pain. Nope, not us. There is only one thing wrong with that idea. It is incomplete, which makes it 100 percent incorrect!

Christians are famous for leaving out parts of Scriptures that don't fit the narrative they are trying to push. In the case of Deuteronomy 28:13, the missing part is, *"If you pay attention to the commands of the Lord your God that I give you this day and carefully follow them."* Many times we forget to read the fine print. Our obedience to His Word is the key. Imagine God's promises as a door. On the front, you read the promise. But as soon as you enter to claim the promise, you turn to see the other side. The "conditions" for fulfillment are listed. You can't have one without the other.

I only know of two professions that start at the top—well-digging and grave digging. In everything else you move from the bottom to the top, not the other way around. The same applies when it comes to living according to biblical principles.

Let's examine the contradictions:
- If you want to be first, be last (Matthew 19:30).
- If you want to lead, first learn to serve (1 Peter 4:10).
- To live, you must die to yourself (Luke 9:24-25).
- If you want to receive, you have to give (Luke 6:38).
- You are not of the world, but you are in the world (John 17:14-18).

There are no shortcuts in the Kingdom of God. Don't try to cut in line to get to the front. It never works.

TROUBLEMAKERS

But when they did not find them, they dragged Jason and some other believers before the city officials, shouting: "These men who have caused trouble all over the world have now come here, and Jason has welcomed them into his house. They are all defying Caesar's decrees, saying that there is another king, one called Jesus" (Acts 17:6-7).

I DOUBT PAUL AND HIS EVANGELISTIC TEAM THOUGHT WHAT THERE WERE doing was causing trouble, yet in spite of their good intentions, they were considered *"men who have caused trouble."* Why? I believe it was because they were teaching a new way of life, not offering a new philosophy or even a new religion. Proclaiming the Kingship of Jesus was not only against Roman law but to declare that Jesus was King and not Caesar would cost you your life!

The Romans were famous for their worship of idols. Whatever the occasion, they had a god to run to and offer a sacrifice. If a soldier was going to war, then Mars was your guy. If a woman wanted children, she would worship at the altar of Juno. And not only did they have a multitude of gods to meet every need, once a year each citizen was obligated to go to the local temple and declare Caesar was god over all the universe.

To follow Christ in our culture may look different from Paul's day, but with each passing year, it is becoming more and more difficult to proclaim God's sovereignty. Many Christians are more afraid of being labeled a troublemaker than seeing their culture changed. The gods of our culture don't go by such names as Neptune, Minerva, or Venus, rather some worship fortune and fame. And if we aren't careful, we can allow "things" to become our gods, thereby replacing the Lord Jesus of His rightful place on the throne of our heart.

Paul was not afraid to declare there is only one God; and for that, he was pursued as a common criminal. We need the same boldness today to trumpet the good news of the Kingdom of God. We need to become more like a thermostat, and less like a thermometer. A thermometer registers the temperature, while a thermostat regulates the temperature based on the instructions you give. Paul was considered a troublemaker because he changed the atmosphere by declaring there is no other King but Jesus. May God give us such boldness to do the same!

FIRST THINGS FIRST

But seek first his kingdom and his righteousness, and all
these things will be given to you as well (Matthew 6:33).

SOME BIBLE SCHOLARS HAVE SUGGESTED THIS PASSAGE IN MATTHEW REPRE-
sents the first sermon Jesus preached. If so, what do you suppose would be
the first thing on His list? Would He teach on the beauties of Heaven? Perhaps
He would spend some time talking about the dangers of hell, or even how to be a
good church member? NO. His first topic was about priorities. He spoke of putting first things first.

Jesus did not come to earth to start a new religion or introduce a modern philosophy. He came to announce the Kingdom of God. The announcement of the
Kingdom was His first and only priority: *"From that time on Jesus began to preach,*
"Repent, for the kingdom of heaven has come near" (Matthew 4:17). Myles Munroe
wrote one of the best definitions I have found on the Kingdom of God: "A kingdom is: The governing influence of a king over his territory, impacting it with his
personal will, purpose, and intent, producing a culture, values, morals, and lifestyle that reflects the king's desires and nature for his citizens."[44]

If we determine to live according to the principles of this definition, then our
actions, not our words will prove it. We live out our daily lives by the choices we
make. If your life is in chaos, then it is painfully apparent your priorities are out
of sync. Stop and consider what is taking your time, money, and energy the most,
and then you will know in short order what is first. Don't make the mistake of
thinking just because you are busy with the daily routine of life you are obedient
to King Jesus. Being busy does not equate to being effective any more than trying to cut your lawn with a vacuum cleaner. Busy, yes. Effective, no!

The secret to stress-free living is to understand the innate power of establishing priorities, based on the *"seek first his kingdom"* principle. If Jesus said there is
something we have to do "first," then what do you think we ought to do first? If
you answered, seek God first, you are correct. If not, then you have work to do.
The best time to get started is now!

FRIDAY

ONLY SEEKERS MAY APPLY

But seek ye first the kingdom of God, and his righteousness; and all these things shall be added unto you (Matthew 6:33 KJV).

THE FIRST THREE WORDS IN THIS VERSE GIVE US THE SECRET TO THE ABUN-dant life in the Kingdom God: *"But seek ye."* Most translations leave out the "you" because it is implied in the command. Jesus is saying, "But *you* seek first, or *you* must take the first step to become a "seeker" of the Kingdom and His righteousness." Jesus said only seekers may apply! If you are a seeker, then and only then, can you have the assurance that all these things will be added to you.

The definition of *seeking* according to Strong's Concordance is "to seek by inquiring; to investigate to reach a binding (terminal) resolution; to search, 'getting to the bottom of a matter.'"[45] The question is—are you a seeker? Are you engaged in a passionate pursuit of the things of God? Seekers possess a burning desire for the very thing they want. Jesus says in Matthew 7:7: *"Ask and it will be given to you; seek and you will find; knock and the door will be opened to you."*

To earnestly desire the Kingdom rule of God in our lives may mean ,we might have to give up something that is interfering with our pursuit. Usually, the choice is not between good and evil, but between what is good and what is best.

One of the first warning signs that we have stopped seeking after the Lord is when we begin to delegate "eternal things" to the back of the line and move the "temporal things" to the front. If the love of having a big bank account is your priority, then all of your energy and passion will be spent on pursuing money. Whatever takes your passion away from seeking after God could potentially become a thief robbing you of the joy of living under the rule of King Jesus. And, it is at that moment the downward spiral into mediocre living begins.

What is your first priority? Is it to seek the Lord with all of your heart? The Lord of the universe is waiting and watching to see who will seek after Him. The psalmist declared, *"The Lord looks down from heaven on all mankind to see if there are any who understand, any who seek God"* (Psalm 14:2).

MONDAY

TREASURES

Do not store up for yourselves treasures on earth, where moths and vermin destroy, and where thieves break in and steal. But store up for yourselves treasures in heaven, where moths and vermin do not destroy, and where thieves do not break in and steal (Matthew 6:19-20).

JESUS ISSUED A COMMAND IN THIS VERSE: *"DO NOT STORE UP FOR YOURSELVES treasures on earth."* It is evident Jesus is pointing out a problem with laying up treasures on earth. Everything that follows is dependent on how we discern the command as it relates to our understanding between material and eternal things.

Jesus did not say it is wrong to have money. If He had meant money, He would have said so. The word "treasure" means "wealth" and has a broader meaning than just how much money we have in our bank account. Our treasure may be houses, cars, or a relationship that we cherish beyond words. Here is the key: *whatever is the most important thing in our life becomes our treasure.*

Two words unlock the meaning: *earth and Heaven.* He warns us that whatever we treasure on earth will eventually fade away. I have been to many funerals for both rich and poor. No matter the economic class of the person in the grave, whatever they accumulated on earth will be left behind, no exception.

You may not be able to take it with you, but you can send treasures on ahead. Jesus said not to hoard or store treasures on earth, but hoard, store, treasures in Heaven. What treasures is He talking about? Paul said to Timothy: *"Command those who are rich in this present world not to be arrogant nor to put their hope in wealth, which is so uncertain, but to put their hope in God, who richly provides us with everything for our enjoyment. Command them to do good, to be rich in good deeds, and to be generous and willing to share"* (1 Timothy 6:17-18).

While things of the earth will pass away, treasures we lay up in Heaven are eternal. Living a life rich with good deeds, coupled with an attitude of giving and sharing with others are just a few of the treasures we can enjoy both on earth, and one day we will benefit from the reward in Heaven.

WHERE THE HEART GOES

For where your treasure is, there your heart will be also. "The eye is the lamp of the body. If your eyes are healthy, your whole body will be full of light. But if your eyes are unhealthy, your whole body will be full of darkness. If then the light within you is darkness, how great is that darkness!" (Matthew 6:21-23)

EARTHLY "TREASURES" CAN HAVE A POWERFUL IMPACT ON OUR LIVES. Whether that treasure is a place, person, or thing, it has drawing power to seize our emotions and hold them in an iron grip. There is nothing wrong with having treasures on earth, as long we don't allow earthly treasures to color our view of what is essential.

When Jesus spoke about the heart, He was referring to the emotional grip that treasures can have. He warned us that our hearts follow after whatever we treasure, therefore we must be careful where we place our affections. Once we fix an emotion to a material thing, a bond is formed that is nearly impossible to break. We will begin to ignore our calling of loving people and use things. Instead, we will love things and use people. If you want to know about someone's spiritual condition, just follow what they love—it will lead you to the treasure every time!

Jesus also pointed out the mind is involved (Matthew 6:22-23). The eye is a symbol of the mind. He is talking about the way we view things. The eye observes, while the mind that perceives, so the one stands for the other. If your eye is set on treasures in Heaven, the body is full of light. Everything is in the right perspective and life is in focus.

A wrong view of treasures will produce a blurred and distorted vision. Herein lies the danger. Whatever the heart is set on, the mind will figure out a way to justify. If anything is drawing your heart away from the things of God, it is time to reevaluate where you have placed your affections. Don't be fooled into thinking that it doesn't matter what you worship during the week, as long as you worship God on Sunday.

Continue to allow the Holy Spirit to transform your mind (see Romans 12:1-2), and you will be able to gain a heavenly view of earthly things. First John 2:17 says, *"The world and its desires pass away, but whoever does the will of God lives forever."*

CHOOSE

No one can serve two masters. Either you will hate the one and love the other, or you will be devoted to the one and despise the other. You cannot serve both God and money (Matthew 6:24).

JESUS IS STILL TEACHING HOW WE VIEW OUR TREASURE. YOUR TREASURE MAY be different from mine, but whatever it is, if it holds my attention more than the things of God, then it is time to make a choice. He has put all of us on notice. He said we could not sit on the fence when it comes to serving God, *"You cannot serve both God and money."* Some translations use the word, *"mammon,"* which is a broader term to describe *material wealth that has an evil influence.* Either way, when what we have is more important than what we are in Christ, it is a stumbling block.

The key word that Jesus used is the action word *"serve."* Our unhealthy attraction to earthly treasure moves us in three ways: first, emotion of the heart; second, justification of the mind; and third, to take action. There is no compromise here. We can't sit down at the negotiating table and bargain with the Holy Spirit. His love for us is a jealous love, and He will not tolerate a rival.

I am reminded of the day that the prophet Elijah put the people to the test. He challenged them to make a decision: *"Elijah went before the people and said, 'How long will you waver between two opinions? If the Lord is God, follow him; but if Baal is God, follow him.' But the people said nothing"* (1 Kings 18:21). Why didn't they have anything to say? They knew they were guilty of idol worship and they developed spiritual lockjaw.

The Lord is calling each of us to make a choice. Frankly, I would rather have someone be honest and say that their god is the pursuit of material wealth than put on an act on Sunday morning. I said it before, and I will repeat it. There is nothing wrong with having material things. Paul told Timothy that God had given us all things richly to enjoy (1 Timothy 6:17). And, there is nothing wrong with earning and having money. *That is not the issue.* The issue is who are we serving with what we have. All of us are serving one or the other, can't be both. Time to choose!

THE MIRACLE OF EXCHANGE

In everything I did, I showed you that by this kind of hard work we must help the weak, remembering the words the Lord Jesus himself said: "It is more blessed to give than to receive" (Acts 20:35).

THERE IS A BIBLE PRINCIPLE THAT WE ALL LIVE BY, BUT VERY FEW PEOPLE understand. This principle affects us in the natural as well as the spiritual. I call it the "miracle of exchange." A simple definition of the word "exchange" is to give or to take in return for another thing. So by that definition, when we exchange something, we can have a reasonable expectation we will receive something in return.

Every farmer knows how the principle works. He must be willing to give up something—seed—to receive something in return—a harvest. Every grocery shopper knows this principle. You fill up your cart with food and stand at the checkout counter. Next, a transaction takes place as you are asked to exchange money for the items you chose. If you go to a place of employment, you exchange your time, skill, and diligence for something at the end of the week—a paycheck.

The principle of exchange also works in the things of God. Some folks have been praying for years for something to happen, and it never does. They sit waiting for God to do something, and all the while God is saying, *"I have done everything for you already, now it is up to you to make the next move."*

For example, when we came to Jesus, this powerful exchange principle kicked into action:

- I exchanged my *sin for His righteousness* (Colossians 1:12-15).
- I exchanged my *sickness for His wholeness* (Isaiah 53:4-5).
- I exchanged my *poverty for His riches* (2 Corinthians 8:9).
- I exchanged my *lack for His abundance* (Philippians 4:19).

I think the prophet Hosea was onto something when he said, *"My people are destroyed for lack of knowledge"* (Hosea 4:6). Don't allow a lack of knowledge to rob you of all that God has in store for your life. Remember, all of God's principles and promises operate on our willingness to take the first step in obedience to His Word (see Deuteronomy 8:1-12).

THE POWER OF "IT"

*Give, and it will be given to you. A good measure, pressed down,
shaken together and running over, will be poured into your lap. For
with the measure you use, it will be measured to you* (Luke 6:38).

THIS IS SUCH A SIMPLE STATEMENT BY JESUS, AND YET THERE IS ENOUGH truth packed into one verse to unleash Heaven's resources to handle any situation. But to realize its enormous power, the first step has to be taken.

Jesus says the first step is to *"give."* That is an all-inclusive command meaning everyone can participate because everyone has something to give. In case you are wondering, He is referring to more than just money. For a person to say they have nothing to give is a misstatement. The word "give" is in continuous tense, meaning to "keep on giving." An act of giving becomes an attitude; an attitude of giving then becomes a lifestyle. When God touches something, He wants you to give, just obey His voice. He promises to take care of the rest, *"and it will be given to you."*

I call this the power of "it." What is it? Whatever you give, fill in the blank, and "it" will be given back to you: *"A good measure, pressed down, shaken together and running over, will be poured into your lap."* The law of sowing and reaping means you reap what you sow. If you sow corn, you reap corn, not tobacco. If you plant an orange tree, you harvest oranges, not apples. Paul says, *"Do not be deceived: God cannot be mocked. A man reaps what he sows"* (Galatians 6:7).

God will never tell you to do something without giving you the ability to do it. With each command of obedience, He gives you the power to carry it out. When we begin to release what is in our hands, God will start to release what is in His hands. And I can guarantee you, His hands are much bigger than ours! So the question is, what do you need? What is your *it?* It may not be money, but whatever it is, starting giving and watch what God will do. And for Heaven's sake do not limit God or hold tight the things God has given you to steward: *"For with the measure you use, it will be measured to you"* (see 2 Corinthians 9:6-8).

WHOSE STUFF IS IT ANYWAY?

Whoever can be trusted with very little can also be trusted with much, and whoever is dishonest with very little will also be dishonest with much. So if you have not been trustworthy in handling worldly wealth, who will trust you with true riches? (Luke 16:10-11)

THE UNDERLYING ISSUE IN THIS PARABLE IS ONE WORD—*TRUST.* PSALM 37 states that we can trust God with everything. The heart of the matter is, *can God trust us to be good stewards of the things He has given us?* Trust is a two-way street. The manager in this story in Luke 16 was confronted with an audit by the owner. I'm sure this guy never thought the owner would have him give an account of the "stuff" he was given charge to oversee (see Luke 16:1-13).

The unwise steward mistakenly thought the stuff belonged to him. The fact is, everything belongs to the Lord. He owns it all, and we just have the privilege of managing it. James 1:17 declares, *"Every good and perfect gift is from above, coming down from the Father of the heavenly lights, who does not change like shifting shadows."* The main issue then becomes: Whose stuff is it anyway?

The conflict has been and will always be, who is in control of my possessions? For example, if you earned one thousand dollars last week, how much of that belongs to God? I guess the answer depends on who you ask, right? A tithing church member will say, *"The first 10 percent belongs to God."* An occasional giver will say, *"I give when I feel like it."* And, the majority says, *"It's all mine. I earned it, and I'm spending it the way I want."* The truth is, *all of it belongs to God!* It is His money in our bank account; it is His house we live in; and it is His car we drive.

The Lord has every right to know how we handle His stuff. So, if the question is a matter trust, how is that measured? It's no secret. He told us, *"Whoever can be trusted with very little can also be trusted with much."* Trust then is measured by what we are doing now with the things He has given us. Just by saying that one day we will take our stewardship seriously is not sufficient. The issue is not what we have, but what we love (see Luke 16:13).

A MATTER OF PERSPECTIVE

So when the people broke camp to cross the Jordan, the priests carrying the ark of the covenant went ahead of them. Now the Jordan is at flood stage all during harvest. Yet as soon as the priests who carried the ark reached the Jordan and their feet touched the water's edge (Joshua 3:14-15).

RIGHT TIMING AND PROPER PERSPECTIVE ARE TWO OF THE MOST NECESSARY ingredients for success. In just about everything we do in life, those two elements are crucial. I have no doubt there have been circumstances when even the most spiritual among us have questioned God's timing. We may not be so brave as to speak them out loud, but those doubts are there just the same. Have you ever thought, *Lord, why did You wait so long to answer my prayer?* Or, *Lord, is it too late now for me to do the thing I could have done twenty years ago?"* I know I have asked those questions, and more.

The children of Israel must have wondered about God's timing as they stood on the edge of the Jordan river. What do they find standing in their way of a promise? The Jordan river is overflowing its banks! I can almost imagine the conversation between Joshua and the Lord:

Joshua: *"You've got to be kidding! Lord, is this a joke?"*

The Lord: *"No."*

Joshua: *"Just no? Did You happen to notice the river is flooded?"*

The Lord: *"Yes, but I am not worried."*

Joshua: *"Lord, we have been going in circles for forty years, and You had all that time to get it right."*

The Lord: *"Change your view and look to the other side and you will see it is harvest time. Just relax and follow My instructions, because on the other side I have a miracle harvest waiting for you."*

You see, my friend, what they needed was a different perspective. God's timing was perfect. He didn't get them there at flood stage—but at harvest time! They needed to change from a "flood" perspective to a "harvest" perspective. They were more concerned about the obstacle than they were about what God had in mind for them. Once we realize there are no accidents with God, then we can take our eyes off of "perceived" roadblocks and look beyond and see a harvest is ready for us to enjoy.

IT'S NOT FAIR

*"Your brother has come," he replied, "and your father has killed
the fattened calf because he has him back safe and sound."
The older brother became angry and refused to go in. So his
father went out and pleaded with him* (Luke 15:27-28).

JESUS TOLD THE STORY OF A FATHER WHO HAD TWO SONS. THE YOUNGEST SON
took his inheritance and rode off into the sunset. He squandered his money
on the party life and when he ended up the pig pen, he "came to himself" and
headed home. But, there was another son who didn't leave. He stayed at home to
work for his father, and yet he demonstrates that you don't have to leave home to
develop a rebellious attitude. Living in the "far country" is a matter of the heart,
not a physical location (see Luke 15:11-31).

When the elder brother heard the sounds of celebration (Luke 15:26), he called
a servant to ask what was all the noise. Hearing that his brother had finally come
home, he became so angry that he refused to join in. The father confronts him about
his attitude, and I can almost hear the offended son shout, "This isn't fair! I've always
been here. I haven't done any of those things, and yet you never gave me a party."

The older brother was under the illusion that everything had to be fair. To be
honest, there wasn't anything about what the young prodigal did that was fair.
He took his father's money, lived like the devil, and had the nerve to ask if he
could be restored. Wow, nothing fair about that. And yet, the father restored him
as a son. The Kingdom of God operates on a different scale, and fairness is not
always in the equation.

Where did we get the idea that life is supposed to fair? Maybe our concept of
fairness comes from a PC (politically correct) culture that says everybody is equal,
there only winners, and everybody gets a trophy. I heard the other day that many
schools were canceling sports. And the sports programs that remained were not
allowed to keep score. The idea is so no one will get their feelings hurt. If we are
not careful, we will begin to judge things the same way as the elder brother. He
ended up angry, isolated, and miserable. He based his judgment on what he saw,
not on what the father was doing. His focus was on himself, and what he considered fair. We must avoid the same mistake at all cost.

BETWEEN A ROCK AND A HARD PLACE

Jonathan said to his young armor-bearer, "Come, let's go over to the outpost of those uncircumcised men. Perhaps the Lord will act in our behalf. Nothing can hinder the Lord from saving, whether by many or by few" (1 Samuel 14:6).

As I HAVE SAID BEFORE, THERE ARE TIMES IN LIFE WHEN THINGS DON'T MAKE sense. Just because someone is a Christian doesn't mean the person won't face the same contradictions of life as those who are not. Jesus said, *"that you may be children of your Father in heaven. He causes his sun to rise on the evil and the good, and sends rain on the righteous and the unrighteous"* (Matthew 5:45). In other words, we are all in the same boat!

Jonathan is faced with a dilemma (see 1 Samuel 14:2-3). King Saul's army was sitting on the sidelines waiting for the him to give the battle plan. Instead of gearing up for the fight and leading the army to victory, Saul was sitting under a tree. There is nothing wrong with sitting under a tree, but the inference was that the king had lost his passion for leading. The result of his inaction caused the army to become bewildered and afraid. On the other side was an enemy determined to pursue and wipe out the Israelites.

Jonathan found himself between a rock and a hard place and yet he pushed on believing that somehow God would grant him a victory. The rest of this story tells how he took action in spite of overwhelming odds and defeated the Philistines (see 1 Samuel 14:4-7). What are we supposed to do when we find ourselves facing overwhelming circumstances?

First, don't judge by what you see. Ask God to give insight into the situation and view the circumstances through Heaven's eyes: *"Don't be afraid,"* the prophet answered. *"Those who are with us are more than those who are with them"* (2 Kings 6:16).

Second, seek God before making any plans to attack the situation: *"Plans are established by seeking advice; so if you wage war, obtain guidance"* (Proverbs 20:18).

Third, make up your mind to take action and leave the outcome to God: *"... Perhaps the Lord will act in our behalf. Nothing can hinder the Lord from saving, whether by many or by few"* (1 Samuel 14:6). I say that is a good strategy for victory!

AMBASSADORS

*that God was reconciling the world to himself in Christ, not
counting people's sins against them. And he has committed to us the
message of reconciliation. We are therefore Christ's ambassadors, as
though God were making his appeal through us. We implore you
on Christ's behalf: Be reconciled to God (2 Corinthians 5:19-20).*

WHEN WE GAVE OUR LIVES TO JESUS CHRIST, WE EXPERIENCED A TRANS-
formation from the inside out. And, by virtue of the new birth (see John
3:3), we became citizens of the Kingdom of God. As citizens of God's Kingdom,
we enjoy certain rights and privileges. Paul said we are now commissioned to represent the King as ambassadors to the nations of the world.

In the natural world, ambassadors are sent from one country to another country to represent the values and policies of the sending nation. Ambassadors do not
act or speak on their behalf, nor do they create policy. Their assignment is to be
the spokespersons for the sending government. When an ambassador speaks, it's
as if the governing power of his or her home nation is talking.

What does it mean to be an ambassador? The definition of "ambassador"
according to Strong's Concordance is "To act as an ambassador: means to act
as an established statesman (diplomat) – a trusted, respected ambassador who is
authorized to speak as God's emissary (represent His kingdom)."[46]

We are called as spiritual ambassadors of the King of kings. We are authorized to speak as God's emissaries! Wow, what an awesome responsibility has
been given to us to represent God on the earth. So, what is the official position of
Heaven and what is the message we are to communicate? Paul says we are to be
ambassadors of *reconciliation,* proclaiming the good news that Jesus Christ has
died for the sins of the world!

Can you think of anyone who needs to hear the message of reconciliation? I'm
not suggesting you have to stand behind a pulpit to share the message of hope.
We are what I call "everyday ambassadors," who live and work among people
who need the news that they can have their sins forgiven and be reconciled to
God. The official position from the throne room of Heaven—the war is over, and
peace has been declared (see Ephesians 2:11-19).

PRAYER—LIFE'S GREATEST ADVENTURE

The greatest adventure man can embark on is prayer. Prayer has the ability to take the deepest thoughts and feelings of man before the Creator. At the same time prayer brings the nature, character, and purposes of God into the heart of man. Prayer can chart and change the course of human history. It can calm the heart in the midst of a raging storm and refresh the weary saint in the battles of life.

SAMMY TIPPIT[47]

DO YOU HAVE YOUR EARS ON?

This is the word that came to Jeremiah from the Lord: "Go down to the potter's house, and there I will give you my message" (Jeremiah 18:1-2).

I REMEMBER BACK IN THE 1970S EVERYONE THOUGHT IT WAS COOL TO HAVE A CB radio. What was necessary equipment for truckers soon became the fad of the year. The most popular phrase was, "Hey good buddy, do you have your ears on?" In layman's terms that meant, "Are you listening? I have something to say."

I find it interesting that the prophet was told to *"Go down to the potter's house."* The Lord had something to say to Jeremiah, and it was time to "put his ears on." In most villages, the potter's house was the center of attention. It was a place where business was conducted. It was not what I would call a place to "be still" and hear God's voice. It would be the equivalent of me saying to you, "Go to the busiest place you can find in the mall and there you can hear God." Doesn't stack up to our traditional thinking about hearing God, does it?

Is it possible that you don't have to go and sit on top of a mountain to hear God's voice? Or join a monastery and isolate yourself to commune with Him? Please understand, I'm in no way suggesting that quiet time with God is to be avoided. But it *is* possible to continue to go about your daily business and be open to hearing God. He is still communicating with His people today. Jesus said, *"My sheep listen to my voice; I know them, and they follow me"* (John 10:27). If you are a Christian, then His promise is that you can hear His voice. And be open, because it may come during the busiest part of your day.

How can we really know someone if we don't listen to the person? I'm afraid for many people, communication with God has become a one-sided conversation. Getting to know your heavenly Father is more than bringing a list of things for Him to do and then walking away before He has a chance to respond. He wants to talk to you. Do you have your ears on?

Give ear and come to me; listen, that you may live. I will make an everlasting covenant with you, my faithful love promised to David (Isaiah 55:3).

AN INVITATION

Call to me and I will answer you and tell you great and unsearchable things you do not know (Jeremiah 33:3).

IF YOU RECEIVED AN INVITATION TO SPEND TIME WITH THE PRESIDENT OF THE United States, how would you react? What if the engraved invitation also stipulated that your time with the president was unlimited. You could discuss any subject without restrictions. I don't know about you, but I would go, regardless of the political party in power. Why? For the simple reason that the most powerful person on the planet asked for my presence, allowing me to spend as much time as I wanted. It's a no-brainer. I would not refuse the invitation.

What if you received another invitation? This invitation might read: *The Creator of the universe desires to spend time with you. Your time is unlimited, and any subject matter may be discussed.* Would you take Him up on His offer? You may never receive an invitation to the White House, but I can tell you without fear of contradiction that God has issued you a personal invitation to meet with Him. It is called prayer, and He is waiting for you to respond.

Throughout Scripture, we are urged to spend time with God. Just a brief sample of Scriptures shows we can call on Him anywhere and at any time:

- Psalm 50:15: *"and call on me in the day of trouble; I will deliver you, and you will honor me."*
- Psalm 86:5: *"You, Lord, are forgiving and good, abounding in love to all who call to you."*
- Psalm 116:2: *"Because he turned his ear to me, I will call on him as long as I live.*
- Isaiah 58:9: *"Then you will call, and the Lord will answer; you will cry for help, and he will say: Here am I…."*
- Isaiah 65:1: *"I revealed myself to those who did not ask for me; I was found by those who did not seek me. To a nation that did not call on my name, I said, 'Here am I, here am I.'"*

Too often we only think of prayer when we get in trouble. If everything is going well, we push prayer to the side, and spend our time on other things. Indeed, we can call on the Lord with our problems, but why wait until we are desperate? Will you take the first step? Will you accept His invitation to meet with Him?

NINE POPULAR EXCUSES NOT TO PRAY

When you ask, you do not receive, because you
ask with wrong motives... (James 4:3).

HERE IS A MIND-BOGGLING THOUGHT: THE KING OF KINGS HAS INVITED US to a private time with Him on a daily basis. Have you ever wondered why people don't take advantage of the privilege? I have heard many so-called reasons why people don't spend time in daily communion with God. The list is endless.

Nine of the most popular excuses:

1. Prayer is boring.
2. I don't have time.
3. I tried it, and it doesn't work for me.
4. My home life is too chaotic.
5. I couldn't find a quiet place.
6. I pray only when I'm in trouble.
7. I pray before meals, isn't that enough?
8. I'm too busy, so it's hard to concentrate.
9. I don't think the Lord is interested in the little things of my life.

There is an attitude about prayer I want to highlight. James nailed it when he said some people *do* pray, but they don't receive anything. Why? If prayer is that important and these folks are praying, what is the problem? James said they ask with *"wrong motives."* He was referring to people who pray only to get something in return: *"that you may spend what you get on your pleasures."* James is referring to selfish praying.

Some people treat prayer like a heavenly slot machine. If they can shove enough coins—prayers—into the machine—the Lord—and pull the handle enough times, they will hit their lucky number. Really? Is that how you want your prayer life to go? I have a news flash. He is not a slot machine or a cosmic Santa Claus sitting on His throne waiting for you to bring your goody list.

How would you feel if your children only talked to you when they wanted something? And they refused to talk to you until you finally gave in. How do you think God feels when we act like spoiled children who only want to talk to Him

153

when we want or need something? I'm not saying God doesn't want us to bring our needs and desires before Him. But prayer is more than spinning the wheel on a roulette table! God is waiting to spend time with you. You might be pleasantly surprised at what He has to say!

SECRET WEAPON

*Very truly I tell you, whoever believes in me will do the works
I have been doing, and they will do even greater things than
these, because I am going to the Father* (John 14:12).

JESUS WAS PREPARING HIS DISCIPLES. VERY SOON HE WOULD OFFER THE ULTI-
mate sacrifice for the sins of all humanity. He was going to be physically
removed from their presence, and they needed to know He was not leaving them
as orphans (see John 14:18-24). This collection of disciples were not super-saints
as some suppose, but humans just like us. They were confused, afraid, and not
sure what to do next.

I can just imagine their shock when Jesus told them they would not only
match the works He did, but exceed them: *"whoever believes in me will do the
works I have been doing, and they will do even greater."* In my mind's eye, I can
see Simon Peter mouthing the words to no one in particular: "Did He just say
what I thought He said?" Yes, Peter, you heard Him correctly. He gave you and
all believers in the generations to come a weapon so powerful that it can change
individual lives, as well as the destiny of nations. What is this weapon Jesus
referred to? It is not an army of men—it is greater than that. It is not some new
type of nuclear bomb. It is more powerful than that. *It is prayer!*

It seems there is a huge gap between what Jesus promised and what we see
going on around us. Who was the first person to convince us that prayer is to be
used only in the case of an emergency? Who told us the promises of God are no
longer valid for today? Prayer has been hung up on the wall encased in glass like
a fire extinguisher: BREAK GLASS IN CASE OF EMERGENCY!

E.M. Bounds observed: "Prayer is the easiest and the hardest of all things; the
simplest and the sublimest; the weakest and the most powerful; its results lie outside the range of human possibilities they are limited only by the omnipotence of
God. Few Christians have anything but a vague idea of the power of prayer; fewer
still have any experience of that power."[48]

May God grant us the wisdom to know the weakest Christian on his or her
knees is more powerful than any weapon satan can bring against us.

WHATEVER YOU ASK

And I will do whatever you ask in my name, so that the
Father may be glorified in the Son (John 14:13).

IT SOUNDS TO ME LIKE JESUS JUST GAVE US A BLANK CHECK WITH HIS SIGNA-
ture already affixed. He said we could ask whatever we wanted and He would
answer. Wow! What a promise. Did Jesus mean what He said? Is there some hidden meaning we aren't seeing? I'm quite sure He would not have said it if He
didn't mean it. The test of His word is not on His end, but ours.

When we examine Scripture, we find "whatever" is attached to the will of
God. First John 5:14 says, *"This is the confidence we have in approaching God: that
if we ask anything according to his will, he hears us."* Do you see it—*"according to
his will"* is the qualifier that opens the door to unlimited praying. For our prayers
to have an impact, we must be willing to pray according to God's will. After all,
we wouldn't want to have anything in our life that was not according to His will,
would we? I believe the reason so many Christians give up on prayer is the confusion surrounding one simple word, *"whatever."*

The late Dr. Adrian Rogers provided insight on the issue: "When you are sur-
rendered to the will of God, focused on the Word of God, then the Holy Spirit
begins to pray in you and through you. He energizes, motivates, and guides your
prayer. One of the greatest lessons I've learned about prayer is this: the prayer
that gets to Heaven is the prayer that starts in Heaven.... The prayer that gets to
Heaven is the prayer that starts in Heaven. Our part is just too close the circuit."[49]

If we are to pray according to His will, we must go to the Word and find out
what it says. If you are confused about it, my suggestion is to find out what God
wants and then pray it back to Him. Prayer is not an add-on at the end of a religious exercise—it is our very life!

And pray in the Spirit on all occasions with all kinds of prayers and
requests. With this in mind, be alert and always keep on praying for all
the Lord's people (Ephesians 6:18).

IN MY NAME

And I will do whatever you ask in my name, so that the
Father may be glorified in the Son (John 14:13).

As Jesus was moving toward the cross, He spent time with His disciples revealing the secret to answered prayer (see John 14–16). The secret is *not* that they can ask anything and it will be done. NO, the real key to answered prayer is *"in my name, so that the Father may be glorified in the Son."* As if to emphasize the point, Jesus repeated the promise at least six times in John's Gospel (see John 14:13-14; 15:16; 16:23-26). Jesus is telling us that when we pray in His name, with the right motives, we can have the assurance of answered prayer. When we pray in Jesus' name, we are acknowledging several things:

First, we are saying Jesus is Lord of our life. To pray in His name is not some secret code, or add-on at the end to make sure our prayer reaches the home office. No, when we pray in Jesus' name, we are saying to the Father that we have the "right" as His children to come before Him in the authority of our elder brother: *"Both the one who makes people holy and those who are made holy are of the same family. So Jesus is not ashamed to call them brothers and sisters"* (Hebrews 2:11).

Second, to pray in Jesus' name is to acknowledge that our prayers are directed according to God's will, not ours. Understanding that prayer is based on what Jesus wants for our lives is far more freeing than the frustration that comes when our prayers go unanswered because we pray selfishness prayers.

Third, the *"whatever you ask in My name"* is not a blank check to spend on whatever feels right at the moment. To pray in Jesus' name is recognition that our prayers are based on one simple premise: will this bring glory to the Father? As with all of God's promises, there is a contingent. In the case of answered prayer, we must ask in faith along with the mindset that whatever we ask, God must be glorified.

Fourth, when we pray in Jesus' name, we are demonstrating our love for Jesus. *"If you love me, keep my commands"* (John 14:15). A genuine test of love is never abusing or misusing someone's name. We keep His commands, not out of fear, but out of love.

BACK TO SCHOOL

*One day Jesus was praying in a certain place. When he
finished, one of His disciples said to him, "Lord, teach us
to pray, just as John taught his disciples"* (Luke 11:1).

CAN YOU IMAGINE BEING INVITED TO A SEMINAR ON PRAYER, ONLY TO DIS-
cover the Lord Jesus is your teacher? Jesus could teach His disciples to pray
because He was a Man of consistent prayer. To Him, prayer was as essential as
breathing, and as necessary as eating and drinking. There were times when Jesus
sought a quiet place to pray (see Luke 5:16). On other occasions, He would pray
for and with other people (see Luke 17:9). He did not consider prayer as a burden,
but a blessing. After observing His prayer life, the disciples asked if He would
teach them to do the same.

I have a sense we don't pray more because we are confused about how it works.
I am reminded of when Peter was arrested and thrown in prison (see Acts 12).
While Peter was in jail, the church was praying for a miracle (Acts 12:12). An
angel appeared and set him free. Peter rushed to the prayer meeting to tell them
the good news. He knocks at the gate and Rhoda, hearing his voice, ran and told
the group, *"I think Peter is at the door."* The prayer leader said, *"It can't be Peter at
the door. Don't you understand, he's in jail, and we are praying for a miracle."* Do
you see the irony here? They were praying for a miracle, and when it happened
they were shocked!

We shouldn't be shocked when our prayers are answered. As one dear saint
said, "Getting our prayers answered should be the rule, not the exception." To
which I agree. Keep in mind that prayer was not an edict handed down by the
apostles during the formation of the first century church. From the beginning of
time, prayer was in God's plan to communicate with His creation. Nothing has
changed as far as I can tell. So, what's the problem? Jesus took His disciples into
the school of prayer. I think it is about time for us to go back to the classroom and
learn from the Master Himself.

DOS AND DON'TS

*And when you pray, do not be like the hypocrites, for
they love to pray standing in the synagogues and on the
street corners to be seen by others. Truly I tell you, they
have received their reward in full* (Matthew 6:5).

IN THE PREVIOUS DEVOTIONAL, THE DISCIPLES ASKED JESUS TO TEACH THEM TO
pray. Looking at Matthew's account in chapter 6, He opens up the seminar
with some dos and don'ts of prayer.

- Don't pray like a hypocrite: How do they pray? *"they love to pray
  standing in the synagogues and on the street corners to be seen by
  others."* We have all witnessed the spiritual showboats who like to
  try to impress others with their pious praying. But once the show
  is over, they reveal themselves for what they are. Jesus called them
  hypocrites. A hypocrite is someone who hides behind a mask or a
  person who pretends to be something he or she is not.

- Do learn the power of private praying. *"But when you pray, go into
  your room, close the door and pray to your Father, who is unseen.
  Then your Father, who sees what is done in secret, will reward you"*
  (Matthew 6:6). I don't think Jesus was saying we shouldn't pray in
  public. But He warns us that if we don't have a private prayer life,
  don't put on a mask out in public just to be seen by others.

- Don't pray like a pagan: *"And when you pray, do not keep on bab-
  bling like pagans, for they think they will be heard because of their
  many words"* (Matthew 6:7). Jesus was referring to something
  they already knew. They had seen it up close and personal. Pagan
  prayers were offered in public and in the temples to the various
  gods.

- Do offer sincere prayers from the heart. The pagans had to be loud
  and repetitious to convince the gods of their needs. The pagans
  thought the more they screamed and repeated themselves, whichever god was in charge would finally give up and answer the
  request. But Jesus said, *"Do not be like them, for your Father knows*

what you need before you ask him" (Matthew 6:8). We don't have to beg God to meet our needs. And we don't have to put on a show for the benefit of others.

Find a place to be alone and talk to your heavenly Father. He already knows your need, but loves it when you ask anyway.

FOLLOW THE LEADER

*In this manner, therefore, pray: Our Father in heaven, hallowed be
Your name. Your kingdom come. Your will be done on earth as it
is in heaven. Give us this day our daily bread. And forgive us our
debts, as we forgive our debtors. And do not lead us into temptation,
but deliver us from the evil one. For Yours is the kingdom and the
power and the glory forever. Amen* (Matthew 6:9-13 NKJV).

MANY HAVE CONCLUDED THAT JESUS GAVE THE DISCIPLES, AND US, A MODEL prayer to pray. It has evolved into the number one "prayer for all occasions." I don't think Jesus intended us to use His words as a prayer to be recited, but more a pattern to follow. He said, *"In this manner, therefore, pray"* (Matthew 6:9 NKJV). Praying the same prayer, over and over again, without understanding the meaning of the words is to be avoided. It becomes nothing more than *"vain repetitions,"* and that is what Jesus warned us about (Matthew 6:7).

The most effective way to begin any prayer is to recognize our relationship to God: *"Our Father in heaven."* To say that God is our Father is to acknowledge that we are part of His family. How do you become part of a family? You are born into one! You don't "join" a family or pay dues to be a member. Likewise, to be a member of God's family requires birth. Jesus said, *"Very truly I tell you, no one can see the kingdom of God unless they are born again* (John 3:3).

There is a false teaching that proclaims the fatherhood of God, and the brotherhood of humankind. The premise is that God is the Father of us all, no matter our belief system. And we are all brothers and sisters in the cosmic family. Only one thing wrong with that philosophy—it's wrong! God is the Creator of us all, and we are indeed connected in many ways to each other. But He cannot become a father to anyone who has not been born into His family. How would you feel if your children called every man in your neighborhood "father"?

I challenge you to start every prayer by following the pattern. Asking for God's will to be accomplished *"on earth as it is in heaven."* When we put His name, His Kingdom, and His will ahead of our own, we move from selfish praying and the "It's all about me" syndrome. Next is to bring our needs and petitions before Him.

ONE MORE THING

For if you forgive other people when they sin against you, your heavenly Father will also forgive you. But if you do not forgive others their sins, your Father will not forgive your sins (Matthew 6:14-15).

JESUS ADDS A "ONE MORE THING" IN HIS DISCUSSION ON PRAYER. IN THESE two verses in Matthew 6 He isn't saying that we have to earn our way to answered prayers by living a perfect life. He is talking about being in harmony with our brothers and sisters. Prayer is a privilege given to all of His sons and daughters, and is not based on a "good works" mentality. Jesus is not suggesting that we have to earn so many gold stars before we can come into God's presence.

I find it virtually impossible to pray when I know that my fellowship is broken with someone. There have been times when I pushed ahead anyway, knowing all along there was something wrong. I tried to fool God and pretend like everything was going great. But when I sensed my prayers weren't get any higher than the ceiling, I decided to do the wise thing. I asked God what was wrong. He impressed on my heart there was something that needed to be dealt with between another brother and me. When I took care of the matter, the lines of communication were wide open again.

Since all believers are part of the same family, then it stands to reason we need to learn to get along with each other. For instance, Peter issued a warning to husbands and wives who are not in fellowship with each other: *"Husbands, in the same way be considerate as you live with your wives, and treat them with respect as the weaker partner and as heirs with you of the gracious gift of life, so that nothing will hinder your prayers"* (1 Peter 3:7).

Forgiveness is a choice, not an emotion. When someone hurts me, I can choose to forgive or not. How can we come before God's presence with praise and adoration while at the same time harbor bitterness in our heart toward a fellow believer? We should be slow to anger and quick to forgive. *"Be kind and compassionate to one another, forgiving each other, just as in Christ God forgave you"* (Ephesians 4:32).

MONDAY

BOLD PRAYING

*After they prayed, the place where they were meeting
was shaken. And they were all filled with the Holy Spirit
and spoke the word of God boldly* (Acts 4:31).

I F YOU TAKE THE TIME TO READ THE ENTIRETY OF THE CONTEXT SURROUNDING
this verse, you will discover the early apostles were facing intense pressure. The
religious establishment told them in no uncertain terms to stop teaching and
healing in the name of Jesus Christ. Peter and John chose to obey God rather
than men. They refused to deny what they had seen and heard. Case closed (see
Acts 4:10-11). Well, not really. They knew more persecution was coming and their
attitude was, *"Lord, give us boldness to handle the pressure."*

You've probably heard the saying, "When the going gets tough, the tough get
going." I'm wondering if that slogan applies to today's believer. In our culture, it
seems better to say, "When the going gets tough, the weak-kneed Christians run
for cover!" Lest we think the early Christians were the only ones to face the pressure of living for Jesus, we need to get our heads out of the sand and look around.
The PC culture is slowly eroding any mention of the name of Jesus Christ from
the public discourse. What was once accepted by Christians is now scorned and
ridiculed as more of a fable than fact.

When these early men and women got down to business, their prayer was simple and to the point, *"Now, Lord, consider their threats and enable your servants to
speak your word with great boldness. Stretch out your hand to heal and perform signs
and wonders through the name of your holy servant Jesus"* (Acts 4:29-30).

If there were ever a time we needed bold praying, it is now. If we want to
impact our society with the Good News of the Gospel, we cannot allow the anti-
Jesus mentality to take root. No doubt the pressure is on us to just "sit down and
shut up" when it comes to a bold witness for Christ. How can we be quiet when
we have both seen and heard mighty things the Lord has done for us? How can
we sit by while the world is running headlong to its destruction?

The Lord answered the prayer with an earth shaking and a fresh infilling of
the Spirit. The result was a new boldness to speak for Christ. I am convinced God
wants to do the same for us if we will just ask!

SHAMELESS AUDACITY

I tell you, even though he will not get up and give you the bread because of friendship, yet because of your shameless audacity he will surely get up and give you as much as you need. So I say to you: Ask and it will be given to you; seek and you will find; knock and the door will be opened to you (Luke 11:8-9).

A WISE TEACHER WILL ALWAYS ILLUSTRATE THE POINT. AFTER HIS SEMINAR on prayer, Jesus told a story to highlight the importance of not giving up too soon. He talked about praying with *"shameless audacity."* A one-word description of this kind of praying is "importunity" or "persistency" that says: I will continue asking and knocking until the door to my answer is opened.

The central figure in this illustration is a man with an emergency. He has shown up on his friend's doorstep and needs shelter and food. Custom dictated that the host take care of the man's needs. So he goes to his best friend's house and starts banging on the door. The sleeping man replies that the hour is inconvenient and he's already in bed with his kids (see Luke 11:7). How does the desperate man react? He keeps on knocking until his friend gives him what he wants. I can imagine, as he hands this persistent friend some food, that he says, "I'm not doing this because you're my friend, I'm doing this so you will go away and leave me alone!" (see Luke 11:8).

There are times when we need to be persistent in our praying. Desperate circumstances call for drastic action. According to Jesus, this kind of attitude will move us from "wishing" God would answer our prayer to the mindset: I know God *will* answer my prayer. What situation have you given up on? Is it a rebellious child? A job situation? Or a pile of bills staring you in the face? Whatever it may be, bring it to the throne, and don't give up. The Lord loves it when His children knock on the door of Heaven.

Psalm 119:147-148 says, *"I rise before dawn and cry for help; I have put my hope in your word. My eyes stay open through the watches of the night, that I may meditate on your promises."*

HOW TO STAND OUT IN A CROWD OF 500

Now Jabez was more honorable than his brothers, and his mother called his name Jabez, saying, "Because I bore him in pain." And Jabez called on the God of Israel saying, "Oh, that You would bless me indeed, and enlarge my territory, that Your hand would be with me, and that You would keep me from evil, that I may not cause pain!" So God granted him what he requested (1 Chronicles 4:9-10 NKJV).

ONE OF THE MOST DIFFICULT THINGS TO DO IS TO KEEP YOUR CONCENTRA-tion when reading through certain portions of the Old Testament. We used to call them the "sticky pages," because they were so little used and the pages would have to be pried apart to read them. A prime example is found in the first book of Chronicles. In the early portions of the book, it has been suggested that over five hundred names with a ton of "begets" are listed. If you want to read and count them all, be my guest, and you are my new hero!

So, I ask the question, "How can you stand out in a crowd of 500?" Like a cup of cold water on a hot day, we are introduced to one man who did stand out: *"Now Jabez was more honorable than his brothers."* It was said that he was more "honorable" than his brothers? What made him honorable? Was it perhaps his big bank account or his job title? We are in the dark about his background, and he is never mentioned again in Scripture.

I believe Jabez's extraordinary attribute was his prayer life. At some point in his life, he decided not to go with the flow but to paddle upstream and reach for the throne of God by boldly asking God for blessings. His name is forever affixed to the "Let's ask God for miracles" hall of fame.

I wonder if people be reading about our prayer life thousands of years from now. Will we leave a legacy of miracles and blessings for future generations to marvel at? If you are tired of running with the pack and decide it's time to soar like an eagle, then pay attention to this Jabez. He has a lot to teach us about the kind of prayers that God loves to answer.

MAKE THE ENDING BETTER THAN THE BEGINNING

Now Jabez was more honorable than his brothers, and his mother called his name Jabez, saying, "Because I bore him in pain" (1 Chronicles 4:9 NKJV).

THE HEBREW CULTURE PLACED A HIGH VALUE ON NAMES GIVEN AT BIRTH. IT was always the hope and prayer that the new baby would live up to the standard the name implied. But in some cases, the name was more reflected in a negative rather than a positive light. For example, the name *Jabez* means pain, sorrow, or trouble. His mother gave him a name that hung around his neck all of his life.

Can you imagine going through your life with a name that says you are nothing but a pain! Life is difficult enough without having to explain to future in-laws that your name is not who you really are. I dare say many adults try to live down the labels some hurtful parent pinned on them at a young age. You know the ones—stupid, fat, dumb, ugly, failure, slow-witted, loser.... How tragic. No parent should ever say such things to their children, and yet it happens every day.

Jabez didn't have a choice about his name. But he did have a choice how he would live. He lived his life in such a way that his legacy was more about the content of his life, not the meaning of his name. You could say his ending was much better than his beginning. If you can identify with Jabez, you have the same choice. You can live a life of bitterness and regret over how you were labeled, or you can live up to what God says about you.

A just small sampling of what God says about you:

- You are My child (John 1:12).
- You are an heir of the Kingdom (Romans 8:17).
- You are accepted in the beloved family of God (Ephesians 1:6).
- You are complete in Christ (Colossians 2:10).
- You were chosen by God from the foundation of the world (Ephesians 1:4).
- You are a new creation in Christ (2 Corinthians 5:17).

If your life is not what you intended it to be, it's time to stop blaming others and make your ending far greater than your beginning!

PRAYING FOR THE "INDEED"

And Jabez called on the God of Israel saying, "Oh, that
You would bless me indeed, and enlarge my territory, that
Your hand would be with me, and that You would keep
me from evil, that I may not cause pain!" So, God granted
him what he requested (1 Chronicles 4:10 NKJV).

EVEN A CASUAL READING OF THE PRAYER OF JABEZ LEADS US TO BELIEVE HE was asking for an abundant blessing from God. You notice he emphasized the intensity of his request by adding the qualifier *"indeed!"* By adding "indeed" at the end of his prayer is equal to our reading an email request from a friend who ends their plea in all caps and exclamation points. To visualize what Jabez prayed it would read, *OH THAT YOU WOULD BLESS ME INDEED!!!!!!!!!*

It's time to recapture the beauty and meaning of the word "bless." The word has become overused to the point we toss it around without considering its true meaning. When Jabez asked God to bless him, he was asking God to confer an abounding favor and pour out on him all things beneficial to his life. I'm afraid as Christians we tend to think that to ask God for tremendous blessings is selfish praying.

It is the feeling that we don't deserve more than we have. In fact, the opposite is true. Jesus said, *"If a son asks for bread from any father among you, will he give him a stone? Or if he asks for a fish, will he give him a serpent instead of a fish? Or if he asks for an egg, will he offer him a scorpion? If you then, being evil, know how to give good gifts to your children, how much more will your heavenly Father give the Holy Spirit to those who ask Him!"* (Luke 11:11-13 NKJV).

What blessings are you missing out on because you have not asked? The favor and blessings of God are there for the asking. Don't settle for just a small blessing when God is ready for you to ask Him for more than you ever dreamed possible.

> *And God is able to bless you abundantly, so that in all things at all times, having all that you need, you will abound in every good work* (2 Corinthians 9:8).

> *Now to him who is able to do immeasurably more than all we ask or imagine, according to his power that is at work within us* (Ephesians 3:20).

MONDAY

MUCH MORE

And Jabez called on the God of Israel saying, "Oh, that
You would bless me indeed, and enlarge my territory, that
Your hand would be with me, and that You would keep
me from evil, that I may not cause pain!" So, God granted
him what he requested (1 Chronicles 4:10 NKJV).

THERE ARE SOME QUESTIONS WE PONDER IN OUR MIND, BUT NEVER HAVE THE courage to ask. For instance, a Christian business person might wonder, *Is it right to ask God to give me more business, or should I be content with what I have?* If someone came to me and asked that question, I would refer them to the prayer of Jabez. He was not afraid or ashamed to ask God for much more.

Jabez lived in a culture that deemed territory, or land, equal to influence, abundance, and responsibility. Asking God for more territory was the same as asking God to enlarge his sphere influence. How could anyone pray such a bold, audacious prayer and expect God to answer, right? Well, if the Bible had not given us the answer, we might surmise that God rejected such an outlandish request. But that is not what happened. The Bible says, *"God granted him what he requested."*

When was the last time you prayed for God to increase your influence? Businessperson, when was the last time you asked God to increase your business? Many Christians believe that to walk with God equals a vow of poverty. Being broke and not paying your bills is not a sign of spirituality, it is a false view of living the abundant life. Jesus says in John 10:10, *"The thief comes only to steal and kill and destroy; I have come that they may have life, and have it to the full."*

You might be thinking, *Brother Paul, why should I ask God for much more?* The answer is not that complicated. *We ask for much more so that we can have a greater impact for the Kingdom of God.* We don't ask God to enlarge our territory so we can brag about it or become selfish. No, we want more, so we can give more. We ask for more so we can spread the good news of Jesus. Do be afraid, go ahead and ask God for *much more!*

CONSIDER THE SOURCE

*And Jabez called on the God of Israel saying, "Oh, that
You would bless me indeed, and enlarge my territory, that
Your hand would be with me, and that You would keep
me from evil, that I may not cause pain!" So, God granted
him what he requested* (1 Chronicles 4:10 NKJV).

JABEZ ASKED A BRILLIANT THING OF GOD, *"THAT YOUR HAND WOULD BE
with me."* He knew that to invite God's blessings without God's hand to guide
him would be a mistake. We would be wise to follow in his footsteps. It is not
uncommon for Christians to enjoy the blessings of God without acknowledging
the Source of the very blessings they enjoy. Think about how we would feel if we
spent a great deal of time, money, and effort on Christmas gifts for our children
without ever receiving so much as a thank you. We would have to conclude they
were more enthralled with the gifts than the giver.

This praying man ended his petition with an extraordinary request, *"that You
would keep me from evil, that I may not cause pain!"* He did not ask God to keep
evil from coming near him. He did not ask to be put in a spiritual bubble so he
would be unable learn how to live an overcoming life. He understood that evil
was all around him, and he needed the wisdom and strength from God to avoid
causing pain to others.

Reading this extraordinary prayer might give us a false idea that God would
never answer such a bold prayer. Some would even say that Jabez was only concerned with himself and he was wasting his breath. Apparently, God delighted in
his prayer because *"God granted him what he requested."*

My dear friend Jack Taylor made the following observation about the prayer of
Jabez: "The life story of Jabez was as simple as that. He knew what he wanted and
went for it. He knew where and who to go for it; he asked for it and he received
it!" He continued, "There are people who seem to get everything they want. They
have learned the simple secret that if they delight in the Lord, He will give them
the desires of their hearts (see Psalm 37:4)."[50]

Make up your mind not to miss all that God has for you by ignoring the very
thing that moves you into the realm of abundance—a life of prayer!

DO THIS FIRST

I urge, then, first of all, that petitions, prayers, intercession and thanksgiving be made for all people—for kings and all those in authority, that we may live peaceful and quiet lives in all godliness and holiness (1 Timothy 2:1-2).

PASTOR TIMOTHY NEEDED GUIDANCE IN MANY AREAS OF MINISTRY, AND PAUL wanted to make sure his protégé understood the importance of prayer in public worship. Paul instructed him that when the saints gathered, to *"first of all"* make sure prayer is the highest priority. In everyday language, he said, "Before you do anything else, make sure you pray!"

I wonder what Paul would think about our worship services today? Would he see prayer as an add-on at different times of the service? Or a quick prayer before the important stuff happens, like taking an offering? In the average church, I would guess if you want to draw a big crowd, just announce some celebrity is going to speak, and there will be free pizza afterward. Nothing wrong with free pizza, but if I wanted to take the spiritual temperature of a congregation, just announce a prayer meeting and see what kind of crowd shows up.

You don't have to be a Bible scholar to see the early church viewed prayer as the fuel that drove the dynamic engine of the church. If you told those early Christians that prayer was just a small part of the overall worship experience, they would probably look at you as if you were an alien from Mars. No, they didn't move an inch without praying first. To them, all that mattered was bringing the issue before God in prayer.

- The first church was birthed in prayer (Acts 1:14).
- When choosing a replacement for Judas, they prayed (Acts 1:24-25).
- They prayed for boldness in the face of persecution (Acts 4:24-30).
- When the potential for a split occurred between the brothers and sisters, they prayed and selected leaders (Acts 6).
- They prayed for miracles of healing (Acts 9:40).
- The church prayed before sending Paul and Barnabas out to establish churches (Acts 13:1-3).

It is possible the lack of power in our churches today is directly related to our lack of prayer. It is time to take the matter seriously. *"Devote yourselves to prayer, being watchful and thankful"* (Colossians 4:2).

WHAT'S ON GOD'S AGENDA?

*I urge, then, first of all, that petitions, prayers, intercession
and thanksgiving be made for all people—for kings and
all those in authority, that we may live peaceful and quiet
lives in all godliness and holiness* (1 Timothy 2:1-2).

WE MUST NEVER FORGET THAT PRAYER IS NOT ONLY WHEN WE BRING OUR petitions before God, it is also an act of worship. We can certainly lay our burdens at His feet, but presenting our needs is just a part, not the whole.

Did you know God has a prayer agenda? Paul instructed Timothy that when the believers come together to remember certain things that are on God's heart. If you ever find yourself wondering what God thinks is important, try praying His list:

- *"for all people"*—Before you give up before you start, Paul is not suggesting we pray for the population of the entire world by name! No, he is saying that we should not limit our praying to just one particular group or class of people. *"All people"* includes those we like and those we don't like. It should take into account even those who have been less than kind to us, or have gone out of their way to harm us. Jesus said, *"But to you who are listening I say: Love your enemies, do good to those who hate you, bless those who curse you, pray for those who mistreat you"* (Luke 6:27-28).

- *"for kings and all those in authority"*—When Paul wrote these words, Nero was the emperor. This cruel man was known for killing Christians, so you can understand why praying for this persecutor of the Church could present a problem. Is Paul saying that God wants us to pray for all those in authority, even if we fear what they might do? Yes, I believe that is what Paul is saying. It also translates to today. Should we pray for the president and all those in authority, even if we don't agree with their political agenda? Yes, even if we don't respect people sitting in authority positions, we should still respect the office they hold.

Living peaceful and quiet lives is the result of praying God's agenda. We may not understand why we are to pray for certain people, but we can rest assured the outcome is up to God not us.

COMMON MAN— UNCOMMON RESULTS

Therefore confess your sins to each other and pray for each other so that you may be healed. The prayer of a righteous person is powerful and effective. Elijah was a human being, even as we are. He prayed earnestly that it would not rain, and it did not rain on the land for three and a half years. Again he prayed, and the heavens gave rain, and the earth produced its crops (James 5:16-18).

WHEN I THINK ABOUT PRAYER WARRIORS, THE NAME ELIJAH IMMEDIATELY comes to mind. To me he was a giant with almost superhuman abilities. This guy challenged the status quo of his day and had no problem standing toe to toe with an ungodly king and his false prophets (1 Kings 18).

In today's Scripture passage, James does two things: *First,* he gives us a quick lesson on how our prayers can be effective and powerful. *Second,* he points to Elijah as his prime example. He was a common man who produced uncommon results. According to James, he was *"a human being, even as we are."* Powerful praying is not reserved for the famous or the favored. Getting prayers answered is not reserved for those who can stop it from raining for three years, or call fire down on the top of a mountain!

How can ordinary common people like us pray just like Elijah prayed and see uncommon results? It requires earnest praying. To pray *"earnestly"* means to be energetic, enthusiastic, and have a never-give-up attitude. Earnest praying doesn't view prayer as a last-ditch effort to move God. Elijah's prayer was not answered because God owed him a favor. Elijah was a man who was subjected to the same desires, shortcomings, and feelings that we are. But the one thing he learned was that prayer could move God into any situation.

God is not looking for supermen and superwomen. I'm sure that stopping the water works of Heaven for three and a half years is not a requirement for effective praying. God is looking for just regular, ordinary people who will stand in faith and pray like Elijah who offer up faith-filled, earnest prayers centered on God's will—not ours—with the calm assurance God will act on our behalf.

What circumstances are you facing today that require an intervention from God? Are you hesitant to ask because it has been awhile since you talked to the Lord? He is waiting to hear from you.

GOLDEN NUGGETS

Through the work of Jesus in His blood shed on the cross, we are reconciled to God. The meaning of the word "reconcile" is "to be restored to our original value." It is going back to the position man was in before he was alienated. Because of Christ's work of salvation, we are taken back to that place. Back to the place before sin entered the picture.

DR. JOE LANGLEY, *Beyond Forgiveness: A Bigger Picture of Salvation*[51]

THE GOD OF THE IMPOSSIBLE

*I am the Lord, the God of all mankind. Is anything
too hard for me?* (Jeremiah 32:27)

THE DEFINITION OF THE WORD "IMPOSSIBLE" IS FAIRLY DAUNTING. AS A MAT-
ter of fact, from a human point of view, it can be downright discouraging.
The most common definition as stated by the Merriam-Webster Dictionary is
"incapable of being or of occurring; felt to be incapable of being done, attained,
or fulfilled; insuperably difficult."[52] Now that pretty much covers everything
many people face on a day-to-day basis. So often we fall into the trap of focusing
on the "impossible" things in front of us and tend to forget victories of the past.

Are you dreading the impossible? God has issued a challenge. He says, *"Is anything too hard for Me?"* As the old saying goes, *"If you've done it, it's not bragging,
it's a fact!"* When it comes to the impossible, God's track record is indisputable.

What impossible situations you facing right now? To be an overcomer, it is
important how you deal with circumstances that seem so imposing that it would
take a miracle to break through. Ignoring them with the hope they fade away is
not the answer. The life of faith in God and a complete trust that He can handle any situation is a much better path. No doubt Jesus had the same thought in
mind in Luke 18:27: *"Jesus replied, "What is impossible with man is possible with
God.""* It is our faith that can stare the impossible in the eye and know God can
turn it around. It is our faith that can see impossible mountains move just at His
command. Walking by faith allows us to see God is bigger than any impossibility standing in our way of breakthrough.

When the impossible shows up, we need to go straight to the Word of God
and seek His face and wait for an answer. Romans 10:17 says, *"Consequently, faith
comes from hearing the message, and the message is heard through the word about
Christ."* Don't leave His presence until you get a word to stand on. You are one
word away from seeing the impossible turned into the possible. One word away
from seeing defeat turned into victory. One word away from seeing that nothing
is too hard for God!

LET GO!

Forget the former things; do not dwell on the past. See,
I am doing a new thing! Now it springs up; do you
not perceive it? I am making a way in the wilderness
and streams in the wasteland (Isaiah 43:18-19).

IN THE ONLINE EDITION OF *FOUNDATIONS* MAGAZINE, THERE WAS A STORY
about how trappers catch wild monkeys that are typically sold to zoos. Some
have perfected the procedure and have become quite successful. It's sad and funny
all at the same time.

According to the article here's how it works:

> It seems that trappers take a small cage out into the jungle. Inside the
> cage they place a bunch of bananas, and then they close it, locking the
> bananas inside. Now a monkey coming along and spotting the bananas,
> will reach through the narrow rungs of the cage and grab a banana. But
> he can't get it out. And no matter how hard he tries—twisting his hand
> back and forth—he can't pull his hand through the rungs while hang-
> ing on to the banana. And even with the approaching trappers, he won't
> let go of the banana. For the trappers, it's simply a matter then, of com-
> ing up and grabbing the monkey. Now if you were standing there in the
> jungle, watching all of this happen, and wanted to save the monkey, you
> might yell in exasperation, "Drop the banana!"[53]

It is sad to think that all the poor monkey had to do was let go of the thing
that was keeping him trapped. Isaiah made it clear; if you want to see the new
thing, you have to be willing to let go of the former things. In my experience,
new things don't cause me pain. It's usually the old and the familiar things that
I keep hanging on to. Holding on to old hurts and painful experiences is not the
best way to live. If we aren't careful, the old things will become chains wrapped
around our hearts, refusing to let us move forward.

I urge you to heed the wisdom of Solomon in Proverbs 4:25-27:

> *Let your eyes look straight ahead; fix your gaze directly before you. Give*
> *careful thought to the paths for your feet and be steadfast in all your*
> *ways. Do not turn to the right or the left; keep your foot from evil.*

IT'S ALL ABOUT THE LITTLE THINGS

"Are not Abana and Pharpar, the rivers of Damascus, better than all the waters of Israel? Couldn't I wash in them and be cleansed?" So, he turned and went off in a rage. Naaman's servants went to him and said, "My father, if the prophet had told you to do some great thing, would you not have done it? How much more, then, when he tells you, 'Wash and be cleansed'!" (2 Kings 5:12-13)

IN 1962, THE RACE TO OUTER SPACE WAS HEATING UP BETWEEN THE AMERI-cans and the Russians. Critical to the program was the launch of the Mariner 1 space probe that would circle Venus to provide necessary information to NASA scientists. Unfortunately, the mission had to be scrubbed barely 294.5 seconds after blast off. The problem was a simple omission in the guidance program. The computer program that guided the craft was missing a simple "overline," or in laymen's terms a "minus" sign. The opportunity to take the lead in the space race was derailed because a small but crucial detail was overlooked.

Consider Naaman. All of his prestige and power did not stop leprosy from attacking his body. I'm sure he thought all he had to do was meet with Elisha and the prophet would take care of the problem. His attitude was "Just wave your hand, and I'll be on my way." Unfortunately for Naaman, the prophet didn't play ball. Instead, the prophet sent a message to Naaman and told him to take a dip in the Jordan River, and he would be healed. Just do this one simple little thing, and God will do a miracle. Instead of running to the river, Naaman pitched a fit. Finally, his servants convinced him to obey the prophet. When he heeded the word of Elisha, he was healed, totally and completely!

Living the Christian life means taking care of the little things as well as the big stuff. The way we handle the small things of life determines to a great extent how we will handle the larger things. We must learn that even the smallest details the Lord presents us may turn out to be the most important. It's called making the most of what you have!

I have discovered that when I'm faithful in the daily routine of life, I'm better equipped to tackle whatever comes my way. I have also learned—the hard way—that when God gives me an instruction to follow, it's better to say "yes" and not worry about the details.

JESUS LOVES ME THIS I KNOW

We love because he first loved us (1 John 4:19).

WE LIVE IN AN UNCERTAIN WORLD. NOT A DAY PASSES WITHOUT NEWS OF another crisis. A terrorist attack in Europe or a financial crisis on Wall Street fills our television screens. Now that we have 24/7 news cycles, we don't have to wait long for bad news. There are days when I just want to hide under the bed and hope it all goes away!

Is there anything about which you can be certain? Yes! You can know for certain one eternal truth, *Jesus loves me this I know, for the Bible tells me so!* Before you say this is just a cute little song you sang in Sunday School, I remind you it is the sum total of the greatest truth known to humankind.

The lyrics of "Jesus Loves Me" were first written as a poem by Anna Warner to give comfort to a dying child. Later, William Bradbury added a melody, along with additional words to complete what we have come to know as the popular children's song: *Jesus loves me! This I know, for the Bible tells me so; little ones to Him belong; they are weak, but He is strong. Yes, Jesus loves me! Yes, Jesus loves me! Yes, Jesus loves me! The Bible tells me so.*[54]

It is possible for us to know the song in our head, but never grasp the truth of its meaning in our heart. I believe the Bible is God's love note to us. The following is just a glimpse of how much He loves you:

Isaiah 49:16—*He engraved your name on the palms of His hands.*

Jeremiah 31:3—*He loves you with an everlasting love.*

Psalm 86:15—*He is abounding in steadfast love and faithfulness.*

John 3:16—*For God so loved the world, that He gave you the greatest gift of all.*

Romans 8:37-39—*You are more than a conqueror through Him who loves you.*

Ephesians 2:4-5—*He loves you even when you were dead in sins, and raised you up in Christ!*

I have good news. It doesn't matter what others think about you, or what you might think about yourself. Here's the truth—*Jesus loves you this I know, for the Bible tells you so!*

IS THERE A LOVE GOD HATES?

Do not love the world or anything in the world. If anyone loves the world, love for the Father is not in them (1 John 2:15).

J OHN LEFT NO ROOM FOR DOUBT ABOUT ONE THING: CHRISTIANS CANNOT love the world and love the Father at the same time. The world and the Father are polar opposites of each other. There is a constant tension between what believers know in their hearts to be true and what they see going on. If you were told that if you become a Christian, you won't have to struggle any longer with problems, stresses, and pressure of the world, they did not tell you the truth!

When John speaks of the *"world,"* what in the world does he mean? He's not talking about the world of nature or the world of people (see 1 Timothy 6:17; Acts 17:24; John 3:16). The word he uses for *"world"* is the same word as our English words "cosmos" or "cosmopolitan." These words mean "to arrange" or to "put in proper order." We get "cosmetic" from the same root. The truth John is warning us about is a "world system" that is arranged in opposition to God.

We use the word "world" almost daily to describe many everyday activities. For example, when the news anchor reports the "world of politics," he or she is not describing some planet in our solar system filled with politicians. Of course, to hear some of them talk you might think they are aliens, but no, he is describing the attitude and activities of people involved in the political system.

When John says not to love the world or anything in the world, what is he saying? He is telling us to be careful not to arrange our life according to the dictates of a system entirely opposed to the things of God. It is not so much about naming certain activities, it is an attitude of the heart. Anything that affects our love and devotion to do the will of God must be rooted out and avoided at all cost (see 1 John 2:17).

TO KNOW HIM IS TO LOVE HIM

That is why I am suffering as I am. Yet this is no cause for shame, because I know whom I have believed, and am convinced that he is able to guard what I have entrusted to him until that day (2 Timothy 1:12).

THERE IS A BIG DIFFERENCE BETWEEN KNOWING *ABOUT* SOMEONE AND knowing them in a *personal* way. One of my favorite characters in history is General George S. Patton. I have read books about him, written papers on his leadership style, but I don't know him. I know some things about him, but I cannot honestly say I can speak from personal experience since I never had the pleasure of his company. I find it impossible to know and love someone I have never met.

You will notice Paul didn't say, *"I know in whom I have believed."* If he had stated that, he would be confessing that he had heard of Jesus, or even read what others had written about Him, but never knew Him in an intimate way. What Paul did say, *"I know whom I have believed."* He is speaking of a close personal relationship that only comes with spending time with a person.

How can we trust and love someone we don't know? The Christian life is not a spiritual pre-arranged marriage, nor is Christ a mail-order bride. Can you imagine a wedding ceremony where the groom says to the bride, "I'm going to marry you, but I still want to live a single lifestyle. I'm not interested in getting to know you, and I'll let you know if I need anything." Most ladies I know would tell him to hit the bricks!

If we don't spend time getting to know Jesus, we will not have the confidence or assurance that He can keep us secure during times of pressure and struggle. I will be the first to admit that I don't know Him as I should. The older I get, the greater my desire to be closer to Him, to hear His voice, and love Him more. I pray the desire of Paul will become our passion as well. He says in Philippians 3:10-11, *"I want to know Christ—yes, to know the power of his resurrection and participation in his sufferings, becoming like him in his death, and so, somehow, attaining to the resurrection from the dead."*

SOLID AS A ROCK

And he brought him to Jesus. Jesus looked at him and said,
"You are Simon son of John. You will be called Cephas"
(which, when translated, is Peter) (John 1:42).

I LIKE TO THINK OF SIMON PETER AS AN "EVERYMAN." HE WAS THE KIND OF man who made us wonder, *What in the world did Jesus ever see in this guy?* This rugged fisherman was known for his big mouth and boisterous attitude. If I had to choose one word to describe him, it would be impetuous. His attitude was, "Go big or go home!" There was no in-between with him.

Something happened to Simon that changed him forever. He met Jesus Christ. There came a day when Jesus said something to him that totally captured his heart, *"And he brought him to Jesus. Jesus looked at him and said, "You are Simon son of John. You will be called Cephas" (which, when translated, is Peter)"* (John 1:42). Do you see what Jesus did? He called Simon Peter, which means *stone*. He changed his name, and with the name change came a new purpose for his life!

For one of the few times in his life, Simon was speechless. The words of Jesus shook him to his core. If there was anything he was not, it was it was a rock. He must have felt that if he was anything at all, he was more like the unpredictable waves of the Sea of Galilee. There was nothing on the outside that would lead anyone to believe this rough and tumble guy could one day be used to shake nations for the Gospel of Christ.

Jesus had a way of looking at the facade and seeing what others could not see. Did Peter buy into what Jesus predicted about his life? I think so. Sure, there were stumbles along the way, no doubt about that. After all, Jesus didn't say he would be perfect. In the end, it was Peter who became the driving force in the early church; and because of him, nations were introduced to Christ. If Jesus can take someone rough around edges and transform him into a person with a purpose, just imagine what He can do with you.

RESURRECTION REACTIONS

When they heard about the resurrection of the dead, some of them sneered, but others said, "We want to hear you again on this subject." At that, Paul left the Council. Some of the people became followers of Paul and believed. Among them was Dionysius, a member of the Areopagus, also a woman named Damaris, and a number of others (Acts 17:32-34).

PAUL WAS NOT ONE TO AVOID A CONFRONTATION OR WASTE AN OPPORTUNITY to preach the Gospel. While waiting for his team to arrive in Athens, he was given an opening to speak for himself to a group of philosophers who said, *"'What is this babbler trying to say?' Others remarked, 'He seems to be advocating foreign gods.' They said this because Paul was preaching the good news about Jesus and the resurrection"* (Acts 17:18). I don't doubt if Paul had given them pious platitudes or a watered-down Gospel, their reaction would have been different. Instead, he closed with a truth that cannot be avoided.

The resurrection of Christ demands a reaction:

1. *Some Denied the Truth.* They *"sneered"* or mocked at the very idea of a physical resurrection. Resurrection deniers have been around for more than two thousand years, but that does not change the reality of its truth. To deny the resurrection of Christ is to deny the empty tomb, (Matthew 28:6); the eyewitness accounts (1 Corinthians 15:5-8), and the multiplied millions of transformed lives.

2. *Some Delayed the Truth.* Others who heard the message said, *"We want to hear you again on this subject."* I'm not sure which is worse—to deny or to delay? Both are dangerous to your eternal soul. Life is short, and all people have an appointment with death. You can delay buying a house or a car, but you cannot delay a decision about eternity (James 4:14; Hebrews 9:27).

3. *Some Desired the Truth.* Not everyone turned their back on the message of Paul: *"Some of the people became followers of Paul and believed."* The word "believed" is a verb or an action word. True belief in the message of the Gospel demands action based on knowledge (Romans 10:14).

Paul imparted the Word of truth and their response was to believe and follow. You cannot be passive when it comes to following Jesus! The Gospel demands a response. What will you do?

JESUS CHRIST IS LORD!

*that at the name of Jesus every knee should bow, in heaven and on
earth and under the earth, and every tongue acknowledge that Jesus
Christ is Lord, to the glory of God the Father* (Philippians 2:10-11).

WHEN PAUL WROTE THIS LETTER TO THE CHURCH AT PHILIPPI, IT WAS NO
small matter to discuss the lordship of Christ. It became a severe test of
their commitment to proclaim the lordship of anything other than the emperor.
The Roman culture was infused with emperor worship, and to declare Christ
as Lord was to deny the deity of the caesar. Failure to proclaim "Caesar is lord"
could mean death. Living the Christian life was serious business for the early
believers.

What am I saying when I declare that Jesus is both Lord and Savior of my
life? It means that Jesus has total control, and that includes my family, my future,
and all my possessions. You cannot say that Jesus is your Savior and deny He is
also Lord. It is the confession of His lordship that brings salvation, *"If you declare
with your mouth, 'Jesus is Lord,' and believe in your heart that God raised him from
the dead, you will be saved"* (Romans 10:9). Declaring His lordship brings a new
awareness of His authority and a willingness to give Him complete allegiance.

I am afraid the average Christian has no real concept of what lordship means.
We tend to put things into two boxes—the sacred box and the secular box. For
some reason, we think that what we do on Sunday—the sacred—and what we
do on Monday—the secular—are two different things. When He is Lord, every
area becomes sacred, not just our activities at church.

Jesus has every right to be our Lord because He paid the price (see Romans
14:9). He purchased our redemption with His blood, *"For you know that it was not
with perishable things such as silver or gold that you were redeemed from the empty
way of life handed down to you from your ancestors, but with the precious blood of
Christ, a lamb without blemish or defect"* (1 Peter 1:18-19).

Jesus conquered death, hell, and the grave; He is more than capable of handling every enemy that comes against us. We can't call Him Savior and not call
Him Lord. The bottom line—*He is Lord over all, or not Lord at all!*

ARE YOU IN THE RIGHT PLACE?

The Lord God took the man and put him in the Garden
of Eden to work it and take care of it (Genesis 2:15).

A FRIEND OF MINE TOLD ME ABOUT AN INCIDENT THAT HAPPENED TO HIM several years ago while attending a pastor's conference:

> We were given a lunch break and I decided to stop at the men's room and freshen up. As I headed that way I met an old friend and we started talking, and the next thing I knew we were in front of the restrooms. Without paying attention, I made a sharp right turn and headed for the first door I saw. I was now in the restroom—the WOMEN'S restroom!
>
> As I stood there, all sense of time stopped. Then my life flashed before my eyes. Somehow I managed to blurt out an apology and back gracefully out of the room. I could hear the roar of laughter from inside, as well from a small group of friends who had gathered in the hall. Needless to say, I was living proof of someone who was in the wrong place at the wrong time!

Finding yourself in the wrong place at the wrong time can have deeper consequences than having people laugh at your miscues. The key to productivity and fruitfulness is found in proper placement. Adam was placed in the Garden to *"work it and take care of it."* God created Adam before He created the Garden (see Genesis 2:7-8). And God gave Adam an assignment of work before He gave him a mate (see Genesis 2:21-22).

Proper placement is God's primary purpose for your life. While reading this, your life may be lacking productivity. Have you considered that maybe it's time to start asking God to point you to your assignment? As mentioned previously, if you take a fish out of water, it will die. Why? The best environment for a fish to thrive is in water, not out of water. Our best environment to thrive is living in God's purpose.

But be aware of one thing, proper placement may be preceded by a season of discomfort. We don't always want to move out of our comfort zone, and yet we realize that we will never change what we are willing to tolerate. If you're going to fly like an eagle, you have to be willing to leave the nest.

MADE

Then I went down to the potter's house, and there he was,
making something at the wheel (Jeremiah 18:3 NKJV).

WHEN GOD DIRECTED JEREMIAH TO GO DOWN TO THE POTTER'S HOUSE, IT was for a divine purpose. The Lord wanted the prophet to see the potter was *"making something at the wheel."* The key word is *"making."* There may be many applications and interpretations of this Scripture, but one thing is clear, the Lord is our Master Potter, and has uniquely created each of us. Your parents may not have planned you, but there are no accidents with God.

The reason many people live lives of frustration is what I call, "the uncertainty of creation, or the "Why am I here?" syndrome. The frustrations of life are better dealt with when we know why God put us on this planet. To put it another way—*frustration ends when your reason for living begins.* Don't misunderstand; I'm not talking about the little everyday things that irritate us. Showing up late for an appointment may be annoying, but it can be easily fixed.

The One who made you knows what you were made to do, so if you don't know—ask! If you live your life wandering around confused about your purpose, you can be sure something will fill the void. It may suffice for a while, but at some point, you will realize whatever you are doing is not God's design for your life.

Take some time and meditate on these wonderful truths:

- Psalm 139:1-6: *You have searched me, Lord, and you know me. You know when I sit and when I rise; you perceive my thoughts from afar. You discern my going out and my lying down; you are familiar with all my ways. Before a word is on my tongue you, Lord, know it completely. You hem me in behind and before, and you lay your hand upon me. Such knowledge is too wonderful for me, too lofty for me to attain.*

- Isaiah 64:8: *Yet you, Lord, are our Father. We are the clay you are the potter; we are all the work of your hand.*

- Jeremiah 1:4-5: *The word of the Lord came to me, saying, "Before I formed you in the womb I knew you, before you were born I set you apart; I appointed you as a prophet to the nations."*

MIRACLES

He performs wonders that cannot be fathomed,
miracles that cannot be counted (Job 5:9).

ILEARNED A LONG TIME AGO IT IS ALWAYS BEST TO DEFINE TERMS WHEN PRE-senting a subject of potential controversy. One issue that comes under this heading is asking people what they believe about miracles. One definition of a miracle that is most commonly used: an extraordinary event manifesting a supernatural work of God. Based on that simple definition, could the issue of miracles be proven true by what has happened in your life?

If I were to ask you if you believed in miracles, what would you say? Would you say miracles only happened in the Bible, and they are not expected today? Or, would you take the more traditional approach and try to explain what appeared to be a miracle in the context of luck or fate? Whether we want to admit it or not, our view of the supernatural work of God is based on what some teacher had to say about the subject. If we sat under someone who taught that miracles are not for today, then more than likely we hold to the same belief system. We must be cautious and not fall into the trap of "unbelieving believers." Jesus said to the religious leaders, the Pharisees, of the day, *"Thus you nullify the word of God by your tradition that you have handed down. And you do many things like that"* (Mark 7:13).

There are no easy answers to the subject of miracles. For instance, why do so many believers who need a miracle never receive one, while other believers seem to live in a constant overflow of the supernatural? It is time to find out what the Bible says about miracles and not leave it up to so-called scholars who try to explain it away.

Bible teacher Crystal McDowell stated, "Miracles still happen. Just because we don't see people raised from the dead on a regular basis doesn't mean that God isn't still in the miracle business. The Lord receives glory from the miracles He does every day in our lives. We must continue to press Him in prayer for the miraculous and not settle so quickly into doubt, anxiety, or fear. Miracles will continue."[55]

To which I say, AMEN!

NEED

*Then they came to Jericho. As Jesus and his disciples, together with
a large crowd, were leaving the city, a blind man, Bartimaeus
(which means "son of Timaeus"), was sitting by the roadside begging.
When he heard that it was Jesus of Nazareth, he began to shout,
"Jesus, Son of David, have mercy on me!"* (Mark 10:46-47)

THE GOSPEL WRITERS RECORDED AT LEAST THIRTY-SEVEN MIRACLES OF
Jesus. But as John wrote in his Gospel about Jesus' miracles, *"…If every one
of them were written down, I suppose that even the whole world would not have room
for the books that would be written* (John 21:25). I want to focus on one miracle in
particular found in Mark 10.

Consider Bartimaeus (see Mark 10:46-52). My first thought about this miracle
is that we will never get a miracle if we don't know we need one. Bartimaeus was
aware he was blind, and for his condition to change there had to be a supernatural act of God. To have a need means "a lack of something requisite or a condition
that requires relief." How do I know that this man knew he had a need? When
Jesus asked him, *"What do you want me to do for you?"* Bartimaeus did not hesitate to answer, *"Rabbi, I want to see"* (Mark 10:51). The blind man could have
said he needed a bigger cup to beg with or a new coat to keep him warm, but he
didn't, he wanted to see.

God has some unusual ways of getting my attention. He never seems to get
my attention through my success, but rather in my distress or need. *"Hear me
when I call, O God of my righteousness: thou hast enlarged me when I was in distress;
have mercy upon me, and hear my prayer"* (Psalm 4:1 KJV). Having a need does
not mean that God is angry at us, but rather it is a signal that God is up to something. Having a need is not a lack of faith or a failure to trust in God's provision.
No, it's an opportunity to build our faith in God's supply.

Paul says, *"And my God will meet all your needs according to the riches of his glory
in Christ Jesus"* (Philippians 4:19) We will never know what Paul said is true without needs. I have discovered that when a need shows up in my life, it is God's way
of telling me to trust Him. Before the need was ever on my mind, the supply was
already on the way!

ATMOSPHERE

*Many rebuked him and told him to be quiet, but he shouted all
the more, "Son of David, have mercy on me!"* (Mark 10:48)

IT IS A FACT THAT NEGATIVE PEOPLE CREATE A NEGATIVE ATMOSPHERE. JUST look at how the religious crowd reacted when they heard this blind man crying out for a miracle. Instead of rooting for Bartimaeus to receive his sight, they tried to shut him up. It did not matter to Bartimaeus, the more they told him to be quiet, the louder he shouted. He determined to place himself in an atmosphere of healing.

The atmosphere we put ourselves in significantly determines many things, not the least of which is our level of faith, and our attitude toward the things of God. The Scripture warns that if we hang around negative people long enough, their negativity will eventually rub off on us: *"Blessed is the one who does not walk in step with the wicked or stand in the way that sinners take or sit in the company of mockers"* (Psalm 1:1).

On more than one occasion, Jesus had to deal with a negative atmosphere. Jesus went to His hometown, and the result of His visit was not what one would expect: *"He could not do any miracles there, except lay his hands on a few sick people and heal them"* (Mark 6:5). If Jesus had the power to heal everyone who was there, why didn't He? Read the context, and you will see how they diminished His ministry and were "offended" at His teaching. The only limit to His power was the negative atmosphere He encountered.

When there is a negative atmosphere, it always focusses on what you think God can't do, instead of what He can do (see John 6). Another aspect of a negative atmosphere is it always regulates miracles to the past, or some future time, but never for today (see John 11). This kind of toxic atmosphere stays focused on past failures, therefore losing hope for the future.

Determine to place yourself in a positive environment. Hang around people who believe the Word of God is true, and stay away from those who would try to convince you that the days of miracles are over. I love what the writer of Proverbs said about the company we keep: *"Walk with the wise and become wise, for a companion of fools suffers harm"* (Proverbs 13:20).

INSTRUCTIONS

Jesus stopped and said, "Call him." So they called to the blind man,
"Cheer up! On your feet! He's calling you." Throwing his cloak
aside, he jumped to his feet and came to Jesus (Mark 10:49-50).

Bartimaeus found himself in the right atmosphere—Jesus was passing by—and now all he had to do was to ask for what he wanted. This was going to be easy, right? Hardly. Reading this story reminds me of two important facts when asking God for supernatural intervention.

First, there will always be *external obstacles* that have to be overcome. In this story, the barriers took the form of the crowd who kept telling Bartimaeus to keep quiet. It was their way of telling him this was not going to be his day for a miracle. In our day, there is always the self-righteous crowd standing around telling you that God just doesn't do miracles anymore. You may even have friends and family members who try to convince you that you shouldn't embarrass yourself with such foolish talk.

Second, there will always be *internal objections* to confront. There is a constant battle between what our brain is telling us, and what we know to be true in our heart. Every time I ask God for a miracle, He gives me an instruction. Miracles are not a product of chance, fate, or the luck of the draw. Miracles are not random actions of an unpredictable God. What I have noticed about God's miracles in the Bible is most of the time His instructions don't make sense to the natural mind.

For instance:

- God told Joshua to march around in circles (a total of thirteen times), and the walls of Jericho would fall. What a strange battle plan!
- Elisha told Naaman if he wanted to be healed to dip seven times in the Jordan River.
- Jesus told the servants to fill up their water pots with water and then draw out the wine.
- Jesus spit on a blind man and then told him to walk two miles and wash his face.

- Jesus took a small lunch and told His disciples to take it and feed everybody.

God will never require you to do something that is impossible. His instructions were actions that anyone could do. So, I ask you, what miracle do you need? What instruction has He given you? Just obey, even if it doesn't make sense!

ACTION

Throwing his cloak aside, he jumped to his feet and came to Jesus. "What do you want me to do for you?" Jesus asked him. The blind man said, "Rabbi, I want to see." "Go," said Jesus, "your faith has healed you." Immediately he received his sight and followed Jesus along the road (Mark 10:50-52).

SITTING AROUND HOPING GOD WILL DO SOMETHING HAS NEVER WORKED FOR me, how about you? The defining moment in this story is when Jesus stopped and called for Bartimaeus. Bartimaeus was then faced with a choice—whether to obey the instruction and take action or just sit there and be miserable. His miracle didn't come while he was sitting by the roadside, but when he took action. I wonder if Jesus would have kept walking if the blind man had kept silent instead of crying out? A real test of our desire for God to intervene in our situation is our persistent pursuit.

God's power is not dependent on our participation. He is perfectly capable of doing whatever He wants to do all by Himself. But He does expect us to obey Him when He gives us instructions to follow. When God releases His Word into our situation, we have a choice. We can respond in faith and take action, or we can sit back and hope something good will happen. The proof of our faith is our actions, not our words. James 2:17 says, *"In the same way, faith by itself, if it is not accompanied by action, is dead."*

Faith is the expression of your confidence in God. He wants you to trust Him, to believe His Word and take action. Your needs do not move God. He is not drawn into your situation based on your tears, pain, or hurt. He only responds to your faith: *"And without faith it is impossible to please God, because anyone who comes to him must believe that he exists and that he rewards those who earnestly seek him"* (Hebrews 11:6). Following His instructions and taking action, no matter how illogical they may seem, is proof that you have total confidence in His Word.

I have learned to never argue or debate with the Source of my miracle. When God gives me an instruction, He has a miracle on His mind. For you too!

CITIZENS

But our citizenship is in heaven. And we eagerly await a Savior from there, the Lord Jesus Christ, who, by the power that enables him to bring everything under his control, will transform our lowly bodies so that they will be like his glorious body (Philippians 3:20-21).

WHEN PAUL WROTE HIS LETTER TO THE CHURCH IN PHILIPPI, THEY UNDER-stood the meaning of citizenship. "Indeed, our English word 'politics,' is a transliteration of this Greek word. Paul exhorts them, 'Only be constantly performing your duties as citizens, worthy of the gospel of Christ.'[56] The meaning has more to do with actions and behaviors of a citizen than a particular political viewpoint.

When the Roman Empire conquered a city, they made that city a colony of the central government. Although Philippi was many miles away from Rome, the issue was not distance, but the law that governed them. These citizens of Philippi maintained the customs and behavior of their citizenship. If you had visited the city, you would have heard them speak the Roman language and dress like Roman citizens. In every way, they were a "Rome away from Rome."

As Christians, we are citizens of Heaven who live on this planet. We have our birth from Heaven (John 3:3), and we are stamped with Heaven's image. We may be physically here, but this world is not our permanent home. We belong to Heaven, and we are always to remember our obligation to bring a slice of Heaven wherever we go. This is what the Lord Jesus did while He was on the earth. He infused every situation with the fragrance of the heavenly world.

Paul said, *"we eagerly await a Savior from there, the Lord Jesus Christ."* He is talking about a tiptoe anticipation of the Savior's return. Historians tell us the greatest event in any Roman colony was the visit of the emperor. The streets were cleaned, and the houses were made ready with decorations. The citizens were not taken by surprised when the sovereign made his appearance. Each of us should live as if Jesus our Sovereign would come back today!

Questions to ponder: Does your life demonstrate the values and principles of Heaven? In your business? Your home? Does your conduct match your words? Do you bring a refreshing breeze from Heaven when you come in contact with others? Something to think about.

DEAD FLIES

*I plead with Euodia and I plead with Syntyche to be of the same
mind in the Lord. Yes, and I ask you, my true companion, help
these women since they have contended at my side in the cause
of the gospel, along with Clement and the rest of my co-workers,
whose names are in the book of life* (Philippians 4:2-3).

PAUL LOVED THE CHURCH AT PHILIPPI. BUT, IN SPITE OF ALL THE GOOD
things the church was doing, there was a problem that needed addressing.
I'm reminded of what the writer of Ecclesiastes says, *"As dead flies give perfume
a bad smell, so a little folly outweighs wisdom and honor"* (Ecclesiastes 10:1). There
were problems in the church, and it was causing a "fly in the ointment."

Two women, Euodia and Syntyche, were not getting along and the result was
a *"bad smell"* in the fellowship. There is nothing like church people having a disagreement to send a message to the community that Christians have issues just
like everyone else. There are no perfect Christians, which means there are no
perfect churches. As the old saying goes, "If you find a perfect church, don't join
it because it won't be perfect anymore!" But to say we are not perfect is not an
excuse to act selfishly.

Paul met the issue head-on with a loving attitude. We don't know all the reasons for their disagreement, but it is obvious to me they were more than just good
Christians. Paul made it clear that they *"have contended at my side in the cause of
the gospel."* In other words, these two put their lives on the line for the Gospel of
Christ. In spite of all the good they did, they had a falling out that was causing a
disruption. It is tragic when Christians can't get along.

The best way to "freshen up" the atmosphere is to *"be of the same mind in the
Lord."* These two were not in harmony with one another. The indication was one
or both of them were out of fellowship with Christ. You can't be in fellowship
with the Lord and be out of sorts with your fellow believers. Jesus said there is one
way to tell if a person belongs to Him, *"By this everyone will know that you are my
disciples, if you love one another"* (John 13:35). If your relationship with another
brother or sister is causing a "stink," it's time to set things right.

PRAISE HIM ANYWAY

*David was greatly distressed because the men were talking of stoning
him; each one was bitter in spirit because of his sons and daughters.
But David found strength in the Lord his God* (1 Samuel 30:6).

NO ONE IS IMMUNE FROM HAVING A BAD DAY. YOU KNOW THE KIND OF DAY
I'm talking about, right? You don't want to crawl back into bed, but crawl
under the bed and hide! If that sounds familiar, take heart, because we are told
about a man who is probably having the mother of all bad days. His name was
David. How he handled the situation is a lesson for all of us.

Get the picture in your mind. David and his men ride into home base (Ziklag),
and discover their arch enemy, the Amalekites, came into the city while they were
gone. They burned, looted, and took captive all the women and children. They
lost it all! If David and his men had any hope of recovering what the enemy had
stolen, it would be by God's wisdom and power and not their own.

Meanwhile, back at camp things are about to go from bad to really bad: *"the
men were talking of stoning him; each one was bitter in spirit because of his sons and
daughters."* They blamed David for the tragedy. Have you noticed when things
are going badly we always find someone or something to blame? It is more convenient to fix blame than to solve the problem. Instead of running to the man
in charge, David, and offering encouragement, his men started complaining
and murmuring. In their twisted logic, they wanted to pick up some rocks and
kill him!

David learned to do something that would benefit all us when faced with
tough times. He praised God: *"But David found strength in the Lord his God."*
Instead of focusing on what his men wanted to do, he started focusing on the
promises of God. It is easy to praise God when things are going well, but learning to praise Him when things are "up in smoke" is when we are on the road
to victory.

Is your life a disaster? Praise Him anyway! Read Psalm 149 and see that praise
is a weapon we can use against all the negative forces that come against us!

BE PREPARED

*When the Philistines heard that David had been anointed king over
all Israel, they went up in full force to search for him, but David
heard about it and went out to meet them* (1 Chronicles 14:8).

I DON'T KNOW HOW MANY TIMES I HAVE HEARD PEOPLE SAY THAT THE CLOSER they get to God the more resistance comes their way. Just look at King David. As soon as the Philistines heard that he was ruling over all of Israel, they decided to wipe him out. Why is that? They knew a united Israel, under an anointed king, was a direct threat. A revival was about to break out and David had to be stopped.

You can mark it down—the closer you get to God, the more the enemy will oppose you. David decided to prepare for the battle before the enemy ever showed up. What did David do when he heard what his enemies were planning?

1. He prayed about it: "so David inquired of God: 'Shall I go and attack the Philistines? Will you deliver them into my hands?' The Lord answered him, 'Go, I will deliver them into your hands'" (1 Chronicles 14:10). What is your first response when you receive bad news? Do you complain and blame God? David had a history of receiving bad news, and each time he demonstrated what was in his heart. He didn't run away in fear, nor did he try to solicit the opinions of others. He talked to God.

2. He obeyed the word: "So David did as God commanded him, and they struck down the Philistine army, all the way from Gibeon to Gezer" (1 Chronicles 14:16). David understood it was one thing to receive a word from God, but that is not enough. He had to put feet to his prayer. I once heard a friend say, "Every defeat I have experienced can be traced to my failure to pray."

3. He realized only God could give the victory: "So David and his men went up to Baal Perazim, and there he defeated them. He said, 'As waters break out, God has broken out against my enemies by my hand'" (1 Chronicles 14:11). It is up to us to obey, and it is up to God to produce the results! Keep your eyes on God, and He will give the victory! *"Our God, will you not judge them? For we have no power to face this vast army that is attacking us. We do not know what to do, but our eyes are on you"* (2 Chronicles 20:12).

FREE INDEED

This day—this very moment—millions are living their lives in shame, fear, and intimidation who should be free, productive individuals. The tragedy is they think it is the way they should be. The have never known the truth that could set them free. They are victimized, existing as if living on death row instead of enjoying the beauty and fresh air of the abundant life Christ modeled and made possible for all of His followers to claim. Unfortunately, most don't have a clue to what they are missing.

—CHUCK SWINDOLL[57]

LOOK AND LIVE

Just as Moses lifted up the snake in the wilderness, so the Son of Man must be lifted up, that everyone who believes may have eternal life in him (John 3:14-15).

J ESUS HAD JUST CONFRONTED NICODEMUS WITH THE TRUTH THAT *"NO ONE can see the kingdom of God unless they are born again"* (John 3:1-8). Nicodemus asked Jesus how can this be? In modern terms, he might have asked, "How is it possible that all of my religion will not gain me access to your Kingdom?" To answer his question, Jesus painted a picture of God's grace from the Old Testament. Salvation is by God's grace, always has been, always will be. It's not about a person striving to make himself or herself acceptable to God.

The event Jesus referred to took place in Numbers 21. The Israelites asked God for help against their enemies and promised God if He would give them the victory, they would destroy all their cities. Once again God answered their prayer. But instead of doing what they said they would do, they started their usual griping and complaining (see Numbers 21:1-5). God had enough of their nonsense: *"Then the Lord sent venomous snakes among them; they bit the people and many Israelites died"* (Numbers 21:6).

Realizing the snake invasion was deadly serious, they repented of their sin and asked Moses to pray for the Lord to take the snakes away. Moses prayed, an in response, *"The Lord said to Moses, 'Make a snake and put it up on a pole; anyone who is bitten can look at it and live.' So Moses made a bronze snake and put it up on a pole. Then when anyone was bitten by a snake and looked at the bronze snake, they lived"* (Numbers 21:8-9).

The people were not told to kill the snakes or to find a way to offer a sacrifice. No! They were told to "look" and "live." The condition of those bitten did not matter. Suppose some had been blinded by the poison and could not "see" the serpent? The instructions were not to "see" but to "look."

God's grace is now on display. The brazen serpent lifted high is a picture of the cross of Christ. Salvation is offered to all who will *look to the cross and live.* Our condition does not preclude us from looking at the cross to receive salvation. No matter how blinded by the poison of sin, the truth is still the same today. Isaiah 42:18 declares, *"Hear, you deaf; look, you blind, and see!"*

AMAZING GRACE

*For God so loved the world that he gave his one
and only Son, that whoever believes in him shall
not perish but have eternal life* (John 3:16).

IT HAS BEEN SAID JOHN 3:16 SAYS EVERYTHING THAT NEEDS TO BE SAID ABOUT God's grace. Packed into one statement is the sum total of God's demonstration of love to all humankind. It is so simple that a little child can understand its meaning.

The opening phrase, *"For God,"* tells us that the Lord is the initiator of our salvation. Before the emergence of sin, there was the emergence of God's grace (1 John 4:9). The simple phrase, *"so loved"* is describing the intensity and the depth of God's love for His creation. The love spoken of here is *agape* love. We hear talk of love on an everyday basis. We use the same word to describe how we feel about our spouses and our love of cars. In the English language, the same word can be used to describe many things. But *agape* is a new kind of love that emanates from the heart of God and reaches down to the lowest sinner. *"See what great love the Father has lavished on us, that we should be called children of God! And that is what we are! The reason the world does not know us is that it did not know him"* (1 John 3:1).

The word John uses for *"world"* is not the world of nature or the world of beauty, but the world of humanity. Jesus did not die for a certain group or a particular country—*all* are included! The offer of salvation has been extended to all, but tragically not all will receive this wonderful gift. I suppose if salvation could be attained by money or works, more people would certainly be attracted to God.

If I were to hand you the keys to a new car, and say, "It's yours, and it's free." Would you ask me, "Brother Paul, is there anything I can do to pay you back for this gift?" My answer would be, "The minute you try to pay me for the gift of the car, it stops being a gift and becomes something you can buy." Likewise, salvation cannot be bought or worked for; it is a gift. God has extended His open hand to give you something you don't deserve. Have you received it yet?

THE GIFT OF ALL GIFTS

*For God so loved the world that he gave his one
and only Son, that whoever believes in him shall
not perish but have eternal life* (John 3:16).

THE WORDS OF JOHN 3:16 GIVE OFF THE SWEETEST SOUNDS THAT COULD EVER be heard. The truth that mortal humans can have intimate fellowship with the One who created them is void of all our understanding, except for one thing. It is God who took the first step in the drama of redemption, not the other way around. God is the prime mover, and the first to give out of a heart of love.

We need to get something straight. People have been led to believe that Jesus died on the cross so God would love humanity. This concept of God has given rise to a false view of His true nature and character. He has been portrayed as vengeful, detached, and ready to rain down fire on unsuspecting sinners. He has been accused of all sorts of evil things, not the least of which is that He is a cruel, bloodthirsty bully who revels in sending people to hell. Whoever takes time to read the Bible discovers that nothing could be further from the truth!

Who among us would allow their only child to die in the place of evil people? A child who never harmed anyone, to be handed over to be savagely beaten and tortured to death. What would you do? In all honesty, I don't think I could. But God did not hesitate to allow His only Son to die in our place. Talk is cheap; it doesn't cost a dime. But real love is expensive and shows itself genuine by its actions. God *so loved* us that He did not just talk about it, but was willing to hand over His Son to evil men to fulfill the divine drama of salvation.

John 3:16 clearly reveals the heart of God for all His children: *"God so loved the world that he gave his one and only Son."* Jesus did not die for God to love us, He died because God already loved us! The Father's loving expression resulted in His giving the best gift the world will ever know, His Son. God took the first step. Before we were looking for Him, He was pursuing us. First John 4:19 says, *"We love because he first loved us."*

WHOEVER MEANS ME

*For God so loved the world that he gave his one
and only Son, that whoever believes in him shall
not perish but have eternal life* (John 3:16).

THE LOVE OF GOD IS NOT RESERVED FOR A SELECTED GROUP OF PEOPLE. NOR is it limited by education, class, or pedigree. Keep in mind the context of the statement *"whoever believes in him."* Jesus was talking to Nicodemus, who was considered one of the religious leaders of his day. This man belonged to a group who kept the rituals and traditions of the Jewish faith. In his conversation with Jesus, he is discovering that all the religion in the world will not gain access to the things of God.

After reading this marvelous verse, I can well imagine someone thinking, *Am I included?* A fair and honest question indeed. The short answer is *yes;* you are included. How do I know with such certainty? I looked up the meaning of *"whoever"* and discovered it means what is says—*whoever!*

All humanity is wrapped up in that statement, no matter how far from God a person may be. His love reaches out to any and all who respond to His overture of grace and forgiveness. To eliminate any doubt or confusion, Paul says, *"But God demonstrates his own love for us in this: While we were still sinners, Christ died for us"* (Romans 5:8).

The greatest most important decision a person will ever make is not who to marry or what kind of career to choose. Sadly, many people spend time worrying about things that have no eternal consequence. James declares, *"Now listen, you who say, 'Today or tomorrow we will go to this or that city, spend a year there, carry on business and make money.' Why, you do not even know what will happen tomorrow. What is your life? You are a mist that appears for a little while and then vanishes"* (James 4:13-14). Our life is compared to the morning fog that appears for only a brief moment.

The most important question you will every answer and decision you will ever make: *"Where will you spend eternity?"* Receiving God's gift of eternal life gives you the assurance of an abundant life here and eternal life there. But, for those who turn their backs on the grace of God face an uncertain future here, and a separation from God's love forever. Don't gamble with your soul.

YOU ARE FREE: NOW WHAT?

*Jesus replied, "Very truly I tell you, everyone who sins is
a slave to sin. Now a slave has no permanent place in the
family, but a son belongs to it forever. So if the Son sets
you free, you will be free indeed" (John 8:34-36).*

I AM OLD ENOUGH TO REMEMBER THE 1960s. THE BATTLE CRY OF THAT GENER-
ation was, *"I WANT MY FREEDOM!"* Whether they were marching in the
streets or showing up by the thousands at a farm in up-state New York (Wood-
stock), the chant never changed. Strangely enough, all the while wanting freedom,
they all looked alike, wore their hair alike, talked alike, and even smelled alike. It
seemed to me it was more about conformity than individuality.

Not understanding the meaning of freedom is not confined to the hippie generation; the lie started in the Garden of Eden, and the same lie has been repeated in
every generation. What is the lie? In essence, satan (the snake) told Eve she didn't
have to trust God and that if she would just "do your own thing," she would be
just like God (see Genesis 3). We all know how that turned out. Freedom is not
doing anything you want without fear of contradiction or consequences.

Jesus said to a group of religious leaders that if they wanted to know what it
meant to be free, it could only be found in a personal relationship with Him, *"So
if the Son sets you free, you will be free indeed."* And a personal relationship with
Christ means experiencing His truth. *"To the Jews who had believed him, Jesus
said, 'If you hold to my teaching, you are really my disciples. Then you will know the
truth, and the truth will set you free'"* (John 8:31-32).

When I gave my life to Jesus Christ, my eyes were opened to the truth that I
was free from the bondage of sin. I was no longer a slave (John 8:34) but a child
in the family God. And, I was free to discover why God put me on this earth.
The unlocking of my potential has been the greatest journey of my life. Freedom
is not found in a book of rules and regulations on how to be a good church member. Freedom means I can be all that God intended me to be. You too!

YOU WANT TO SUPERSIZE THAT?

Moreover the law entered that the offense might abound. But where sin abounded, grace abounded much more (Romans 5:20 NKJV).

I WAS ORDERING A COMBO MEAL AT THE LOCAL FINE DINING HAMBURGER ESTAB-lishment when the young man behind the counter looked at me and said something I had never heard before, "You want to supersize that?" I was naturally intrigued, so I responded, "I have no idea what you mean." He explained that for a few dollars more I could "supersize" my order. Wow, to have more than I need may be a new concept for buying burgers, but it is certainly not new with God.

Using fast food lingo, we could say that God's grace has "supersized" our salvation to go above and beyond any need we might have. If we take Paul literally, and I do, we might translate Romans 5:20 as, "Where sin was in abundance, God's grace was in super abundance." A limited understanding of abundant grace has led to a faulty belief that God's grace is in short supply. Do we think that God has limited His supply of grace? Nothing could be further from the truth. God's deep reservoir of grace is more than sufficient to meet any and all difficulties, hardships, trials, and temptations we might face.

Take a moment and ponder the following: The moment you gave your life to Christ you were justified freely by God's grace. Romans 3:23-24 tells us, *"for all have sinned and fall short of the glory of God, and all are justified freely by his grace through the redemption that came by Christ Jesus."* What does it mean to be justified? When God looks at you, He doesn't see your past sins or hold you to a judgment at some future time. No, Jesus took care of that at the cross. He died *for* you, but more importantly, He died *as* you!

How do I know it is true? Paul says, *"I have been crucified with Christ and I no longer live, but Christ lives in me. The life I now live in the body, I live by faith in the Son of God, who loved me and gave himself for me"* (Galatians 2:20). The next time you feel your life is spiraling out of control and you have gone so far away from God that there is no way back, remember you have a heavenly Father who operates in "supersize" grace!

COME AND DINE

*Jesus replied: "A certain man was preparing a great banquet
and invited many guests. At the time of the banquet he
sent his servant to tell those who had been invited, 'Come,
for everything is now ready'"* (Luke 14:16-17).

IMAGINE FOR A MOMENT THAT YOU WERE INVITED TO JOIN THE PRESIDENT OF the United States on a trip to visit the Queen of England. How would you respond? Would you say, *"Sorry Mr. President, I can't find time in my schedule for such a long trip."* Or, would you jump at the chance for a once-in-a-lifetime opportunity?

Jesus loved to illustrate God's grace through parables. This parable in Luke 14:16-24 is a picture of a banquet where everyone was invited. Believe it or not, some who received the invitation decided it was not important enough to warrant their attention. God's grace is freely given to all who will respond, but the tragedy is not all will come and dine at the King's table!

Jesus said, *"A certain man was preparing a great banquet and invited many guests."* Much to the dismay of the host, the invited guests gave excuses as to why they could not come. I could almost understand if they had been invited to a funeral or a boring lecture on microeconomics by professor Dry Dust from Boring University. But this wasn't that—it was something special, a great supper, a banquet table for all to enjoy! Who could turn down this invitation?

The first person said, *"I have just bought a field, and I must go and see it. Please excuse me."* Really? If he had already purchased it, the deal is done, why the rush to see it now? Why can't he see it another time?

Now, the second one said, *"I have just bought five yokes of oxen, and I'm on my way to try them out. Please excuse me."* I don't know anybody who buys something like this without first making sure they can do what is advertised.

And the third one is my personal favorite. He says, *"I just got married, so I can't come."* You can fill in the blank on this one. I think you get the point Jesus was trying to make. Let's face it, all of our excuses are just like that! They all are nothing more than what they appear to be—*excuses*. If you have made up your mind to reject God's offer of grace, any old excuse will do!

AN USUAL GIFT

Even if I should choose to boast, I would not be a fool, because I would be speaking the truth. But I refrain, so no one will think more of me than is warranted by what I do or say, or because of these surpassingly great revelations. Therefore, in order to keep me from becoming conceited, I was given a thorn in my flesh, a messenger of Satan, to torment me (2 Corinthians 12:6-7).

THE AGE-OLD QUESTION, "WHY DO CHRISTIANS SUFFER?" WILL PROBABLY never be answered completely on this side of Heaven. Whether we like it or not, pain and suffering are part of life. What is clear is there are times when we bring suffering on ourselves. If someone has poor eating habits, is overweight, and has high blood pressure, whose fault is that? It is certainly not God's. And they can't blame the devil for eating that last piece chocolate pie. No, it's the person in the mirror's fault.

Consider the experience of Paul. This hand-picked soldier of the cross was by no means a man of weak faith, nor was he doing things to bring self-inflicted pain. No, it seems that God had a redemptive purpose in mind. Notice he said it was God who gave him this unusual gift, *"I was given a thorn in my flesh."* Some teachers have speculated it was his poor eyesight (see Galatians 6:11); while others say it was the religious establishment who were trying to discredit his ministry. Whatever it was, it was painful, and Paul wanted it removed.

The bottom line: God allowed the devil to *"torment"* him to keep his pride and ego in check. Yes, there are times when God will allow painful experiences to afflict us to keep us from sinning. The Father has some unusual "pins" to burst the bubble of our self-inflated egos. The word *"thorn"* means a "sharp pointed object" and the word *"torment"* means to "punch, or hit with a fist." It was as if Paul was saying this messenger of satan was constantly giving him a sucker punch, and it was painful!

When suffering comes our way, we can get angry and bitter; or like Paul, we can know that nothing will happen to us that God did not allow. Paul may not have liked the pain, but he was willing to accept God's strength to get him through.

GOD'S GRACE TO SEE YOU THROUGH

Three times I pleaded with the Lord to take it away from me. But he said to me, "My grace is sufficient for you, for my power is made perfect in weakness." Therefore I will boast all the more gladly about my weaknesses, so that Christ's power may rest on me (2 Corinthians 12:8-9).

WHAT IS THE ONE THING WE WANT TO HEAR WHEN PAIN SHOWS UP ON OUR doorstep? Trust me, it's not another sermon or some well-meaning Christian reminding us we have to grit our teeth and bear it. Paul had a "thorn" in his flesh, and three times he begged God to remove it. He called this "pain" a messenger from satan. Was Paul wrong to ask God to remove his suffering? Is it wrong for us to ask God to stop the hurting? For me, it is simply a human response to pray for the pain to stop. Paul did the human thing; he prayed about it, and the answer was not what he wanted to hear.

God had a message for Paul. It was a message of "supersized" grace, *"My grace is sufficient for you."* God's abundant supply of grace was more than enough to meet every need in Paul's life. And, the good news is His ample supply of grace to meet every need in our lives. I once heard a teacher say that grace and mercy are two sides of the same coin. He said, "Grace is God giving us something we did not deserve, and in mercy, God was not giving us what we did deserve! John 1:16 tells us, *"Out of his fullness we have all received grace in place of grace already given."*

It was also a message of "supersized" strength: *"for my power is made perfect in weakness."* Paul didn't ask for God's power to overcome his thorn in the flesh. He asked God to take it away. God said He would do something even greater than removing our pain. He said He would give us strength to endure and overcome so that *His* name would be glorified. Paul didn't know how strong he was until he was at his weakest moment.

The message for us—when suffering comes our way, get a word from God. Get still and let Him speak to our heart. Once Paul understood what God was up to, he could move ahead with the assurance that the Lord had not abandoned him.

GRACE GIVING

But since you excel in everything—in faith, in speech, in knowledge,
in complete earnestness and in the love we have kindled in you—see
that you also excel in this grace of giving (2 Corinthians 8:7).

IN THIS VERSE, PAUL IS REMINDING THE CHURCH AT CORINTH OF SOMETHING he shared with them more than a year ago. There was a famine in Jerusalem, and they had committed to helping by taking an offering. Now they needed to follow through on their promise. The apostle Paul was not shy about teaching on giving. Wherever he planted churches he made it a top priority to instruct the people of God on the importance of being good stewards of their time and their treasure.

He did not view giving as a burden, nor did he use scare tactics to motivate people to give. Paul said that *"grace giving"* is birthed out of a heart filled with God's love. Giving then becomes something we do because we love Jesus, not because of some regulation that says we have to give to please God. In the modern church, there is a continual tension between two extremes when it comes to the subject of giving.

On the one hand, there are those who teach that giving is the only way to garner God's blessing. The impression is the more you give, the more God will approve of you. These hucksters will use every carnival trick in the book to manipulate money out of your wallet into their pocket. Using tactics such as promising that if you give them a certain amount (usually one thousand dollars), God will pay off all of your debt. If those tactics don't work, then they are not above using guilt and shame. The other extreme developed because of an overreaction to the manipulators. The idea is: "We don't take offerings, we don't talk about giving, and if you want to give we will make it as difficult as possible." This extreme wants us to believe that teaching people about good stewardship and money management has no place in ministry.

Balance is needed! When the Holy Spirit motivates our giving, we enter into the joy of "grace giving." Then we understand Paul's statement, *"remembering the words the Lord Jesus himself said: 'It is more blessed to give than to receive'"* (Acts 20:35).

A Good Example of Grace Giving

And now, brothers and sisters, we want you to know about the grace that God has given the Macedonian churches. In the midst of a very severe trial, their overflowing joy and their extreme poverty welled up in rich generosity (2 Corinthians 8:1-2).

PAUL WAS URGING THE CHURCH AT CORINTH TO MAKE GOOD WHAT THEY HAD promised. *"Now finish the work, so that your eager willingness to do it may be matched by your completion of it, according to your means"* (2 Corinthians 8:11). It was evident they had good intentions, but for some reason, they had not kept their word. This would not be the last time someone or some group got caught up in the emotion of an appeal and made a commitment.

A fast way to discredit our word is to make a promise we don't intend to keep. Somehow these folks in Corinth had the idea because they excelled *"in every-thing"* (2 Corinthians 8:7), they could excuse their lack of giving. Paul was glad they had all the gifts of the Spirit but warned them not to neglect *"this grace of giving."*

One of the best ways to demonstrate a truth is using a real-life example. So, he pointed to the churches of Macedonia as living examples of grace giving. If we want to see grace-giving in action, just look at the experiences of the churches in Macedonia. They were in a pressure cooker of trials and extreme difficulties. In spite of *"a very severe trial"* they gave with *"overflowing joy."* Their difficulties resulted in *"extreme poverty."* The word Paul used for *"poverty"* means a beggar. These folks were in dire straits, and yet they didn't allow their difficulties to become roadblocks or excuses for not giving. They did not complain, gripe, or blame bad breaks; they opened their hearts and gave. Likewise, when we experience the grace of God, we will refuse to use difficult circumstances as an excuse not to give to meet the needs of others.

Too many times we have based our giving on circumstances and not on what the Lord is telling us. I determined years ago not to allow my balance sheet to have any influence over what I do or don't do when it comes to obeying the Lord. I have learned to trust and obey, for there is no other way to be happy in Jesus!

215

ACTIONS SPEAK LOUDER
THAN WORDS

I am not commanding you, but I want to test the sincerity of
your love by comparing it with the earnestness of others. For
you know the grace of our Lord Jesus Christ, that though he
was rich, yet for your sake he became poor, so that you through
his poverty might become rich (2 Corinthians 8:8-9).

PAUL WAS QUICK TO POINT OUT THAT HE WAS IN NO WAY USING PRESSURE TAC-
tics to motivate their giving. Grace giving does not issue out of a guilty
conscience, but comes from a willing heart: *"For if the willingness is there, the gift*
is acceptable according to what one has, not according to what one does not have"
(2 Corinthians 8:12).

How can a person prove the sincerity of their words? Paul said the only way
to demonstrate the sincerity of their commitment was by actions: *"I am not com-*
manding you, but I want to test the sincerity of your love by comparing it with the
earnestness of others" (2 Corinthians 8:8). What he was saying is their actions will
match their words. There is a huge difference between the attitude of "I intend
to give," and "I will follow through" with my commitment. I am afraid there are
times when the mouth speaks one thing, but the heart says something entirely
different. Grace giving starts in the heart and ego giving starts with the mouth.

The Bible has much to say about the importance of keeping our word. Deuteronomy 23:21-23 says, *"If you make a vow to the Lord your God, do not be slow to*
pay it, for the Lord your God will certainly demand it of you and you will be guilty
of sin. But if you refrain from making a vow, you will not be guilty. Whatever your
lips utter you must be sure to do, because you made your vow freely to the Lord your
God with your own mouth."

Paul not only pointed out the sacrifice of others, but he wanted to show the
greatest proof of sacrificial giving known to humankind. *"For you know the grace*
of our Lord Jesus Christ, that though he was rich, yet for your sake he became poor, so
that you through his poverty might become rich" (2 Corinthians 8:9). Even though
Jesus was rich in all things, He willingly laid aside the garments of glory to provide salvation for a spiritually bankrupt humanity.

WELCOME TO GRACE-LAND

For the law was given through Moses; grace and
truth came through Jesus Christ (John 1:17).

WHEN I SPEAK OF "GRACE-LAND," I'M NOT TALKING ABOUT THE HOME OF the late king of rock and roll, Elvis Presley. No, I'm talking about living in freedom from the bondage of sin and a miserable life of trying to please God with religious rules and regulations.

When Jesus arrived on the scene, the number one religious group of the day were the Pharisees, followed closely by the Sadducees. These two groups, along with the scribes, were the "turf shepherds" of the law of Moses. Using the law, along with an added list of rules and their own interpretations, they regulated the day-to-day life of every Jew. They made it clear to average Jews that if they had any hope of seeing God in the afterlife, they better conform to their rules. These self-appointed guardians of the faith believed they were acting as the voice of God to the people (see Matthew 23).

Living under the law was a dismal and hopeless situation. How difficult it must have been to know that no matter what you did, you are guilty until proven innocent! When the legalistic approach to God was burned into the culture, it became man's attempt to gain salvation by an outward conformity to what others said, not what God said.

When *"grace and truth came through Jesus,"* the religious world was turned right side up. Jesus taught that a person did not have to live under the crushing load of a religious yoke. He said taking His yoke would bring peace and rest, not shame and guilt. *"Take my yoke upon you and learn from me, for I am gentle and humble in heart, and you will find rest for your souls. For my yoke is easy and my burden is light"* (Matthew 11:29-30).

Establishing moral standards and self-discipline is good and necessary; but it is not a substitute for a personal relationship with Christ. Everything Jesus said pointed to the heart, not the head. And while the common folk loved and followed Him, the religious crowd hated Him. Why did they want to silence Him? It was because He said all the rules and regulations in the world would not save us. Living in *grace-land* is not a license to sin, but the freedom to become all that God created us to be.

BATTLE STATIONS!

I am astonished that you are so quickly deserting the one who called you to live in the grace of Christ and are turning to a different gospel—which is really no gospel at all. Evidently some people are throwing you into confusion and are trying to pervert the gospel of Christ (Galatians 1:6-7).

DURING WARTIME WHEN A SHIP IS ABOUT TO COME UNDER ATTACK, THE CAPtain would sound an alarm. Every sailor knew when the alarm sounded it was time to "man the battle stations" because the enemy is close at hand. When Paul wrote his letter to the churches in Galatia he sounded the alarm—the enemy is near!

Certain individuals came later and started teaching a doctrine that Paul viewed as a perversion of the true Gospel. Their "false" gospel was a mixture of law and grace, and Paul would have none of it. He issued a warning: *"If anybody is preaching to you a gospel other than what you accepted, let them be under God's curse!"* (Galatians 1:9).

These "enemies" of the Gospel were teaching that if you are a real true Christian, you will not only put your faith in Christ, but you must also keep the law of Moses. In other words, faith in Christ alone is not enough. To the Ephesians, Paul wrote, *"For it is by grace you have been saved, through faith—and this is not from yourselves, it is the gift of God—not by works, so that no one can boast"* (Ephesians 2:8-9).

Paul was not playing around—there was too much at stake. Following strict religious rules will not make you holy, they will make you miserable! The only way to come to Christ is through faith, plus nothing. You cannot buy or work your way into the Kingdom of God.

When Paul left these folks, they were walking in freedom and living in peace. Now they are in a state of confusion and unrest. That is what believing a lie will produce. The devil uses lies to keep people in bondage, but God uses the truth to set people free. Living in peace and assurance is the result of trusting Christ alone. Never allow anyone to steal your freedom in Christ!

PEOPLE PLEASER OR GOD PLEASER?

*Am I now trying to win the approval of human beings, or of God?
Or am I trying to please people? If I were still trying to please
people, I would not be a servant of Christ* (Galatians 1:10).

I FIND IT INTERESTING AND ALMOST COMICAL THAT PAUL WAS ACCUSED OF being a people pleaser. When you read some of his thoughts concerning those who were twisting the Gospel you would have to surmise he was not using people skills to win friends. He did not set out to be offensive, he just told the truth, and his enemies had to find a way to discredit him.

In his letter to the Thessalonians he addressed the issue this way: *"On the contrary, we speak as those approved by God to be entrusted with the gospel. We are not trying to please people but God, who tests our hearts. You know we never used flattery, nor did we put on a mask to cover up greed—God is our witness. We were not looking for praise from people, not from you or anyone else, even though as apostles of Christ we could have asserted our authority"* (1 Thessalonians 2:4-6).

Jesus spoke about the danger of wanting to please others at the expense of pleasing God: *"I do not accept glory from human beings, but I know you. I know that you do not have the love of God in your hearts. I have come in my Father's name, and you do not accept me; but if someone else comes in his own name, you will accept him. How can you believe since you accept glory from one another but do not seek the glory that comes from the only God?"* (John 5:41-44).

I don't know of anyone who starts out in ministry or in business with the attitude of trying to make people dislike them. On the contrary, it would be more along the lines of going overboard to be liked by everybody, even to the point of exhaustion! Are you a people pleaser or a God pleaser? If I am pleasing God, then I won't have to worry about pleasing others. Those who love the Lord will extend grace even when we mess up or make a mistake. As far as others are concerned, well, that's another story.

GRACE GREATER THAN OUR SIN

In him we have redemption through his blood, the forgiveness of sins, in accordance with the riches of God's grace (Ephesians 1:7).

THE PROBLEM OF SIN HAS BEEN WITH US SINCE ADAM AND EVE DECIDED they had a better plan than God. Unfortunately for them, and us, their faulty wisdom opened the door to the sin problem that is still plaguing us today. What can we do with our sin? Is God's grace truly greater than our sin?

In reality we have only two choices: First, we can try to deny our sins: *"If we claim to be without sin, we deceive ourselves and the truth is not in us* (1 John 1:8). Just to deny that something is not real, does not make it any less true. *"Whoever conceals their sins does not prosper, but the one who confesses and renounces them finds mercy"* (Proverbs 28:13).

When you pick up the Bible and read the stories of some of God's greatest men and women, you will see they had issues with sin. Consider Moses. The law-giver was considered the greatest leader and motivator in the Old Testament, and yet he sinned. You can read where his sin of disobedience disqualified him from going into the Promised Land. Simon Peter, who preached the first sermon on the day of Pentecost and was in Christ's inner circle, he even denied that he knew the Lord Jesus! It is possible that we can win the victory over sin, so pretending it is not an issue is wrong.

The second option: we can bring our sins to the cross and confess them. *"If we confess our sins, he is faithful and just and will forgive us our sins and purify us from all unrighteousness* (1 John 1:9). The word *"confess"* just means to "agree" or to "say the same thing." So, when we confess our sin, we agree with God. Calling sin what God's calls it is the first step to victory. Here is the promise: *"he is faithful and just and will forgive us our sins and purify us from all unrighteousness."* How is God able to do that? *"in accordance with the riches of God's grace"* (Ephesians 1:7). Yes, my friend, God's grace is truly greater than all our sin!

"FREE FROM THE LAW—O HAPPY CONDITION"

Now then, why do you try to test God by putting on the necks of Gentiles a yoke that neither we nor our ancestors have been able to bear? (Acts 15:10)

I LOVE THAT OLD HYMN, "FREE FROM THE LAW, O HAPPY CONDITION." BUT what does it mean to be free from the law? Does it mean as Christians we don't have to be aware of God's standards as set out in the law of Moses? Does it mean we can live any way we want, and excuse our lifestyle because we are free from the law? I don't think that is what the Bible is teaching, nor what the hymn is suggesting.

To be free from the law is to acknowledge that our salvation and relationship with the Lord are not based on the law, but on God's grace. A crisis developed in the early church over the issue of Gentiles coming to Christ. The burning question: "Do the Gentiles have to become Jews and observe the law as well as receive Christ's work on the cross?" The legalists argued the cross was a necessary first step, but it was still not enough. In their wisdom, the elders declared that they could not put people under a yoke that even their ancestors were not able to bear.

Why is the law like a yoke? Because yokes were used to control animals and the law was given to control humans. The law of God was never intended to change anyone, but to reveal the righteous nature of God. It was only when Jesus Christ took on Himself the yoke of sin and bore the yoke of the law that humanity was set free (see Galatians 3:13).

When Christians put themselves under the law, they deny the freedom that Jesus purchased on Calvary. In essence, we are taking off the yoke of liberty and putting on the yoke of slavery: *"It is for freedom that Christ has set us free. Stand firm, then, and do not let yourselves be burdened again by a yoke of slavery"* (Galatians 5:1).

When we become Christians, we exchanged one yoke for another. We now have the yoke of God's love flooding our hearts. Now that is something to shout about!

Free from the law, O happy condition,
Jesus hath bled, and there is remission;
Cursed by the law and bruised by the fall,
Grace hath redeemed us, once for all.[58]

EVEN BARNABAS

The other Jews joined him in his hypocrisy, so that by their hypocrisy even Barnabas was led astray (Galatians 2:13).

BARNABAS WAS THE KIND OF GUY EVERYBODY WANTED ON THEIR TEAM. HE was loyal and determined to go the extra mile when it came to the spreading of the Gospel. But he was human and fell into the age-old trap of following a leader who played the hypocrite. Faithfulness to the team and loyalty to a leader can only go as far as your liberty in Christ will take you.

The leader that caused Barnabas to step over the line is a very familiar figure. He was a close disciple of Jesus and received a revelation from God that *all* people are on equal footing when it comes to a need for salvation. When the door was opened, he shared the Gospel with Gentiles (see Acts 10). His name was Simon Peter, but when the opportunity to stand for liberty was presented, he crumbled like a house of cards.

The church at Antioch was populated with Gentile converts. When Peter came to the church, he had no problem eating and fellowshipping with the new Christians. I can imagine he was right in the middle of the men's prayer breakfast on Saturday morning, scarfing down as much bacon as the next man. But, when *"certain men"* showed up from Jerusalem, he allowed fear to rob him of his freedom.

As we say in Texas, Paul and Peter had a "dust-up." *"When Cephas came to Antioch, I opposed him to his face, because he stood condemned. For before certain men came from James, he used to eat with the Gentiles. But when they arrived, he began to draw back and separate himself from the Gentiles because he was afraid of those who belonged to the circumcision group"* (Galatians 2:11-12).

I have often wondered why Paul was so hard on his co-laborer. He even called him a hypocrite to his face. Paul's attitude was, there are certain things worth fighting for, and liberty in Christ is one of them. He also knew that people would follow their leaders and that makes this misstep a double tragedy. Peter's actions caused other people to stumble: *"even Barnabas was led astray."* Every time legalism reared its ugly head, Paul would take the sword of the Spirit and cut it off.

You do not have to sacrifice your liberty just to please others (see Galatians 2:14-16).

WHAT JESUS KNEW

*After he had said this, he went on to tell them, "Our friend
Lazarus has fallen asleep; but I am going there to wake
him up." His disciples replied, "Lord, if he sleeps, he will
get better." Jesus had been speaking of his death, but his
disciples thought he meant natural sleep* (John 11:11-13).

I LOVE "FEEL-GOOD" STORIES, DON'T YOU? WHEN JESUS CAME TO BETHANY, IT
did not appear that this story was going to have a happy ending. Jesus received
an urgent message that his dear friend Lazarus was at death's door (see John
11:1-14). Instead of rushing to the home, Jesus did the unthinkable, He delayed.
Then the crushing news was delivered that His friend had died. Hope for a positive outcome was buried in a tomb.

What was Jesus thinking? Could it be that He didn't worry about the outcome because He already knew what He was going to do? He told His disciples,
*"and for your sake I am glad I was not there, so that you may believe. But let us go to
him"* (John 11:15).

How many times have we decided the outcome was going to be negative, even
before we asked God for His wisdom? The sisters of Lazarus had already decided
that nothing good could come out of this tragedy. Their brother was dead, and
there was nothing more to say, with one exception; if Jesus had come when they
asked Him, things would have turned out differently. That is not the end of the
story. Mary and Martha had a change of attitude and placed the final say in the
Lord's hands. What a novel approach (see John 11:22-32).

The next time we are faced with a negative situation, we need to stop and ask
the Lord, "Father, what do You know about this that I don't?" Wouldn't it be
wonderful if every time we faced difficulty the Lord would allow us to see things
from His perspective? If He did, it would not require any faith on our part. I have
found the best approach is to understand that no matter what the outcome may
be, the Lord is still in control of my life. *"The Lord is my strength and my defense;
he has become my salvation. He is my God, and I will praise him, my father's God,
and I will exalt him"* (Exodus 15:2).

LET THAT MAN GO

The dead man came out, his hands and feet wrapped with
strips of linen, and a cloth around his face. Jesus said to them,
"Take off the grave clothes and let him go" (John 11:44).

I'M SURE YOU HAVE HEARD THE OLD EXPRESSION, "GRAVEYARD DEAD." SUCH was the case of Lazarus. When Jesus called him out of the grave, there was something else that needed to be done. When the Lord acts, He doesn't do half a job. Giving His friend life was just the start of the miracle. Lazarus had life but, but no freedom. His feet were tied, he couldn't walk. His hands were tied, he couldn't work. His face was covered, he couldn't witness. So what did Jesus do? He saw the situation and declared, *"Take off the grave clothes and let him go."* As with everything Jesus did, there are lessons to learn.

First, everyone who responds to the Word of Christ has been given eternal life: *"Whoever believes in the Son has eternal life, but whoever rejects the Son will not see life, for God's wrath remains on them"* (John 3:36). Jesus promised not only life but life more abundant (see John 10:10).

Second, not everyone walks in the freedom they could enjoy. Abraham Lincoln signed the Emancipation Proclamation on January 1, 1863, freeing the slaves. The sad truth—even though the paper was signed and carried the full force of the United States government, most slaves did not have a clue what their freedom meant. Many slaves continued to work the fields just as before because they did not comprehend the meaning of liberty. Many Christians are still working the same fields as before because they do not understand what Jesus did when He set them free.

And *third,* many believers are still bound with the grave clothes of the old life. Somehow we have the impression that when we gave our lives to the Lord, the issues of the past life were gone. While it is true we became new creations in Christ (see 2 Corinthians 5:17) and our sins were forgiven, the fact remains that we still wear the grave clothes of the old life: *"But now you must also rid yourselves of all such things as these: anger, rage, malice, slander, and filthy language from your lips"* (Colossians 3:8).

It is time for us to get rid of the smelly grave clothes and enjoy our freedom!

HOME SWEET HOME

HOME SWEET HOME

Mid pleasures and palaces though we may roam,
Be it ever so humble, there's no place like home;
A charm from the sky seems to hallow us there,
Which, seek through the world, is ne'er met with elsewhere.
Home, home, sweet, sweet home!
There's no place like home, oh, there's no place like home!
An exile from home, splendor dazzles in vain;
Oh, give me my lowly thatched cottage again!
The birds singing gayly, that come at my call—
Give me them—and the peace of mind, dearer than all!
Home, home, sweet, sweet home!
There's no place like home, oh, there's no place like home!

JOHN HOWARD PAYNE[59]

ESTABLISHING THE PATTERN

*So the Lord God caused the man to fall into a deep sleep;
and while he was sleeping, he took one of the man's ribs
and then closed up the place with flesh. Then the Lord God
made a woman from the rib he had taken out of the man,
and he brought her to the man* (Genesis 2:21-22).

GOD DOES EVERYTHING ACCORDING TO A PATTERN. IF YOU WANT TO KNOW God's ideal, you have to go to the original design. The very first institution created by God was not the church, synagogue, or the government. No, it was the family unit. God chose the family to bring revival and blessings to the nations of the earth (see Genesis 12:3).

From that day to this, the forces of hell have been doing everything in its evil power to destroy the home. For example, the despicable tragedy of slavery was a successful attempt to divide and destroy the family unit. As horrible as it is to think that owning another human is morally acceptable, is the fact that slavery was the devil's scheme to eliminate the family unit from the face of the earth.

While it is true every generation has faced its own set of difficulties, it seems that in the 21st century the lines of decency have been erased. Even though Isaiah was writing in a different age, his warnings could have been issued in this very hour: *"What sorrow for those who say that evil is good and good is evil, that dark is light and light is dark, that bitter is sweet and sweet is bitter. What sorrow for those who are wise in their own eyes and think themselves so clever. What sorrow for those who are heroes at drinking wine and boast about all the alcohol they can hold. They take bribes to let the wicked go free, and they punish the innocent"* (Isaiah 5:20-23 New Living Translation).

If you want to know how to build a godly home, go to the owner's manual—the Bible—and follow the pattern: *"But if serving the Lord seems undesirable to you, then choose for yourselves this day whom you will serve, whether the gods your ancestors served beyond the Euphrates, or the gods of the Amorites, in whose land you are living. But as for me and my household, we will serve the Lord"* (Joshua 24:15).

READ THE FINE PRINT

*The man said, "This is now bone of my bones and flesh of my
flesh; she shall be called 'woman,' for she was taken out of man."
That is why a man leaves his father and mother and is united
to his wife, and they become one flesh* (Genesis 2:23-24).

THERE ARE NO PERFECT MARRIAGES. HENCE, THERE ARE NO PERFECT HOMES. The reason is simple: there are no perfect people! To build a godly home in an ungodly world is one of life's greatest challenges. If you are determined to build a godly home, then let's look at some of the fine print.

First, when a marriage takes place between a man and woman, there are some things to *learn: "…and they become one flesh"* (see Ephesians 5:31). Marriage presents a new math: 1+1 equals *one flesh*. Becoming "one" does not mean losing your own identity or personality, but it does mean putting someone's else needs and desires above your own. More than one marriage has been doomed because of selfishness. We are living in a culture that stresses "me first," and it's killing our homes. Keeping your word and sacrificing for the greater good of the home are concepts that are rarely heard today, even among Christians.

Second, there are some things to *leave: "That is why a man leaves his father and mother and is united to his wife."* The Lord is not just referring to a physical location. I believe He is talking about specific relationships. He's not saying we can't have a relationship with our parents, not at all. He's saying the relationship with your spouse will overshadow all other relationships by comparison.

Third, there are some things to *cleave: "and is united to his wife."* The literal translation of the word "united" or "joined" is a picture of gluing something together. In other words, when you said "I do," you were superglued to your mate! There may be days when things are not going so well in the home. We must remember that love between husband and wife is more than an emotion, it's a commitment. Emotions are like soap bubbles, they will burst with the slightest movement; but the commitment to one another is the strong foundation that will stand the test of time.

THREE BUILDING BLOCKS

*By wisdom a house is built, and through understanding
it is established; through knowledge its rooms are filled
with rare and beautiful treasures* (Proverbs 24:3-4).

OVER THE YEARS I HAVE BEEN INVOLVED IN EVERY ASPECT OF HELPING COU-
ples achieve their maximum potential in their home. Starting out, I don't
think most couples have the idea that their marriage will not be healthy and
happy. But according to the latest statistic, one out of every three marriages end
in divorce. Those are not very good odds, but it doesn't have to be that way.

The issue is not "Will we be problem-free," but "What can we do to ensure
the marriage will last?" Let me suggest three things that will at least give you a
fighting chance.

First, for a marriage to last requires a full-on total commitment of both spouses.
Making a commitment also includes having the lines of communication open at
all times. Trouble usually starts when one spouse decides that talking is a waste
of breath. In counseling couples, one of the most common complaints I hear
are wives saying, "He doesn't talk to me." Commitment and communication go
hand in hand and will help ensure that no problem is too big to solve.

*Second, for a marriage to last requires making the Lord the Head and not the
tail.* The numbers don't lie. The odds of success are much higher when a home is
built on Christian principles. That's just a fact, not fiction. The psalmist declares,
"Unless the Lord builds the house, the builders labor in vain" (Psalm 127:1). Trying to build a healthy, happy, and productive marriage without the wisdom of
the Lord is like trying to a build a house without any blueprints. You may build
something called a house, but it will never be as good as it could have been using
proper instructions.

Third, for a marriage to last requires dealing with conflicts in a fair manner. Yes,
there will be conflict. As I have said before, no marriage is perfect, and no home
is without the challenge of disputes, problems, and difficulty. The most common
mistake I have seen is ignoring small issues. Hiding under the covers and hoping
the problem goes away is dangerous because we might wake up one day and find
what was once small is now a full-blown crisis.

THE BUCK STOPS HERE

*For the husband is the head of the wife as Christ is the head of the
church, his body, of which he is the Savior* (Ephesians 5:23).

FOR THE PAST NUMBER OF YEARS, A CULTURAL SHIFT HAS BEEN TAKING PLACE,
and the most affected are our homes. A concerted effort has been launched
to blur the lines between the roles of husband and wife. God designed the family unit to function according to His pattern, not humankind's idea of what it
should be.

God's design for the home starts with the man. The Word says the husband is
to be the leader in the home. In every organization, there is a leader of some kind.
It is the attitude of Harry Truman who put a sign on his desk that read, "The
Buck Stops Here!" His meaning was clear; I am the leader, and I take full responsibility for the final decision. Likewise, the husband must take full responsibility
to lead and guide his family. When the man refuses to lead, the result will always
be confusion, chaos, and uncertainty.

As the leader, not dictator, in the home, the Bible gave the man specific instructions. He is to be the *provider* for the home (see 1 Timothy 5:8). I quickly add that
Bible does not prohibit the wife from working, but that is not the issue here. The
point is for a man to make sure his family is provided for, not only by his physical presence but by his hard work.

The husband is to be the *priest* in the home (see 1 Timothy 3:5). Long before
the tabernacle was built in the wilderness and the temple was constructed in Jerusalem, godly men would build an altar and lead their family in worship. It's up to
the husband to take his family and lead them into the presence of God.

And the husband is to be the *protector* of the home (see 1 Corinthians 16:13-14).
I'm not just talking about physical protection. Sir, you can build a spiritual hedge
of protection around your family. You can pray, teach, and lead them in the
things of God. And in so doing, you are standing against the forces of hell sent
to destroy your home. What our nation needs is men of faith to rise up and demonstrate what real leadership is all about. Will you be one?

SIR, ARE YOU LIVING WITH YOUR WIFE?

*Husbands, in the same way be considerate as you live with
your wives, and treat them with respect as the weaker
partner and as heirs with you of the gracious gift of life, so
that nothing will hinder your prayers* (1 Peter 3:7).

YOU MIGHT THINK THE QUESTION, "ARE YOU LIVING WITH YOUR WIFE?"
makes no sense. After all, if you are married, of course, you are living with
your wife. But just because you eat and sleep under the same roof doesn't mean
you *"live"* there. The meaning of the word brings it into focus; and, it makes
perfect sense. The word *"live,"* is the same word "dwell," and it means to "settle
down," or "to be at home." Peter is not talking about living in the same house, at
the same address. He means to be completely at home or to experience a deep-
down togetherness.

It is entirely possible to be somewhere physically, and still not be there emo-
tionally. The sad truth is many women feel their husbands live with the motto:
"I'll bring home the bacon, and it's up to you to cook it"; or, "I do to my job at
the office, and your job is to take care of the home." Can you believe some men
spend as much time as they can at work so as not to be home with their family?
For our homes to be what God intended, men must do more than expend all of
their energy on the job, and leave nothing in the tank for their family.

Peter says husbands are to dwell with their wives *"according to knowledge."*
Where do we find the knowledge or consideration we need when it comes to our
mates? Does this kind of knowledge come from watching Dr. Phil or Oprah?
Can we find it on television or at the movies? What about the latest book on how
to have a happy wife? Not all of those things are wrong, but we are given a better place to find the knowledge we need. Go to the Bible and discover the tools
needed to provide wives with the honor, love, and respect they deserve.

Sir, if God has given you a wife, you have found *"what is good"* (see Proverbs
18:22). For Heaven's sake and your children's sake, don't take her for granted!

SIR, ARE YOU LOVING YOUR WIFE?

Husbands, love your wives, just as Christ loved the church and gave himself up for her to make her holy, cleansing her by the washing with water through the word (Ephesians 5:25-26).

I F I AM TO LOVE MY WIFE AS CHRIST LOVED THE CHURCH, HOW CAN I DO THAT if I don't know how to "dwell" with her in knowledge and understanding? In other words, how can I love someone I don't actually know? I don't think it can be done just by living in the same house and sleeping in the same bed. More than one man has tried to unlock the secret of how a woman thinks, feels, and acts— only to discover the best way to gain knowledge is to go to the One who created her.

Here is just a small sampling of what the Bible says about women:

- Proverbs 11:16: *A kindhearted woman gains honor, but ruthless men gain only wealth.*
- Proverbs 14:1: *The wise woman builds her house, but with her own hands the foolish one tears hers down.*
- Proverbs 22:14: *The mouth of an adulterous woman is a deep pit; a man who is under the Lord's wrath falls into it.*
- Proverbs 31:10-12: *A wife of noble character who can find? She is worth far more than rubies. Her husband has full confidence in her and lacks nothing of value. She brings him good, not harm, all the days of her life.*
- Proverbs 31:30: *Charm is deceptive, and beauty is fleeting; but a woman who fears the Lord is to be praised.*
- First Timothy 3:11: *In the same way, the women are to be worthy of respect, not malicious talkers but temperate and trustworthy in everything.*

Husbands, please listen up. Coming home and flopping down in the lounge chair until bedtime is not recommended if you want to gain knowledge of your spouse. Your wife longs to be understood, so don't close her out and shut her down. After many years of marriage to my wonderful wife, Billie Kaye, I now know the joy we have experienced has been in direct proportion to my knowledge and understanding of her. Through the years my love for her has grown as I determined to learn what not only her fears and disappointments are, but her expectations and dreams. It has been an incredible journey.

SIR, ARE YOU LIFTING UP YOUR WIFE?

Your wife will be like a fruitful vine within your house; your children will be like olive shoots around your table. Yes, this will be the blessing for the man who fears the Lord (Psalm 128:3-4).

IF I AM TO BE THE KIND OF HUSBAND GOD WANTS ME TO BE, I MUST NOT ONLY love my wife (see Colossians 3:19), but also lift her up. I'm talking about an attitude of gratitude for all that she does. I don't know anyone who wants to live with a complainer, do you? Some guys are so hard to please that it puts his wife in a constant state of stress. Let's get this straight—God did not give you a wife to be your servant or your maid.

The psalmist describes the way a husband should view his mate—as *"a fruitful vine."* I know enough about growing grapes to know that a vine will not produce the best ingredients for winemaking if it is not properly cared for. The vinedresser must be vigilant to lift up a drooping vine lest it dries up and dies.

You can lift up your wife by recognizing her value. First Peter 3:7 (NKJV) says, *"giving honor to the wife."* When you give honor to someone, you say the person is a priceless treasure, valuable and costly. You honor your wife when she knows that she is first on your list of priorities. We can never assign enough value, humanly speaking, to what a Christian woman can add to the life of a home and to the foundation of a nation. It has been rightly said that the history of any country will be determined by the virtue, character, and moral fiber of its women.

The pages of the Bible are filled with women who had a profound capacity for the things of God. As Jesus was heading toward the cross, it was a woman who anointed his head and feet in preparation for his burial. While Jesus was dying for the sins of the world, the big tough disciples, except John, were in hiding. It was a small group of women who stood by Him until He drew His last breath. And it was women who shouted the announcement, "HE IS ALIVE!"

Years ago I saw a sign that read: *"The greatest gift a father can give to his children is to love their mother."* To which I say, AMEN!

KING KONG OR KING JESUS

Submit to one another out of reverence for Christ. Wives, submit yourselves to your own husbands as you do to the Lord. For the husband is the head of the wife as Christ is the head of the church, his body, of which he is the Savior (Ephesians 5:21-23).

I HAVE FOUND A QUICK WAY TO START A FIGHT; JUST BRING UP THE WORD "SUB-mission" in a group of women. There are not many subjects that have caused as much controversy in the church and outside the church as what the Bible means regarding the role of women in the home.

Three crucial biblical facts about submission:

1. *Paul was writing to Christians, not non-Christians.* I cannot find one time where women are told to submit themselves to all men everywhere, at all times. *"Wives, submit yourselves to your own husbands as you do to the Lord."* Paul is establishing the divine order of a home. He is not suggesting that women are in any way inferior or less capable than men. For a wife to recognize her role does not lower or otherwise diminish her in any way.

2. *Both husband and wife are to submit to the lordship of Christ.* And then mutually submit to each other. Paul is not saying that one is better than the other; each person has a place in the divine pattern. When a Christian woman submits herself to the lordship of Christ and is willing to follow the leadership of her husband, the chances of a happy home have increased exponentially. I have found one thing to be true—a wife who knows her husband is following after Christ has no trouble following his lead.

3. *Headship is not equal to dictatorship.* Some men have taken the statement, *"Wives, submit yourselves to your own husbands as you do to the Lord"* to mean they are the dictator in the home. Twisting Scripture to suit one's agenda is not new, it has been going on since the days of Adam and Eve. I have personally watched homes fall apart because the husband thought he was King Kong. He felt he had the right to bark orders, bully his wife, and treat her as his personal slave.

It's King Jesus, not King Kong. Sir, the Lord did not give you this precious gift to be your doormat, but your helpmate and your partner in establishing a godly home.

CHILDREN ARE GIFTS, NOT BURDENS

Children are a heritage from the Lord, offspring a reward from him (Psalm 127:3).

IT WOULD BE A FAIR STATEMENT TO SAY THAT WHEN GOD BLESSED US WITH our first child, everything changed. There is nothing to compare with the first time you look into the face of that small baby and realize that you had been given a precious gift. The Bible says, *"Children are a heritage from the Lord."* For just a short period, God allows us to mold and shape this piece of eternity. Many young couples view having children as a burden to bear, but God says they are gifts to receive.

I once heard a preacher say that before he had children, he was an expert in child psychology. He said he preached some of the best sermons ever heard on how to raise kids. But the day he and his wife brought home that bundle of joy, he realized just how little he knew. I suppose he is not the only first-time parent who realized that telling someone else how to raise children is easier than doing it yourself. In raising children, we don't get "do-overs," so we plow ahead praying every day.

The imperative to pray for our boys and girls has never been more evident than in today's culture. Young people are facing pressures that you and I could have never imagined. It would appear that the Information Age has turned the generation gap into the generation canyon. As soon as they wake up in the morning, they are bombarded with a high-speed information freeway that links them to everything via their iPad, cell phone, and in-school computer. Raising godly children in an ungodly world is a serious challenge even for the most conscientious parents.

Fortunately, we have the best Book ever penned on how to train up our children in the way they should go (see Proverbs 22:6). This Book is found in every bookstore, and in most homes. It has outsold every book that has ever been on *The New York Times* bestseller list. It's the Bible. Inside this Book are timeless principles that help navigate us through the shifting sands of an ever-changing social, political, and moral climate. Pick up a Bible, open it, read it, and learn the wisdom needed to lead your children.

COMMANDMENT WITH A PROMISE

*Children, obey your parents in the Lord, for this is right. "Honor
your father and mother"—which is the first commandment
with a promise—"so that it may go well with you and that
you may enjoy long life on the earth"* (Ephesians 6:1-3).

PAUL OUTLINED THE ROLES OF EACH MEMBER OF THE FAMILY UNIT. HUSBANDS
are to love their wives, *"even as Christ loved the Church and gave himself for it."*
Wives are to submit and follow the husbands, *"as unto Christ."* And young people
are to obey and honor their parents *"in the Lord, for this is right."* As the young
people listened to the words of Paul, I can almost hear them murmur under their
breath, *"Why should we obey our parents? They don't understand our generation. We
have all the answers to life…we don't need any help!"* The truth is, young people
don't have all the answers and they do need help to navigate through the grow-
ing-up years.

- Children and teenagers should obey because they are Christians:
  "obey your parents in the Lord, for this is right." It is right because
  saved people have been given new hearts, new homes, and a new
  outlook on life. Rebellion and anarchy are the attitudes and
  actions of the children of darkness, not the children of light (see
  Ephesians 5:8; 1 Thessalonians 5:5).

- Children and teenagers should obey because God commands it.
  When Paul quoted the fifth commandment, he wasn't putting
  youth back under the law. The law was not given as a means to
  salvation, but to show the righteous standards of the Lord. When it
  comes to dishonoring and disrespecting parents, it is just as wrong
  today as it was when the law was given. To honor parents is a step
  above obeying them. It is showing respect and love, even if you
  think they are wrong or out of touch with your feelings and needs.

There is a promise attached to the commandment: *"so that it may go well with
you and that you may enjoy long life on the earth."* I would say to every young person, if you want to live a happy and fulfilled life, start by obeying and honoring
your parents. It's the right thing to do!

MONDAY

SHOOT STRAIGHT

*Like arrows in the hands of a warrior are children
born in one's youth. Blessed is the man whose
quiver is full of them…* (Psalm 127:4-5).

THE PSALMIST PAINTS A LOVELY PICTURE OF HOW PARENTS ARE TO VIEW their children. He likens the children to arrows in the quiver. He is saying that when we bring children into the world, a great responsibility has been laid on our shoulders. Parents launch their children into the future as they aim for a distant yet unseen bull's-eye.

Some parents take their responsibility seriously and direct their children toward a future target. Unfortunately, some arrows are fired from unsteady bows, because parents are ambivalent about where they come from and are uncertain of their aim. They tragically prove the adage, "If you aim at nothing, you will hit it every time." Arrows must be adequately cared for and protected from harm, or they will not fly straight. It doesn't matter how skillful the warrior may be, an arrow out of balance will never hit its intended mark.

Have you thought about what you are investing in those precious young people? Is your deposit significant enough to carry them through to the next generation? I realize some parents only think in terms of how much money and how many material things they can pass on to their children. I get it, and there is nothing wrong with wanting our kids to have more than we did growing up. But I'm talking about a spiritual heritage that will far outlast any amount of money in a trust fund.

There's no greater joy in the world than to point your children in the right direction and shoot them wisely into the next generation. The wisdom writer wrote, *"Start children off on the way they should go, and even when they are old they will not turn from it"* (Proverbs 22:6). You notice he doesn't say we should start them off on the way "we think" they should go. Nor did he say we should try to relive past failures through our children.

As parents, our mission is to discover the gifting and talent that God has placed inside each child. We can then invest the necessary time and resources to make sure they are taking advantage of every opportunity and open door. It is a big responsibility, but it is well worth the effort. Take careful aim and shoot straight—you only get one shot at it!

DAD: DON'T PROVOKE YOUR CHILDREN

And you, fathers, do not provoke your children to wrath, but bring them up in the training and admonition of the Lord (Ephesians 6:4 NKJV).

I DON'T KNOW ANY FATHER WHO BRINGS A CHILD INTO THIS WORLD TO DELIB-erately mistreat them. Most men I know have every desire to see their children grow up to be happy and healthy. Paul's admonition to fathers is a stark reminder of their importance in the training and discipline of their children. The definition of *"provoke"* is "to arouse to a feeling or action: to incite to anger: to stir up purposely as to provoke a fight."[60]

Is it possible for a father to provoke his child even when he is not trying to cause tension and confusion in the home? I believe it is. I don't have all the answers, and I don't claim to be an expert on the subject. The only thing I can attest to are personal experiences I have encountered as a dad. Here are three things I advise against:

1. Don't tell your children *not* to do something and then turn around and do it yourself. I don't know if God created all children with "hypocrite" radar or not, but a child can pick up on the *"Don't do as I do, do as I say"* type of parenting pretty quickly. I know it's hard sometimes, but consistency between words and actions go a long way in establishing trust with your children.

2. Never, ever, make a promise you don't intend to keep. How many times have we told our kids we are going to _____ (fill in the blank), and then not follow through? Some parents use the idea of a promise to placate their kids. If you do that often enough, they will cease to believe you about anything else.

3. Do try to be even-handed when it comes to discipline. A sure source of discouragement for any child is to see a parent showing favoritism to one child over the other. We are to *"bring them up in the training and admonition of the Lord."* Our responsibility is to bring discipline with love; and in so doing, strive for consistency with a heavy dose of impartiality. When children feel the love and encouragement of a father, they will be more inclined to listen, learn, and obey.

HOW TO SPEAK TO AN ANGRY PERSON

When Abigail saw David, she quickly got off her donkey and bowed
down before David with her face to the ground. She fell at his
feet and said: "Pardon your servant, my lord, and let me speak to
you; hear what your servant has to say" (1 Samuel 25:23-24).

A S I WAS READING THROUGH DAVID'S ENCOUNTER WITH NABAL AND ABIGAIL (see 1 Samuel 25), I saw something I had never seen before. Keep in mind, David was in transition. He is caught between two worlds—the world of promise and the world of reality. It has been thirteen years since he was anointed king and he is still on the run, moving from cave to cave.

David sent his men to a sheepherder named Nabal with a simple request for something to eat. Instead of granting his request, Nabal sends David a message filled with insults. David did not take it very well. He told his men to *"strap on your sword,"* which interpreted in any language means, "Let's go kill the dude!" David's response might have been a little over the top (1 Samuel 25:4-12). His anger and frustration were about to cause him to cross the line. Something happened to change his mind. What was it?

Enter Abigail. What did she do to diffuse the situation? *First,* she went out to meet David, but she did not go empty-handed (1 Samuel 25:18). She prepared a meal and gently explained why her husband acted the way he did. She did not berate David but used *"A gentle answer turns away wrath"* (Proverbs 15:1).

Second, she spoke to the king inside of David instead of the fool he was about to become. She called him *"my lord"* (1 Samuel 25:24). How we address someone goes a long way in determining how they will act. Calling your spouse an idiot, stupid, or lazy just adds fuel to a simmering fire. Take Abigail's approach and speak to the person's anointing, not their mistakes. Whichever one you speak to will significantly determine who they become.

Third, she became a dream restorer. She spoke to his future, not his past: *"Please forgive your servant's presumption. The Lord your God will certainly make a lasting dynasty for my lord, because you fight the Lord's battles, and no wrongdoing will be found in you as long as you live*" (1 Samuel 25:28). Everyone needs an Abigail in their life who will speak to their future, not constantly remind them of their past failures.

FATHERS HAVE THEIR DAY TOO

*Blessed are all who fear the Lord, who walk in obedience
to him. You will eat the fruit of your labor; blessings
and prosperity will be yours* (Psalm 128:1-2).

ATTENTION FATHER—LEST YOU MISUNDERSTAND, WE STILL RANK SECOND behind our wives even on a day that is supposed to be ours. I'm referring to Father's Day. I read a few statistics that said: approximately $8 billion would be spent on Father's Day gifts, while almost $10 billion will be spent on Mother's Day gifts. And, while 72 percent of Americans will honor dads on his day, around 80 percent will honor moms on her day. The bottom line—we may be in second place on special days, but we have been given a first-place responsibility to lead our families.

The psalmist painted a thumb-nail sketch of an ideal father. I realize there are no "ideal" dads because after all, no one is perfect. But that is no excuse for any man to stop striving to reach a higher level, to be the best he can be.

You cannot look to Hollywood or the secular media to gain an accurate picture of the biblical role of the father in the home. In today's culture, the dad is most times portrayed as a bumbling fool. I saw one television commercial that showed a man who was so stupid he couldn't figure out how to open a box of cereal. Most sit-coms that revolve around the family picture the dad as either fat, lazy, or just plain ignorant. For example, watch a rerun or two of the *King of Queens,* and you will see what I mean.

In the 1970s, the church thought the best way to reach dads was to reach the kids. The thought being that if the kids were involved the church, dads would soon follow. All over America buses and vans were bought to go out and pick up the neighborhood children. But the opposite happened. In many instances, instead of dads following their kids, they were more than happy to put their kids on a bus and let the church babysit them while they played golf or did whatever they wanted to do.

The key to reaching a family runs straight through the heart of the father. Psalm 128 gave three characteristics of a godly dad. Turn the page, and find out what they are.

THE IDEAL DAD (PART 1)

*Blessed are all who fear the Lord, who walk in obedience
to him. You will eat the fruit of your labor; blessings
and prosperity will be yours* (Psalm 128:1-2).

IF YOU WANT TO KNOW WHAT THE IDEAL DAD LOOKS LIKE, YOU WON'T FIND out from Hollywood, but from God's Word. Psalm 128 gives us three characteristics of a godly dad.

First of all, *he must give close attention to his faith.* The faith of this ideal dad is expressed in what he loves, *"Blessed are all who fear the Lord."* Here is a picture of a man living and loving the Lord with all of his heart. When he uses the word *fear,* he is talking about respect, reverence, and awe of the Lord. The Bible teaches, *"The fear of the Lord is the beginning of wisdom, and knowledge of the Holy One is understanding"* (Proverbs 9:10). The most significant decision a dad will ever make is giving his life to the Lord Jesus Christ.

The faith of an ideal dad is also seen in his *labor* for the Lord. *"You will eat the fruit of your labor; blessings and prosperity will be yours."* There is something noble about a man who takes the responsibility of providing for his family. There is nothing wrong with hard work; long before Adam sinned, God put His blessing on laboring with your hands.

There is an adage that says, *"As the home goes, so goes the church, and as the church goes, so goes the nation."* I would add, *"as the dad's go, so goes the home."* A pastor friend told me about an experience he had several years ago. He said one day he was out witnessing to a family who had visited his church. The mom and her four children were all seated on the sofa, and then the dad walked in the room. The pastor got to the point of decision and asked the dad first, "Sir, will you give your heart to Jesus?" The man paused and said, *"No not now, I have too many things going on!"* My friend then looked at the mom and kids and asked the same question. All of them had the same reply, *"If dad will, we will."* Therefore, none did.

My friend told me a few months later the dad was shot dead in his driveway. Come to find out he was a major drug dealer and chose a life of crime over leading his family in faith! Sir, above all else, lead your family in faith, it's the right thing to do.

THE IDEAL DAD (PART 2)

Your wife will be like a fruitful vine within your house; your children will be like olive shoots around your table. Yes, this will be the blessing for the man who fears the Lord (Psalm 128:3-4).

THERE ARE NO PERFECT FATHERS. WE ALL HAVE OUR PARTICULAR FLAWS. IF you are not sure about that, just ask your wife. But that should not stop us from striving to reach the biblical standard.

The second characteristic of an ideal dad found in Psalm 128 *is he will pay close attention to his family.* Here he talks about the home and the importance of family. Dad, let me ask you a question. What is it like living in your house? If I would talk to your wife and children, what would they say? Would they tell me that when you are physically home your mind is still at work? Or would they say you are physically, mentally, and spiritually present even when you are zoned out in your favorite chair?

Sir, take a good long look at your mate. To a great extent, what she has become is a reflection of your involvement in her life. I don't care if you are considered a leader at the church or not, if you aren't leading your mate in spiritual things, you're missing the point. It is the height of hypocrisy to put on a show at the church on Sunday, and then go home and treat your wife like dirt. I don't care how loud you shout during the praise service at church, if all you do is criticize everything she does at home. The husband is to be a wall of protection and love for his wife; and therefore she can become *"a fruitful vine within your house."*

The psalmist also talks about the children. The Living Bible version says, *"And look at all those children! There they sit around the dinner table as vigorous and healthy as young olive trees."* An olive tree can produce for five hundred years; and in some cases, grow to be 50 feet tall. A father can impart such a legacy of faith to his children that they will carry it forward for many generations!

There is much more to being a father than contributing to their conception. Just because you have brought them into this world does not mean your responsibility is finished. As a matter of fact, your responsibility has just started.

THE IDEAL DAD (PART 3)

May the Lord bless you from Zion; may you see the prosperity of Jerusalem all the days of your life. May you live to see your children's children—peace be on Israel (Psalm 128:5-6).

THE PSALMIST HAS ALREADY SAID THAT AN IDEAL FATHER WILL PAY ATTENtion to his faith and his family. But there is more thing that an ideal dad can do.

The *third characteristic* of an ideal dad is that *he will pay close attention to his future.* When the psalmist refers to Zion and Jerusalem, he is letting us know his central message is to the men of Israel. But the application can be made for all men who will follow and honor the Lord: *God has promised all fathers who will put their faith in the Lord, and be the kind of men they ought to be, that a national blessing will be the result.* It is essential because as the men of a nation go, so goes the nation. When men take their rightful place as leaders, the spiritual, ethical, and moral standards of a country are lifted to a whole new level.

Let's be honest. Some children grow up thinking that Christianity is just for women and kids. More than one man has demonstrated by his actions that spiritual things belong to the women. They see their role as taking care of the material needs of the family, and the women can do the rest. Nothing could be further from the truth. You don't have to sacrifice one for the other. Sir, we can do both.

And there is a personal promise, *"May you live to see your children's children."* This is about living long enough to enjoy our grandchildren. I thought having children was life-changing, but when our children had children, well that's a whole new level of special.

The responsibility of a man is not only to enjoy his children and his children's children, but to make sure his and their spiritual future is secure in the Lord. There are multitudes of children being brought into this world by men who don't care for the things of God. Can you imagine how many boys and girls will grow up following in the footsteps of a disbelieving father who cares not for their eternal destiny? Sir, they will follow your steps—make sure they lead to Christ!

HOW TO GET A NEW HUSBAND

*Wives, in the same way submit yourselves to your own husbands
so that, if any of them do not believe the word, they may be
won over without words by the behavior of their wives, when
they see the purity and reverence of your lives* (1 Peter 3:1-2).

THIS IS FOR THE WOMAN WHO WISHES GOD WOULD DO SOMETHING TO change her husband. I'm not talking about trading him in for a newer model, but a biblical approach to improving the one God gave you. Before you get too excited about the prospect of a new husband, let me give you this thought: *Every time I prayed for God to change someone, the Lord always started with me.*

Peter said wives need to win over their husbands by their *"behavior." "Wives, in the same way submit yourselves to your own husbands."* We looked at submission before, so let me just say again that wives are not to be doormats or slaves to their husbands. Nor are wives to be submissive to anyone else's husband. Submission expresses itself in godly actions and behaviors that demonstrate the lordship of Christ. Submission is a mark of security and should never be based on fear or insecurity. Nowhere does the Bible teach that a wife has to live with a monster who abuses her or her children.

Some wives view their role in the home as conditional. They say, "I'll be the kind of wife I should be as long as he is the kind of husband he should be." What can you do if your husband is not living for the Lord or is not the leader he should be? Peter says your actions and the way you live can speak louder than your words: *"if any of them do not believe the word, they may be won over without words by the behavior of their wives, when they see the purity and reverence of your lives."* By the way, pinning Bible verses on his pillow or shaming him into going to church is not what Peter is referring to. It might work for a little while, but when you stop, so will he.

I don't know many husbands who have changed for the better by being badgered about their lack of spiritual depth. You are not responsible for improving him, that's God's job. If you want to change the atmosphere in your home, start by changing yourself. You are responsible for one person, *you!*

UNFADING BEAUTY

Your beauty should not come from outward adornment,
such as elaborate hairstyles and the wearing of gold jewelry
or fine clothes. Rather, it should be that of your inner self,
the unfading beauty of a gentle and quiet spirit, which
is of great worth in God's sight (1 Peter 3:3-4).

Let's go ahead and talk about the elephant in the room. Is Peter suggesting that God is against women wearing makeup, jewelry, fancy hairstyles, or nice clothes? Some religious organizations use this Scripture to enforce strict rules to prevent women from wearing jewelry and makeup. Some have even gone a step further and said if women are going to join they cannot cut their hair.

I don't think that is what these verses are teaching at all. Yes, it is true that Peter could be warning women not to look like certain loose females who would congregate around the pagan temples to entice men to pay them for sexual favors. It was no secret how these women would cover themselves with all kinds of adornment. And what was true then is true today. You can find women in every city in almost every country who wear heavy makeup and skimpy clothes just to entice men to sin. Does that mean women should not try to look their best? Absolutely not!

I believe Peter is pointing to a balance between what you see on the outside, versus what is real on the inside. You can't hide internal issues by focusing solely on the outside appearance. He is encouraging women not to work on one while excluding the other. You can look good and walk with God all at the same time. Whether we like it or not, people will treat us based on how we present ourselves. People notice how you are dressed before you open your mouth. That may not be fair, but it's the truth.

Holiness starts on the inside and works its way out, not the other way around. The Lord places value on, *"your inner self, the unfading beauty of a gentle and quiet spirit."* Proverbs 31:30 declares, *"Charm is deceptive, and beauty is fleeting; but a woman who fears the Lord is to be praised."* This is a picture of a godly women who is living with quiet elegance and dignity. Beauty may only be skin deep, but the inner beauty of a *"gentle and quiet spirit"* reaches all the way to the throne of God!

FIGHT FOR YOUR FAMILIES

After I looked things over, I stood up and said to the nobles,
the officials and the rest of the people, "Don't be afraid
of them. Remember the Lord, who is great and awesome,
and fight for your families, your sons and your daughters,
your wives and your homes" (Nehemiah 4:14).

NEHEMIAH KNEW THERE WAS A CONCERTED EFFORT TO STOP THE REBUILD-
ing of the wall around Jerusalem. One of the tactics of the enemy was to
separate families. Nehemiah gathered the leaders together and implored them to
"fight for your families!"

Even though we live in the 21st century with all of the attending conveniences,
the plan and tactics of the enemy have not changed. The battle cry of the forces
of hell is still, "Destroy the family at all cost!" These attacks on homes are coming
in all shapes and sizes, designed to fool even the wisest among us. Lack of time
and space allow me to mention only two:

1. *An ever-increasing focus on materialism to the exclusion of spiritual things.*
Make no mistake about it, there is a constant drive to have the biggest and best
of everything. I'm not suggesting we return to a time when we didn't have instant
access to everything; but to be honest, there are times when I long for a simpler
day. If we aren't careful, we will be more concerned about what Apple is doing
with the latest version of the iPhone to the exclusion of what God wants to teach
us. There is nothing wrong with living in a big, beautiful house. But it takes more
than brick, wood, and paint to make it a home. Without Christ at the center, a
house is just a structure where people live.

2. *A new morality, which is not new at all, that's disguised by different names.* We
have moved from a Judeo-Christian ethic to new morality about which one evangelist said it is neither new nor moral. It is merely the old immorality brought up
to date. We are being told the traditional home is outdated and must be thrown
on the trash heap of history. The simple truth is the institution of the home is not
obsolete; the problem is with the people who live inside.

The challenge of Nehemiah must ring out in this hour: *"Remember the Lord,*
who is great and awesome, and fight for your families!" Will you fight for yours?

IN EVERYTHING GIVE THANKS

WE GATHER TOGETHER

We gather together to ask the Lord's blessing;
He chastens and hastens his will to make known;
The wicked oppressing now cease from distressing,
Sing praises to his name: He forgets not his own.

Beside us to guide us, our God with us joining,
Ordaining, maintaining his kingdom divine;
So from the beginning the fight we were winning;
Thou, Lord, wast at our side, All glory be thine!

We all do extol thee, thou leader triumphant,
And pray that thou still our defender wilt be.
Let thy congregation escape tribulation;
Thy name be ever praised! O Lord, make us free!
Amen.

TRADITIONAL THANKSGIVING HYMN
Translation by THEODORE BAKER (1851-1934)[61]

FAMILY, FOOD, FOOTBALL, AND GIVING THANKS

Give thanks to the Lord, for he is good; his love endures forever (1 Chronicles 16:34).

THANKSGIVING DAY HAS BEEN CELEBRATED IN ONE FORM OR THE OTHER since the Pilgrims landed in the New World. The first celebration lasted three days; and according to some historical records, it was attended by both Native Americans and approximately fifty-three Pilgrims. Moving forward, some states observed Thanksgiving in some form, but it was in the midst of the Civil War that it was recognized as a national observance. On October 3, 1863, Abraham Lincoln issued a proclamation which reads in part: "I do therefore invite my fellow citizens in every part of the United States, and also those who are at sea and those who are sojourning in foreign lands, to set apart and observe the last Thursday of November next, as a day of Thanksgiving and Praise to our beneficent Father who dwelleth in the Heavens."[62]

It is a tradition in many families that Thanksgiving is celebrated with a sumptuous feast followed by large helpings of football, and of course the afternoon nap. Nothing wrong with any of that. There is a lot right with families coming together to enjoy each other's company. The one aspect of Thanksgiving that we must not overlook is the reason we celebrate this special day. As Lincoln proclaimed, it is "a day of Thanksgiving and Praise to our beneficent Father who dwelleth in the Heavens."

What are you thankful for during the Thanksgiving season? If you are not sure where to start, let the writer of First Chronicles 16:34 offer a suggestion, as well as James and Jeremiah.

- *For God is good* – The very core of God's heart is goodness. We can be thankful because everything we have or hope to have is because He is good. *"Every good and perfect gift is from above, coming down from the Father of the heavenly lights, who does not change like shifting shadows"* (James 1:17).

- *God's love endures forever* – His love could not be bought or earned; it was a gift. *"The Lord appeared to us in the past, saying: 'I have loved you with an everlasting love; I have drawn you with unfailing kindness'"* (Jer. 31:3).

Enjoy your family, but remember to give thanks for all He has done for you!

TOO BLESSED TO BE STRESSED

When anxiety was great within me, your
consolation brought me joy (Psalm 94:19).

O NE DAY JESUS WAS SHARING WITH HIS DISCIPLES ABOUT UPCOMING EVENTS. He must have noticed worry and anxiety in their mood. He said to them, *"Peace I leave with you; my peace I give you. I do not give to you as the world gives. Do not let your hearts be troubled and do not be afraid* (John 14:27). You see, even the most devoted followers of Jesus knew what it was like to feel stress and anxiety.

The medical profession has designated stress as the "silent killer." The human body is not built to handle stress for very long. Most doctors agree that uncontrolled stress can bring on ulcers, backaches, migraines, insomnia, and even some types of cancer. If you allow stress to eat you up inside, you could end up with a dreary life, too sick and miserable to do anything about it.

What is it about the holidays that causes so much stress and worry? For some, the holiday season is just a reminder of loved ones who are no longer with them. I get that. Each birthday I celebrate is a reminder that many of my family and friends have already shifted from earth to Heaven. But for others, it is the painful memories of broken relationships. The list is endless. No one is immune from facing stress and anxiety, but it is what we do with it that matters.

The Lord said He would handle your worry and stress if you release it to Him: *"your consolation brought me joy."* The word "consolation" means to give comfort. Pay close attention, the psalmist is trying to tell you something. The Lord will give relief from stress, and in exchange will give you joy in your soul. Therefore, if you are full of worry brought on by stress, why haven't you turned the situation over to the Lord? What's holding you back?

If you are a child of God and the holidays make you crazy with worry and stress, it's time for you to declare, "I'M TOO BLESSED TO BE STRESSED!" He is more than able to handle whatever comes your way. Give it a try. It sure beats being miserable during the holidays!

PSALM 100—A MODERN-DAY VERSION

Shout for joy to the Lord, all the earth. Worship the Lord with gladness; come before him with joyful songs (Psalm 100:1-2).

WE ARE COMPLAINERS BY NATURE. IT JUST COMES NATURALLY TO MOST OF us. Have you noticed that it is a lot easier to complain than to praise? When our children were growing up, I don't remember a time when we had to sit them down and teach them how to complain. They just figured it out all by themselves.

Psalm 100 has been viewed as the "crème de la crème" of Old Testament praise hymns. Packed into a few verses, it contains everything we want or expect when praising and extolling the goodness and mercy of God. Several years ago, I decided to update Psalm 100 based on my many years of observing people. I call it a "Modern Day Version of Psalm 100." I will give you the New International Version followed by the Modern Tsika Version (MTV) in italics.

- Verse 1: **Shout for joy to the Lord, all the earth**. *Make a pitiful groan to the Lord and make sure everybody around you knows you're having a bad time* (MTV).
- Verse 2: **Worship the Lord with gladness; come before him with joyful songs.** *Serve the Lord with sadness, come before him with complaining and your latest frustration* (MTV).
- Verse 3: **Know that the Lord is God. It is he who made us, and we are his; we are his people, the sheep of his pasture.** *Therefore, don't blame me for my bad moods, outbursts of anger, or my general moody pessimistic disposition. He made me this way so take it up with God* (MTV).
- Verse 4: **Enter his gates with thanksgiving and his courts with praise; give thanks to him and praise his name.** *I don't have any trouble being thankful as long as I get what I want or desire, especially during the holidays* (MTV).
- Verse 5: **For the Lord is good and his love endures forever; his faithfulness continues through all generations.** *I don't have*

any issues with this statement as long as it doesn't cramp my lifestyle (MTV).

Praise is a choice, an act of the will. Let's examine Psalm 100 and see what happens when we choose to praise Him for what we have instead of complaining about what we don't have.

SCHOOL OF PRAISE, LESSONS LEARNED

Shout for joy to the Lord, all the earth. Worship the Lord with gladness; come before him with joyful songs. Know that the Lord is God. It is he who made us, and we are his; we are his people, the sheep of his pasture (Psalm 100:1-3).

PRAISE IS A CHOICE, AN ACT OF OUR WILL. WE SHOULD NEVER TAKE FOR granted the privilege we have when entering into God's presence. Just because He has invited us in, does not mean we should treat Him with disrespect or a nonchalant attitude.

We approach Him with a *"Shout for joy."* This phrase means to "blast with a trumpet." Those who think church is supposed to be a place of hushed whispers are challenged by this statement. The Lord is saying when we come into His presence we should announce our arrival with a gleeful exclamation of praise, not barge in like a herd of buffalo!

First, when we praise Him, we can know others better. *"Shout for joy to the Lord, all the earth."* You notice the psalmist did not say, "Shout for joy to the Lord, all of Israel." Instead he said, "all the earth." The joyful shout of praise is not confined to one group or class of people. People of all race, place, and background are included. Praise is a universal language, and favors no person. It doesn't matter where you are or in what country you live, praise can break down walls and remove obstacles (Revelation 7:9-10).

Second, when we praise Him, we will do our work better. *"Worship the Lord with gladness; come before him with joyful songs."* The word for *"gladness"* is the word for "mirth." Serving the Lord is not supposed to be hard or boring. There are times when a Sunday morning service looks more like a funeral than a celebration. Serving the Lord is something we get to do, not something we have to do.

Third, when we praise Him, we will know ourselves better. Here is what I know about myself: I am not God, and I'm glad! It is God who made each of us unique and special. That means we have a purpose and destiny, and He has promised to lead and guide if we will only let Him. Sheep need a shepherd to protect and guide them to the "still waters" and "green pastures" (see Psalm 23).

WHAT HAPPENS WHEN WE PRAISE HIM?

Enter his gates with thanksgiving and his courts with praise; give thanks to him and praise his name. For the Lord is good and his love endures forever; his faithfulness continues through all generations (Psalm 100:4-5).

IF WE CONFINE OUR OFFERING OF "GIVING THANKS" TO SOMETHING WE DO once a year followed by a big meal, we miss the point completely. It should become an attitude of gratitude year-round. I often think we only view praise and worship as a "Sunday morning thing." It should become a lifestyle, not an afterthought. What happens when we get serious about praise?

When we offer praise, God gets involved.

"But You are holy, enthroned in the praises of Israel" (Psalm 22:3 NKJV). Paul and Silas were bound and beaten in the Philippian jail, but it did not stop them from offering praise and thanksgiving. I can imagine as God was listening to the sweet sounds of praise He decided to get in on the action. As the old-time preachers used to say, "When God heard the singing He started tapping His toe, and the result was an earthquake that shook the prison to its foundation" (see Acts 16:25-26).

When we praise Him, joy fills our heart, and supernatural strength is released.

"Then he said to them, 'Go your way, eat the fat, drink the sweet, and send portions to those for whom nothing is prepared; for this day is holy to our Lord. Do not sorrow, for the joy of the Lord is your strength'" (Nehemiah 8:10 NKJV). He is not talking about a strength that comes from building up your muscles. This kind of strength transcends the natural and moves us into the spiritual realm that enables us to face whatever challenges come our way.

When we praise Him, the enemy is defeated.

"Let the saints be joyful in glory; let them sing aloud on their beds. Let the high praises of God be in their mouth, and a two-edged sword in their hand (Psalm 149:5-6 NKJV). Praise flowing from the lips of even the weakest believer becomes a powerful weapon to defeat the enemy (see 2 Chronicles 20:20-22).

When we meditate on His Word and offer praise and thanksgiving, our hearts open up to a new appreciation that *"the Lord is good and his love endures forever."*

FOR BELIEVERS ONLY

Rejoice always, pray continually, give thanks in all circumstances; for this is God's will for you in Christ Jesus (1 Thessalonians 5:16-18).

IF I TELL YOU A CERTAIN THING IS GOD'S WILL FOR YOUR LIFE, YOU HAVE EVERY right to pray, seek counsel, and study God's Word for confirmation. It is the right thing to do. You should never just take off in any direction without hearing from God, right? In Paul's letter to the folks in Thessalonica, he said three things were God's will*: 1) Rejoice always; 2) pray continually; and, 3) give thanks in all circumstances.* Paul was operating in apostolic authority, and what he said to them, and us, carries the weight of Heaven.

To be honest, the first time I read his words I thought he had lost his mind! There is no way under Heaven that any person could do those things on a continual basis. And to top it off, he said it was God's will for my life! Are we supposed to live our lives with our head in the clouds and pretend that there are no challenges that would test our faith? Should we act like happy-clappy Christians without a care in the world? I don't think that is what he is telling us at all.

Here's what we need to know: *First,* Paul is addressing believers, not non-believers. His words are meant "For believers only." *Second*, God will never command us to do anything that He doesn't also with the command give us the enablement to accomplish His purpose. *Third*, it's only by the inner empowerment of the Holy Spirit that any believer can walk in an attitude of joy, prayer, and giving thanks. In short, trying to live out these admonitions is fruitless without the power of God!

Did you notice at the end of verse 18 a key was given that unlocked the possibility of obeying this Scripture? Everything revolves around three words—*in Christ Jesus*. What does it mean to be *"in Christ Jesus?"* It says we are new creations, and the Holy Spirit of God now lives inside us (see 2 Corinthians 5:17; Ephesians 2:10). It also means we are able to realize God's awesome plan for our lives (see Ephesians 1:3-4; 2 Timothy 1:9). In the next few pages, we are going to dig a little deeper and see some awesome truths behind Paul's words.

REJOICE ALWAYS

Rejoice always, pray continually, give thanks in all circumstances; for this is God's will for you in Christ Jesus (1 Thessalonians 5:16-18).

T HERE ARE SOME THINGS ABOUT GOD'S WILL THAT YOU AND I WILL NEVER understand. For instance, if you are thinking about quitting your job and starting a new business, it might be difficult to find a Scripture reference to give you a clear-cut answer. Sure there are principles and concepts presented, but nothing definitive. Yet in First Thessalonians 5:16-18, Paul left nothing to the imagination. He said three things are God's will for our lives: *1) Rejoice always, 2) pray continually, 3) give thanks in all circumstances.*

Let's take them one at a time.

Rejoice always. Does this mean we are never to experience a bad day or deal with a sad situation? Is he telling us to just "grin and bear it" when life suddenly falls apart with an unexpected tragedy? Are we to develop a "fake it till you make it" attitude that gives an impression of insincerity?

If Paul wants us to deny reality and pretend that evil is not running rampant, then why did he say in Romans 12:15, *"Rejoice with those who rejoice; mourn with those who mourn."* Or why did James encourage believers to *"Consider it pure joy, my brothers and sisters, whenever you face trials of many kinds, because you know that the testing of your faith produces perseverance"* (James 1:2-3).

There seems to be confusion over the difference between happiness and joy. Happiness is an emotion that responds to circumstances. If things are going well, all the bills are paid, and life is smooth, then we are happy. But if the car breaks down or a child brings home a bad report card, then we are down in the dumps. Real joy is based on an inner relationship with Christ, regardless of circumstances. To rejoice always in all things is a spiritual attitude developed on a daily basis as we spend time with the indwelling Holy Spirit: *"But the fruit of the Spirit is love, joy, peace, forbearance, kindness, goodness, faithfulness"* (Galatians 5:22).

Only when we walk with the Lord, do we get a proper view of circumstances, good or bad. Everything we need to face life with a joyful heart is found in: *"Rejoice in the Lord always. I will say it again: Rejoice!"* (Philippians 4:4).

PRAY CONTINUALLY

Rejoice always, pray continually, give thanks in all circumstances; for this is God's will for you in Christ Jesus (1 Thessalonians 5:16-18).

IT IS THROUGH THE VEHICLE OF PRAYER THAT WE DISCOVER WHO WE ARE IN Christ, and this discovery leads to the strength to face life. One of the most common questions about Paul's statement to *"pray continually"* is: Are we supposed to be on our knees twenty-four hours a day to obey this command? The short answer is no, that is not what he means. If that were the case, then no one would ever go to work or feed the children. We would all just stay home and pray.

The phrase *"pray continually"* means, "something that is constantly occurring." It is the idea that our prayer life should not be a "hit and miss" proposition, but an ongoing, inner dialogue with God. He knows our heart, and there are times when a silent prayer spoken in the front seat of our car is just as effective as a prayer uttered in church on Sunday morning (see Psalm 10:17).

I see an analogy between praying continually and breathing. You don't command your lungs to breath; they just do it automatically. What breathing is to the natural human (it keeps us alive), prayer is to the spiritual human. The Lord Jesus is the most excellent example of Paul's admonition. He started His ministry in prayer, and His last word from the cross was a prayer (see Luke 3:21; 23:46). Jesus prayed early in the morning and late at night (see Mark 1:35; Luke 21:37). He prayed before, during, and after public ministry. Jesus is the example we should follow.

The most significant antidote to worry and stress is to make prayer a constant occurrence, not something done when there is an emergency. I find it most difficult to worry and pray at the same time. We need to be persistent and consistent, much like the widow Jesus talked about in Luke 18. He said there was a widow who kept coming to the judge demanding justice against her enemy. At first he refused, but he finally granted her request because she would not stop until he relented and gave her what she wanted (see Luke 18:1-8). We need a prayer life like that!

GIVE THANKS IN ALL CIRCUMSTANCES

Rejoice always, pray continually, give thanks in all circumstances; for this is God's will for you in Christ Jesus (1 Thessalonians 5:16-18).

WALKING WITH GOD IS ALWAYS ABOUT CHOICE. WE CAN CHOOSE TO LIVE with a joyful attitude, and we can choose to pray on a consistent basis. But one of the most challenging things to do is to give God thanks in all circumstances. It would be more comfortable for me if Paul said we could offer thanks for just the good things, but he said *in all things.*

Two things Paul didn't say:

1. *He didn't say all circumstances were good.* I don't think there can be any disagreement here. There is evil all around us, and it would seem that it is getting worse. Too often we see or hear about another mass shooting, terrorist attack, or some natural disaster claiming lives. The key for us is to realize that no matter how bleak or dark things seem, the brightness of God's glory will always shine brighter (see Isaiah 60:1-3).

2. *He didn't say we would understand all circumstances.* God never told me that I'm owed an explanation for anything He does or allows. Years ago I heard someone say, "Never put a question mark where God puts a period." I'm convinced there are some things we will never fully understand until we see Him face to face. If we are not careful, we can develop a *whatever happens will happen mentality* at best or a *victim mentality* at worst. We are never told that it is wrong to pray for circumstances to change, but at the end of the day, whether they do or not, the attitude of a thankful heart is God's will for my life.

Walking with God involves trust that He knows the end from the beginning. One verse we love to quote is Romans 8:28: *"And we know that in all things God works for the good of those who love him, who have been called according to his purpose."* We will never know the truth of that verse until we are faced with circumstances that we don't understand. I will choose to trust Him to make those circumstances work for my good and His glory. If I can trust Him, then I can thank Him, no matter what the circumstances are.

BE LIKE THE ONE

*Jesus asked, "Were not all ten cleansed? Where are the
other nine? Has no one returned to give praise to God
except this foreigner?" Then he said to him, "Rise and
go; your faith has made you well"* (Luke 17:17-19).

ONE DAY AS JESUS PASSED THROUGH A CERTAIN VILLAGE, TEN LEPERS HOPED
against hope that this was their day for a miracle. Mosaic law banned
these men from any contact with a healthy person. If someone should inadvertently approach them, they were to loudly declare themselves, "UNCLEAN,
UNCLEAN!" So, all they could do was stay the proper distance and cry out
to the Lord. He heard them and responded. He spoke the word, and they were
healed. Next, He told them to go and show themselves to the priests (see Luke
17:11-16).

It is painfully obvious that something is missing in this story. *"Jesus asked,
"Were not all ten cleansed? Where are the other nine?"* When Jesus inquired about
the "nine," He wasn't asking for purposes of receiving money for their miracle.
Nor did He have a television crew on standby to film their glowing testimony
to use in promoting upcoming healing crusades. Only one man came back and
offered praise to God. The other nine went to the priest and didn't give any
thought of going back to Jesus. How sad.

Why didn't they return? We are not told the reason why; each had a choice to
make and they made it. We can't be too hard on them because they reflect what
many of us have done. I have seen it happen more than I care to remember. We
get in a crisis or a time of desperation, and we cry out for God's help. After the
crisis is passed and all is well again, we tend to forget who to thank for the rescue.
My prayer is that we will never become so busy or caught up in the holiday spirit
that we forget the source of our blessings.

Let us return continually and offer praise and thanksgiving to the God who
rescued us from sin and gave our life meaning. I cry out with the psalmist who
says, *"He lifted me out of the slimy pit, out of the mud and mire; he set my feet on a
rock and gave me a firm place to stand"* (Psalm 40:2). Be like the one, not the nine!

MONDAY

BLACK FRIDAY, CYBER MONDAY, AND THANKFULNESS

*So then, just as you received Christ Jesus as Lord,
continue to live your lives in him, rooted and built up in
him, strengthened in the faith as you were taught, and
overflowing with thankfulness* (Colossians 2:6-7).

WHO CAN REMEMBER THE GOOD OLE' DAYS? YOU KNOW, THOSE DAYS WHEN we celebrated Thanksgiving on the fourth Thursday in November, and the Christmas season started in early December. Now, thanks to the fine folks on Madison Avenue, we have things all meshed together into one hodgepodge of merchandising madness. These days, if you don't start Christmas shopping by September, you feel left behind. Not to worry, you can always get up before dawn and join in the chaos of Black Friday. Or you can wait and get in on Cyber Monday. Either way, you are going to give up some cash, so just ahead and make peace with your bank balance.

I don't have anything against any of the things just mentioned, as long as we keep the right perspective. My concern is we have replaced an attitude of *"overflowing with thankfulness"* with a spirit of selflessness that borders on the insane. Thankfulness and gratitude are the opposite of a self-centered, me-first mentality that is killing the spirit of the holidays. Thanksgiving is supposed to be about giving thanks to the Lord for His many blessings. And Christmas is intended to celebrate the birth of Christ, not an excuse to overindulge ourselves.

I'm not suggesting that all believers have gone over the line; but to be honest, we are fast approaching a day much like the days of Ruth. *"In the days when the judges ruled, there was a famine in the land. So a man from Bethlehem in Judah, together with his wife and two sons, went to live for a while in the country of Moab"* (Ruth 1:1). Do you see it? Naomi and her family lived in Bethlehem in Judah, which means "House of Bread and Praise." This was supposed to be a land of milk and honey, instead there was a famine in the house of bread!

We in the United States have been a house of bread for many years. We have every reason to be overflowing with thankfulness. Let's not take for granted the good things the Lord has done for us and end up in a famine, not of bread, but of spiritual dryness.

BEWARE OF DISCONTENTMENT

*Keep your lives free from the love of money and be content
with what you have, because God has said, "Never will I
leave you; never will I forsake you"* (Hebrews 13:5).

LEARNING TO BE CONTENT WITH WHAT YOU HAVE IS SOMETHING MANY PEO-ple desire. The Bible warns us of the dangers of discontentment; and if we aren't careful, it will lead to mistrust of God's promise to provide for our every need. Go back several thousand years and see what discontentment did to the children of Israel. It seemed no matter what God did for them they were never satisfied. He gave them His presence in a cloud by day and a pillar of fire by night, and that didn't satisfy them. He provided food, water, along with everything they needed, and they still complained.

A big mistake some make is hoping that contentment will be found in material things. It's true that God gives us all things to enjoy (see 1 Timothy 6:17), but we must remember those things will never replace a personal relationship with Christ. The apostle Paul revealed the secret to living a life of contentment in Philippians 4:11-12: *"I am not saying this because I am in need, for I have learned to be content whatever the circumstances. I know what it is to be in need, and I know what it is to have plenty. I have learned the secret of being content in any and every situation, whether well fed or hungry, whether living in plenty or in want."*

Paul didn't discover the secret of contentment by hearing a teaching on success or reading a book about *how to be happy with your stuff.* No, he said, *"I have learned to be content whatever the circumstances,"* which means he graduated from the school of personal experience. He had to live it and learn from it before he could reveal it!

Don't allow the world's idea of success to influence your attitude toward living a contented life. I heard about a man who was asked how he lived a life filled with great contentment. He replied, *"I have learned to cooperate with the inevitable."* This man learned that no matter his condition, he would still love and praise the Lord. A good place to be!

ARE YOU DOING IT YOUR WAY?

*I can do all things through Christ who strengthens
me* (Philippians 4:13 NKJV).

ONE OF THE MOST POPULAR SONGS EVER RECORDED BY FRANK SINATRA WAS
entitled, "My Way." The premise of the song was to proclaim to the world
that he didn't need anyone or anything to face the challenges of life. What about
you? Are you still trying to figure out life on your own and do it your way, or are
you willing to allow God to infuse you with His strength and wisdom and do
things His way?

Paul had a clue as to the source of his strength. He said, *"I can do all things
through Christ who strengthens me,"* He never used the language of a pessimist
who says, "I don't think it can be done." Nor the optimist who says, "I'm sure
there is a way to get things done." Paul uses the language of the overcomer who
says, *"I just did it, with Christ's help!"*

We must avoid the thinking that we can run our own lives without the inner
strength of Christ. Paul spoke the language of hidden power when he said, *"I
can—through Christ."* One of the most popular philosophies of our day is: *"I am
the captain of my ship, the master of my fate."* Really? Is that the best way to go
through life, or are we willing to recognize that unless Christ is our Source of
strength and contentment, we are nothing but a shell?

The world of nature is dependent on resources you can't see. Take a tree, for
example; the tree sends its roots down deep into the earth to draw up water and
the necessary nutrients for its growth. You can't see the roots, so how do you
know they are there? You don't have to dig them up, just look at the tree as it
grows taller and stronger. The external evidence points to its internal resource
of strength.

The most significant part of Paul's life was the part that only God could see.
He knew to fulfill his purpose and finish his race with confidence was to draw on
the resources of a relationship with Christ. The Living Bible translates his statement this way: *"for I can do everything God asks me to with the help of Christ who
gives me the strength and power."*

IS PLANNING FOR THE FUTURE A SIN?

*Now listen, you who say, "Today or tomorrow we will go to
this or that city, spend a year there, carry on business and make
money." Why, you do not even know what will happen tomorrow.
What is your life? You are a mist that appears for a little while
and then vanishes. Instead, you ought to say, "If it is the Lord's
will, we will live and do this or that" (James 4:13-15).*

OCCASIONALLY I HAVE BEEN AROUND PEOPLE WHO BELIEVED IT WAS A SIN TO plan for the future. They thought things like life insurance and savings accounts were of the devil. And Lord help you if you brought up any goals or plans beyond the next day!

So, the age-old question is still around: *Is it sin to plan for the future?* Isn't that what James is teaching? No, James is *not* teaching it is a sin to plan ahead. And for those who want to shirk their responsibilities to take care of their families, you will have to find somewhere else to justify your lack of concern.

The Bible does not condemn planning or practicing sound and honest business principles. There are plenty of Scriptures to back me up: see Genesis 41:35; Proverbs 6:6-8; Acts 11:29; and Colossians 3:23. If that is the case, then what is James condemning? He is condemning living our lives without the consideration or reference to the Lord. He is talking about the sin of presumption, or taking the future for granted without bothering to get the Lord's counsel.

Keep in mind James is talking to Christians. Yes, it is possible for believers to commit the sin of presumption and live like practical atheists. A practical atheist says, *"I believe in the Lord, but I will plan and live my life as if God did not exist."* Presumption keeps us from being ready to face adversity. I don't care who you are, there will always be events and circumstances that demand preparations. Making plans and setting goals is not sinful as long as we recognize that God must be the center.

The proper attitude concerning the future should be, *"If it is the Lord's will, we will live and do this or that."* Our life is like a mist, here today and gone tomorrow. Therefore, it is dangerous to live out from under the leadership and authority of the Lord. It's not worth the gamble.

ONE THING YOU CANNOT IGNORE

We must pay the most careful attention, therefore, to what we have heard, so that we do not drift away. For since the message spoken through angels was binding, and every violation and disobedience received its just punishment, how shall we escape if we ignore so great a salvation? This salvation, which was first announced by the Lord, was confirmed to us by those who heard him (Hebrews 2:1-3).

WHO HASN'T BEEN SO BUSY AND STRESSED OUT THAT WE IGNORED THE VERY reason we celebrate special times of the year? There are some things in life that if ignored could cost a great deal of pain and heartache. Ignoring the well-being of a child or the needs of your spouse or job requirements are just a few examples. I think you get the idea that in life it is not advisable to ignore or neglect certain responsibilities.

The Bible warns us about the ultimate danger of ignoring something that will take the color out of life and turn everything into a thick fog. I am referring to *"This salvation, which was first announced by the Lord."* The writer of this Scripture was not warning them or us about "rejecting" salvation, but of simply ignoring what they had already received. The word *"ignore,"* or "neglect" means to "make light of something," or more literally "not to care."

The picture here is of a ship missing a rudder drifting on the ocean without direction. It is very easy to get caught up in the hustle and bustle of the holidays and put the "spiritual stuff" on the shelf for another day. Drifting along on the current of mindless daily activities puts us in danger of ignoring the greatest gift anyone has ever received. What should we do? The writer tells us to *"pay the most careful attention."* He is telling us to give our undivided attention to our devotion to the Lord and not be distracted by all the noise coming at us from every direction.

My prayer for you is found in Colossians 1:9-10 from The Living Bible: *"So ever since we first heard about you we have kept on praying and asking God to help you understand what he wants you to do; asking him to make you wise about spiritual things; and asking that the way you live will always please the Lord and honor him, so that you will always be doing good, kind things for others, while all the time you are learning to know God better and better."*

DON'T THROW AWAY YOUR CONFIDENCE

So do not throw away your confidence; it will be richly rewarded.
You need to persevere so that when you have done the will of God,
you will receive what he has promised (Hebrews 10:35-36).

HAVE YOU EVER HAD ONE OF THOSE DAYS WHEN YOU WANTED TO THROW IN the towel, cash in your chips, and call it a day? As the ole' timers used to say, "If it weren't for bad luck, I wouldn't have any luck at all!"

What is the writer trying to tell us when he says, *"So do not throw away your confidence"?* The best analogy of throwing away our confidence is the picture of soldiers in the heat of battle. When the arrows start flying and the enemy is getting closer, they throw away their shields and run for cover. These once brave soldiers are now convinced that the battle is lost. We need to understand that no person and no devil can take away what God has put in us. He has blessed us with favor, including the confidence we need to live a life of fruitfulness.

Loss of confidence is directly related to our view of who we are. If we listen to the lies of the devil long enough, we will start a belief pattern that affects how we view life. What we believe on the inside always translates to how we live on the outside. On the other hand, if we believe what our heavenly Father says about us, then we will walk with confidence and realize that our God is bigger than any challenge we might face.

There is one characteristic that becomes the difference maker between those who are faithful in life, and those who are not. The faithful ones are willing to endure the pain and persevere even when the battle is raging. Failure is never an option, and quitting is not in their vocabulary. While the quitters are looking for a place to hide, the faithful are looking for the next mountain to claim!

I encourage you to copy the following verse of Scripture and tape it to your mirror so you can look at it every morning: *"No, in all these things we are more than conquerors through him who loved us"* (Romans 8:37).

PEACE LIKE A RIVER

*Peace I leave with you; my peace I give you. I do not
give to you as the world gives. Do not let your hearts
be troubled and do not be afraid* (John 14:27).

I REMEMBER WE USED TO TEACH A LITTLE CHORUS TO THE KIDS ENTITLED, "I'VE
Got Peace Like a River." It was a simple song, but it packed a powerful meaning. Is it possible to have peace like a river in our souls? Many define peace as the
absence of conflict. A cemetery is peaceful, and there isn't any conflict there, but
is that the peace Jesus is offering? Every day we are being told that if we eliminate war, poverty, and suffering, then peace will rule and reign. You can search
for peace in success, pleasure, possessions, and even pills—but you will come up
empty.

I could go through all the ways the world defines peace, but let's cut to the bottom line. Jesus says, *"I do not give to you as the world gives,"* meaning you won't
find what you're looking for out there in some magic land called peace. The word
for *"peace"* used by Jesus means, "quietness or rest." Jesus wanted His disciples,
and us, to know that it is possible to live in the *quietness of the soul* that is not
found in any other source.

God's peace is not the absence of anything, but the presence of Someone! And
that Someone is the Prince of Peace, the Lord Jesus Christ (see Isaiah 9:6). Paul
says in Philippians 4:7, *"And the peace of God, which transcends all understanding,
will guard your hearts and your minds in Christ Jesus."* The peace of God will stand
guard in your heart to protect and defend against anything that would try to rob
you of peace.

You may be thinking that this kind of peace is not possible in such a turbulent
world. I have good news for you. Not only is it possible, but it is yours for the asking. Jesus says, *"Do not let your hearts be troubled and do not be afraid."* He knows
that fear will rob you of the quietness of soul, and the only way to overcome fear
is to partake of His peace. A proper connection to Jesus is the first step to real
lasting peace. He says, *"my peace I give you."*

DOES YOUR LIVING SACRIFICE CRAWL OFF THE ALTAR?

Therefore, I urge you, brothers and sisters, in view of God's mercy, to offer your bodies as a living sacrifice, holy and pleasing to God—this is your true and proper worship (Romans 12:1).

NO DOUBT MANY BELIEVERS HAVE HAD THE OCCASIONAL LAPSE IN DEDICA-tion to the Lord that would require a solemn time of reflection and rededication. That's all well and good, but what I read in Paul's statement is a once-and-for-all offering of ourselves to the Lord *"as a living sacrifice."* I can't find an escape clause anywhere in this admonition.

The word *"offer"* or "present" is a word that leaves no wriggle room. It means to give yourself once and for all as a *"living sacrifice"* to the Lord Jesus Christ. The best analogy of this word is a marriage ceremony. As the bride and groom stand before God, they are making a covenant commitment to give themselves to each other in holy matrimony. The marriage covenant doesn't say, "You are commit-ted to each other until you can find a better deal!" Or, "Give it a year or two and see if it works out."

The Old Testament presents us with many types of sacrifices, but all them had one thing in common—they were all dead. Paul is talking about a sacrifice that involves the death to self and giving the Holy Spirit control and use our body to glorify Christ. As a living sacrifice, we recognize the old self is dead, and the new self is alive in Christ (see Romans 6:13).

The most excellent example of what it means to offer yourself as a living sac-rifice is the Lord Jesus. To pay for the sins of the world it was necessary for Him to die on the cross, but He rose as a "living sacrifice," and He is in Heaven plead-ing our case before the throne of God (see 1 John 2). If your living sacrifice keeps crawling off the altar, maybe it's time to reevaluate your commitment to the Lord. A good place to start is to make the words of Galatians 2:20 the capstone of your life: *"I have been crucified with Christ and I no longer live, but Christ lives in me. The life I now live in the body, I live by faith in the Son of God, who loved me and gave himself for me."*

HE WANTS YOUR MIND TOO

*Do not conform to the pattern of this world, but be
transformed by the renewing of your mind. Then you
will be able to test and approve what God's will is—his
good, pleasing and perfect will* (Romans 12:2).

IN RECENT YEARS, THE SUBJECT OF MIND CONTROL HAS BEEN A HOT TOPIC.
There have been so-called Christian cults like the Peoples Temple and the
Branch Davidians whose leaders used mind control to convince their members
that society was the enemy and they were the Messiah. In the case of the believer,
it is not mind control, but *mind transformation* the Lord is after.

The world system wants to control how we think, feel, and where we find pleasure (see Ephesians 4:17-24; Colossians 3:1-11). The world wants to exert pressure
on our mind from the outside to mold it into its belief system. To be *"conformed"*
to the *"pattern of the world"* is to be shaped much like dough placed in a cookie
cutter. When they come out of the oven, they all look and taste the same. If you're
not sure how it works, I urge you to pay close attention to the pressure that is our
placed on our minds during the holiday season. Promotions and advertising are
designed to do one thing—make us spend money on things we don't need but
have to have anyway!

The Lord also has designs on our mind. It starts when we yield ourselves to
the inner working of the Holy Spirit. The commonly used definition for the word
"transformed" means to "change from within." In our English vocabulary, the
word "metamorphosis" is used to describe the same event. The Holy Spirit wants
to transform our mind from within, which in turn enables us to discern the good
and perfect will of God. It should be our desire to keep out anything that is contrary to His will for our lives. This can only be done as we yield our mind, will,
and body on the altar of sacrifice.

How does this spiritual metamorphosis take place? It starts by spending time
in God's Word and making room for interacting with the Holy Spirit on a daily
basis. It is in listening and yielding to God that we will find a slow but sure transformation take place. These spiritual changes don't take place by using human
willpower, but by God's power!

PASS THE BATON

*You then, my son, be strong in the grace that is in Christ
Jesus. And the things you have heard me say in the presence
of many witnesses entrust to reliable people who will also
be qualified to teach others* (2 Timothy 2:1-2).

THE PHRASE "PASS THE BATON" DID NOT ORIGINATE IN THE OLYMPIC GAMES. Many historians believe the idea of passing the baton started much earlier when vital information had to be transmitted over great distances. The modern relay race seen in the Olympic games is just a recreation of those ancient methods of communication.

Many relay races have been lost not because the losers were the slowest, but because they missed making a smooth transition. One of the most notable examples is from the 2004 Summer Olympic Games in Athens, Greece.

Pastor Bryan Wilkerson shared the following account:

> In the 2004 Summer Olympic Games in Athens, Greece, the American women's 4 x 100 relay race was favored to win the gold medal. The team featured Marion Jones, a sprinter who had won four gold medals at the previous games in Sydney. The American team was already off to a strong start when Jones took the baton for the second leg of the race. She gained ground as she ran her 100 meters and approached Lauryn Williams, a young speedster who would run the third leg. Williams began running as Jones drew near, but when she reached back to receive the baton, they couldn't complete the handoff. Once, twice, three times Jones thrust the baton forward, but each time it missed William's hand—she couldn't seem to wrap her fingers around it. Finally, on the fourth try, they made the connection. But by that time, they had crossed out of the 20-yard exchange zone and were disqualified. Everyone knew they were the fastest team on the track. The night before, they'd had the fastest qualifying time. But when they couldn't complete the handoff, their race was over.[63]

Ponder this thought: With each passing year, we are that much closer to the end of our journey on planet Earth. Just as Moses passed the baton to Joshua,

Elijah to Elisha, and Paul to Timothy, we must also pass the baton to the next generation. Solid preparation and a smooth transition are the keys to making sure we don't lose the generation that is following in our footsteps.

IMMANUEL (GOD WITH US)

O Come, O Come, Emmanuel
O come, O Bright and Morning Star,
and bring us comfort from afar!
Dispel the shadows of the night
and turn our darkness into light. Refrain
O come, O King of nations, bind
in one the hearts of all mankind.
Bid all our sad divisions cease
and be yourself our King of Peace.
Rejoice! Rejoice! Emmanuel
shall come to you, O Israel.

A CHRISTMAS HYMN
A translation by JOHN MASON NEALE (1818-1866)[64]

THE REASON FOR THE SEASON

She will give birth to a son, and you are to give him the name Jesus, because he will save his people from their sins (Matthew 1:21).

IMAGINE IT IS THE MORNING OF YOUR TENTH BIRTHDAY. YOU AWAKEN EARLY with anticipation of a day filled with cake, balloons, and gifts. Your mother comes into your room and says, "Good morning sweetheart, it's a wonderful day. I just came in to tell you that to celebrate your special day, your dad and I are going to the children down the street and celebrate your birthday with them." As you sit in stunned silence, she continues, "Don't worry, we will mention your name several times, but all the food and gifts will be for the other kids to enjoy." You say that is ridiculous, and would never happen. You're right; it probably wouldn't.

Although the Bible never commands us to do so, we have been celebrating the birth of Christ in the United States for at least two hundred years. In 1870, December 25 was declared a national holiday. It seems with each passing year we are going further and further away from the day's original intent. Don't misunderstand, I love the holidays with all the food, family gatherings, lights, and the trimmings of Christmas; but if we aren't careful, we will regulate the Christmas story as just an addendum to pages of history.

Before He was born, the angel said, *"you are to give him the name Jesus."* Why that name? It was a common name among the Jews, but Jesus took something that was common and made it special. His name to speaks to His purpose: *"because he will save his people from their sins."* The name "Jesus" means "Jehovah is salvation." Only through Jesus can a person truly know the reason for the season. In the name of Jesus, we can live lives of purpose and meaning. No other name can do that! *"Salvation is found in no one else, for there is no other name under heaven given to mankind by which we must be saved"* (Acts 4:12).

If you are dreading another Christmas because you have no reason to celebrate, I have good news for you. Whatever need you have, Jesus can meet you at the point of your desperation. Acts 2:21 tells us, *"And everyone who calls on the name of the Lord will be saved."*

IMMANUEL... "GOD WITH US"

The virgin will conceive and give birth to a son, and they will call him Immanuel (which means "God with us") (Matthew 1:23).

JOSEPH HAD A SERIOUS PROBLEM. HE WAS ENGAGED TO A GIRL WHO TOLD HIM she was pregnant, and he was not the father. What would you have done? Before answering, you need to consider the cultural norms of the day. Jewish society was plain-spoken when confronted with these issues. Joseph would need to break the engagement and send her away (see Matthew 1:18-19).

Before Joseph could finalize his decision, an angel of the Lord paid him a visit in a dream. The words from Heaven were so powerful that it brought peace to Joseph. He now had the assurance that he and Mary were part of a divine plan (see Matthew 1:20-21). The angel quoted Isaiah 7:14 and pointed to Jesus as the fulfillment of the prophecy: *"Therefore the Lord himself will give you a sign: The virgin will conceive and give birth to a son, and will call him Immanuel."*

What does *Immanuel* mean? It is proof positive that Jesus was much more than a good teacher or a mighty prophet. In spite of what liberal religion might teach, Jesus was God who came in the flesh to live among humankind. Jesus never denied the fact that He considered Himself God. The fact that He said He was God is the underlying reason the religious establishment wanted to kill Him (see John 14:8-9; 19:7). Why claim something and risk death over a lie?

Immanuel also tells us that God is not some distant deity who has no desire to be involved in the affairs of His creation. The ancients viewed their gods as aloof and uncaring. In God's brilliant plan, the Savior of the world came to earth in an unexpected way. While the Jewish nation was looking for a mighty warrior riding on a white horse with lightning shooting out of his eyes to judge the world, God sent a tiny baby. He was born in a stall surrounded by his mother and father and a few animals. The devil and no one else saw that coming!

More than anything else, I find this time of the year a celebration of His presence. We have His assurance to walk with us no matter what we face. How can we be sure? He is *Immanuel, "God with us"* (see Psalm 23:4; Isaiah 41:10).

WHERE IS HE?

After Jesus was born in Bethlehem in Judea, during the time of
King Herod, Magi from the east came to Jerusalem and asked,
"Where is the one who has been born king of the Jews? We saw his
star when it rose and have come to worship him" (Matthew 2:1-2).

MUCH HAS BEEN WRITTEN, OR OTHERWISE PORTRAYED IN CHRISTMAS PAG-
eants concerning these Magi or wise men. I'm afraid what makes for a
good Christmas play may not be backed up by Scripture. We know they came
from the East and were looking for *"the one who has been born king of the Jews."*
Based on Matthew's description, these wise men were most likely educated men
who studied the stars.

Take note that these men were not Jews, but Gentiles. Why is that important?
The purpose of Jesus was to be the Savior of the world, not one race of people. He
did not come to die for the well-educated, wealthy, or the upper crust of society.
Our social standing does not get us one inch closer to the Kingdom of God. On
the contrary, Jesus died for all people, regardless of race, place, or income level.
First John 2:2 declares, *"He is the atoning sacrifice for our sins, and not only for ours*
but also for the sins of the whole world."

I find it interesting the religious establishment already knew the details of
where and how the Messiah would be born (see Micah 5:2), and yet they were
more interested in currying favor with Herod than obeying the Scripture.

These strangers from the East followed the star, and when they found Jesus,
they worshipped Him! Then they proceeded to do a beautiful thing. They presented gifts of *gold, frankincense, and myrrh* (see Matthew 2:11). Some have
suggested that the gifts were not only emblematic, but they also met an impeding
need. It would be soon that Joseph and Mary would take young Jesus and flee to
Egypt, and the gifts could be used to finance the trip. How awesome is God, who
knows what we need before we do!

The Magi did not return the same way they came (see Matthew 2:12). No one
who worships the King of kings will ever be the same. You always leave His presence different from the way you came.

TIME TO LEAVE

When they had gone, an angel of the Lord appeared to Joseph in a dream. "Get up," he said, "take the child and his mother and escape to Egypt. Stay there until I tell you, for Herod is going to search for the child to kill him" (Matthew 2:13).

THE MAGI WERE WORSHIPPING, AND KING HEROD WAS FUMING. HEROD'S trick play didn't work, and his evil intent was exposed. He wanted to know the location of Jesus, not to go and worship, but to eliminate this potential rival to his power. I am reminded of what Jesus said about the devil. He called him a murderer and a liar, and from his actions, I would say that description perfectly fits this wicked king (see John 8:44). Herod lied to the Magi and proceeded to order the murder of babies.

The Lord, who knows the end from the beginning, was not taken by surprise when the king tried to kill Jesus. The Magi had provided the funds with their gifts, and the angel appeared to Joseph with the plan. It was time to leave Bethlehem, which means "house of bread," and move to Egypt where safety and security could be provided.

There are times in our lives when obeying the Lord looks strange to those around us. I can imagine the neighbors coming over and asking the young couple why they were moving to a foreign country. History tells us that Egypt had a contingent of Jews living there, but it was still the last place any self-respecting Jew would want to live. All Joseph could say was, "I am obeying the Lord." Joseph and Mary were under divine orders to trust God, not to try to figure out the details.

I have learned the only thing God asks of me in trying times is to trust Him. When I don't understand why things are happening, I know this is not the time to live in fear and doubt. And during dark days is not the time to argue with the Source of my supply. I'm so thankful Joseph did not try to come up with what *he* thought was a better plan. I can guarantee the soldiers of Herod would have found them eventually. When in doubt—trust God. When nothing makes sense—trust God. And when He tells you to move—obey Him and *move!*

AVOID THE INNKEEPER SYNDROME

*And she gave birth to her firstborn, a son. She wrapped
him in cloths and placed him in a manger, because there
was no guest room available for them* (Luke 2:7).

I URGE YOU TO AVOID FALLING VICTIM TO THE "INNKEEPER SYNDROME" AT ALL cost. What is that you ask? It is when we become so preoccupied with the busyness of the Christmas season that we miss out on the meaning and reality of Christmas altogether.

The innkeeper was the first to fall into the trap. I'm sure if we had the opportunity to talk to this man he would tell us it wasn't his fault. He might say something like, "What could I do? There was a census taking place, and the city was overflowing with people. Every room in my inn was booked. I was being pulled in every direction. I just didn't have time to think about this young couple who needed a place to stay."

I don't think the busy innkeeper was trying to be difficult or hostile to Mary and Joseph. He was just so preoccupied with all the activities going on around him that he missed the joy of watching the most significant event in human history take place, the birth of the Savior. I'm not too hard on this guy. He represents millions of people in today's world who are so busy they just want the whole thing to be over.

A few thoughts to help you avoid the *Innkeeper's Syndrome:*

- Set aside a daily time to read the Christmas story. No matter how many times you have read the story, there will always be something new that will jump off the page.
- Don't fill up your schedule with meaningless activities and miss out on the most meaningful moments. Here at our ranch, we love spending time putting up lights, cooking food, and making the time to enjoy our family.
- If you start to feel stressed out, stop what you're doing, take a deep breath and smile. This is supposed to be a happy time of the year, so enjoy it!

- Most of all, offer thanksgiving for the greatest of all Christmas gifts, the Lord Jesus Christ!

THEY SHOULD HAVE KNOWN BETTER

*When King Herod heard this he was disturbed, and all
Jerusalem with him. When he had called together all the
people's chief priests and teachers of the law, he asked them
where the Messiah was to be born* (Matthew 2:3-4).

THE INNKEEPER WAS NOT THE ONLY ONE WHO MISSED OUT ON THE BIRTH OF the Savior. When Herod wanted to know more details about the birth of this one called *"The King of the Jews"* he turned to the most logical source of information, the religious establishment. I find it interesting that these *"chief priests and teachers of the law"* researched and knew the details of where and how the Messiah would be born.

Think about it; when it came to matters of religion, these leaders were the sharpest minds of the day. And yet they discounted what the prophets had foretold (see Micah 5:2). They missed out because of religious pride; nothing more, nothing less. Their self-righteous attitude blinded them to the coming of the Savior of the world. The birth of a baby certainly did not fit their agenda. Many years later, their hatred for Jesus knew no bounds, even to the point of siding with evil men to plot His death.

These so-called experts of the Scripture were just a few miles from where God's glory was being revealed, and decided it wasn't worth their time to take a walk. They should have known better.

How reflective of today's world. There are people today who know all the facts of the Christmas story, and decide that it is not worth the effort to discover the joy of a personal relationship with Jesus. To acknowledge a Savior is to admit to being a sinner in need of salvation. When people are filled with self-righteousness, they don't see a need to be saved. If you don't know you are sick, then you won't find the cure.

So who *did* respond to His birth? Out of the thousands of people in the city of Jerusalem, the Lord chose to reveal the Savior's birth to a handful of Gentiles from the East, some lowly shepherds, an older couple named Anna and Simeon (see Luke 2). Isn't that just like the Lord to bypass the high and mighty and show His glory to those who will come and worship the newborn King!

BEHIND THE GLITTER
OF CHRISTMAS

*The one who does what is sinful is of the devil, because the devil
has been sinning from the beginning. The reason the Son of
God appeared was to destroy the devil's work* (1 John 3:8).

THERE IS A GAP BETWEEN HOW THE WORLD VIEWS THE BIRTH OF THE SAVIOR
and what the Bible teaches. Much of society only view Christmas through
the glitter of the season, while the Bible goes behind the scenes, and reveals the
real reason Jesus was born.

At every turn, the devil tried to stop God's redemptive plan. As Jesus was
being born, a plan was devised to find the newborn and kill him. That plan
failed, along with all other schemes. The final battle erupted as Jesus hung on the
cross. No doubt the forces of hell were celebrating His death. As they laid His
lifeless body in the tomb, they thought they had finally stopped Him. But Colossians 2:15 declares, *"Having disarmed the powers and authorities, he made a public
spectacle of them, triumphing over them by the cross."* The devil, once and for all,
was defeated at Calvary!

Here is the backstory. Two times in Scripture the word "destroy" is used concerning the devil. In Hebrews 2:14 (NKJV) it says, *"that through death He might
destroy him who had the power of death, that is, the devil."* The word *"destroy"* here
means to put out of operation. The price Jesus paid on the cross put the devil out
of business. We no longer have to fear the *sting* of death, because Jesus pulled the
stinger out once and for all (see 2 Timothy 1:10).

The second time we see the word *"destroy"* is in First John 3:8. The purpose
of His coming was *"to destroy the devil's works."* The meaning here is to disinte-
grate, or to remove any vestige of the devil's power over the believer. But you say,
"Wait a minute, I see the devil's handiwork all around me." My friend, the devil
has been defeated, and the only power he has over anybody is what he is allowed
to have. Christmas is a reminder of how Jesus rendered the devil powerless. No
wonder the enemy of our souls wants to deflect, obscure, and distract from the
real meaning of Christ's birth!

MEET THE NAZARENE

*and he went and lived in a town called Nazareth. So
was fulfilled what was said through the prophets, that
he would be called a Nazarene (Matthew 2:23).*

AFTER THE DEATH OF HEROD, THE ANGEL OF THE LORD TOLD JOSEPH IT WAS time to go back to Israel (see Matthew 2:19-20). Instead of going back to Bethlehem, where Jesus was born, or to Jerusalem, the site of the temple, they settled in Nazareth. It was here that Jesus spent most of His life, and it was from here that He launched His public ministry. When He was identified as *Jesus of Nazareth,* it was not because there was confusion about His hometown. It was deeper than that.

The first time we see this title used is in a conversation Philip had with Nathanael in John 1:45-46: *"Philip found Nathanael and told him, 'We have found the one Moses wrote about in the Law, and about whom the prophets also wrote— Jesus of Nazareth, the son of Joseph.' 'Nazareth! Can anything good come from there?' Nathanael asked...."*

Did Nathanael say something negative about Nazareth? He did. Why? The city of Nazareth was, to put it tactfully, not the most inspiring place to live. Nazareth was a hodgepodge of Jews and Gentiles, and a hotbed for criminals, religious zealots, and anarchists. To be identified as a "Nazarene" was to be lumped in with the dregs of society—it was not a compliment.

So, why did Jesus allow the tag to stick? Look at His ministry, and you will find the answer. He was always identified with the lowest of the low, the outcasts of society. On more than one occasion the accusation against Him was that He hung out with sinners. Mark 2:16-17 tells us, *"When the teachers of the law who were Pharisees saw him eating with the sinners and tax collectors, they asked his disciples: 'Why does he eat with tax collectors and sinners?' On hearing this, Jesus said to them, 'It is not the healthy who need a doctor, but the sick. I have not come to call the righteous, but sinners.'"*

Jesus took the title and transformed it into something worthy of glory. He identified with those who needed Him then, and continues to do so today. Hallelujah!

A PROPHET WITHOUT HONOR

Jesus said to them, "A prophet is not without honor except in his own town, among his relatives and in his own home." He could not do any miracles there, except lay his hands on a few sick people and heal them. He was amazed at their lack of faith... (Mark 6:4-6).

I'M SURE YOU HAVE HEARD THE SAYING, "FAMILIARITY BREEDS CONTEMPT." That statement was never truer than when Jesus announced His public ministry. It was in His hometown of Nazareth, the place where He grew up. It was here He became strong in the spirit, and the grace of God was upon Him (see Luke 2:39-40).

After three decades of preparation, Jesus was ready to reveal what His Father had called Him to do. The reaction from the people was shocking. In the Tsika paraphrase, they said, *"We know who You are, where You live, and all about Your family. This must be some kind of joke. You are from the wrong side of tracks, just like us!"* Jesus answered, *"A prophet is not without honor except in His own town, among His relatives and in His own home"* (see Luke 4:16-30). The people were so offended at Jesus they tried to throw Him off a cliff and kill Him.

Sadly, the people missed out because their familiarity with Jesus bore the fruit of unbelief. Their lack of faith produced a toxic atmosphere that prevented Him from doing all that He wanted to do. I see a danger here, especially for those of us who are Christians. We must be careful not to allow the story of the coming of Jesus into the world to become so familiar that we tune out and go numb during this season of celebration. Years ago, I heard someone say, "Some people have heard so many Christmas stories that their familiarity with the truth of Christmas has potential to breed a stony heart." Familiarity with spiritual truth will always choke conviction and stunt our growth.

There is a long list of why so many people miss out on the joy and excitement of Christmas. But the underlying cause is one word—*unbelief!* It was unbelief that stopped the ministry of Jesus in Nazareth. John 1:10 says, *"He was in the world, and though the world was made through him, the world did not recognize him."* But, the good news is, *"Yet to all who did receive him, to those who believed in his name, he gave the right to become children of God"* (John 1:12).

MORE THAN A BABY

*Jesus went throughout Galilee, teaching in their synagogues,
proclaiming the good news of the kingdom, and healing every
disease and sickness among the people* (Matthew 4:23).

WHEN CONSIDERING THE BIRTH OF CHRIST, A COMMON MISTAKE PEOPLE make is to leave Him in a manger. Some never seem to grasp the fact that He grew up, and at age 30 launched a public ministry that is still reverberating today. The devil would love to keep people thinking that a harmless baby could never heal the sick or take away the sins of the world.

There is one aspect of His ministry that is often downplayed, or otherwise regulated to the dustbins of the first century. It goes something like this: "Oh, yes I know that Jesus was a healer, but that was in Bible days, and we **all** know the Lord doesn't do that anymore." A question that has stirred division and controversy among Christians: does Jesus still heal today? From my study and many decades walking with God, I believe two things about the matter.

First, from the earliest days of recorded history, God made provision for the healing of His people. If you don't think so, watch what happens the next time you break a bone! The Gospels record at least forty-one instances of physical and mental healings by Christ. And He commissioned His ministry to His disciples (see Mark 6:13; Luke 10:9; Acts 2:43; James 5:14-16).

Second, I believe that God heals out of compassion and mercy. He is the same yesterday, today, and forever (Hebrews 13:8). Our physical well-being is an important part of the "good news of the Kingdom" as the spiritual part (3 John 2). When it comes to the subject of healing, no one understands everything there is to know. I don't understand how electric current works, but that doesn't mean I'm going to sit in the dark!

So, yes, He does heal today; and since He is God, the means and methods are up to Him. I don't believe it is wrong to pray if we get sick and ask God to touch us. If He uses a doctor to partner with Him in our healing, all the better. Either way, we should give Him the praise and glory!

WHAT'S IN A NAME

For to us a child is born, to us a son is given, and the government will be on his shoulders. And he will be called Wonderful Counselor, Mighty God, Everlasting Father, Prince of Peace (Isaiah 9:6).

NAMES ARE IMPORTANT TO GOD. IN THE WESTERN CULTURE, NAMING A child is more about "what's popular" than any other consideration. But in the Hebrew culture, the purpose of giving a child a specific name was intended to speak to their character and point to their destiny.

One of the more famous lines from William Shakespeare's *Romeo and Juliet* is Juliet's question, *"What's in a name? That which we call a rose by any other word would smell as sweet."*[65] Yes, William, I suppose you could call a beautiful rose a stinkweed and it would smell just as sweet, but as it relates to people, and especially the Lord, not so much.

One day the disciples came to Jesus and asked if He would teach them something. They didn't ask if they could learn how to do heal the sick, cast of demons, or debate with the Pharisees. No, they asked if He would teach them how to pray. He said, *This, then, is how you should pray: "Our Father in heaven, hallowed be your name (Matthew 6:9).* To "hallow" someone's name is to show honor and respect to that name. If we don't know their character, it is impossible to do.

If we want to know more about God, the best way is to find out is to study His names written in the Bible. The more we study His names, the more we discover about His character. When faced with life's ups and downs, we need comfort, strength, and a fortified tower that offers protection from the evil one. We have that and more bound up in the names of our God. Proverbs 18:10 tells us, *"The name of the Lord is a fortified tower; the righteous run to it and are safe."*

I know many people by name, but that doesn't mean I know their character. I have discovered if I really what to know someone, I have to make an effort to spend time with them. We will never really know about God's character by just reading about Him in a book. Making an effort to spend time in worship and prayer is the secret to the revelation of who He is.

WHO'S YOUR DADDY?

For those who are led by the Spirit of God are the children
of God. The Spirit you received does not make you slaves,
so that you live in fear again; rather, the Spirit you
received brought about your adoption to sonship. And
by him we cry, "Abba, Father" (Romans 8:14-15).

D O YOU REMEMBER HOW THRILLING IT WAS WHEN YOUR BABY UTTERED HIS or her first words? Hearing those first utterances is something every parent encases in the memory book of their heart. Can you imagine what would happen in the delivery room if a newborn baby would look up and say, "Hi, Daddy, how's it going?" Probably everyone in the room would faint! Nope, that's not going to happen. But, newborn Christians can start talking to their heavenly Father the moment they are born into the Kingdom of God (see Galatians 4:6).

The term *"Abba Father"* is an Aramaic term of endearment and respect. I must admit that the first time I heard anyone suggest we call God our "Poppa," I was concerned. It almost sounded disrespectful, and something I shouldn't do. It wasn't until I saw how Jesus taught His disciples to pray that I understood what it meant to address God in that manner. Jesus told His disciples to begin their prayers with, *"Our Father in heaven"* (Matthew 6:9). Suddenly, it was clear. I have the right and the privilege to call on the God of all creation as my *Abba Father*. I show respect by calling Him my *"Father,"* and enjoy intimacy by calling Him "Poppa."

In the natural, a genuine dad may disappoint his children. But, at the end of the day, he will sacrifice and go to any lengths to make sure his children are cared for. Jesus said, *"Which of you fathers, if your son asks for a fish, will give him a snake instead? Or if he asks for an egg, will give him a scorpion? If you then, though you are evil, know how to give good gifts to your children, how much more will your Father in heaven give the Holy Spirit to those who ask him!"* (Luke 11:11-13).

Remember, we didn't earn the right to call Him our dad. Never take it for granted. It would be sad if we missed out on such a wonderful opportunity to spend time with our *heavenly Daddy*.

RELAX—HE ALREADY KNOWS YOUR NEED

So Abraham called that place The Lord Will Provide.
And to this day it is said, "On the mountain of the
Lord it will be provided" (Genesis 22:14).

WE WILL NEVER KNOW THAT GOD CAN PROVIDE ALL OF OUR NEEDS UNTIL our backs are against the wall. If you read Genesis 22, you will see that Abraham was facing one of those "backs against the wall" moments. The Lord told him to take his son and offer him as a burnt offering (see Genesis 22:1-2). I would hope and pray that if God asked me to do something like that, I would saddle up my donkey, gather the supplies, and head out to offer my son on the altar.

As Abraham and Isaac neared the place of sacrifice, Isaac wanted to know one thing, *"The fire and wood are here," Isaac said, "but where is the lamb for the burnt offering?"* Now notice the language of faith in Abraham's response, *"Abraham answered, 'God himself will provide the lamb for the burnt offering, my son.' And the two of them went on together"* (Genesis 22:6-8).

Just as Abraham was about the plunge the knife into his son, the angel of the Lord stopped him. Abraham looked up and saw a ram caught in a thicket. He offered the ram instead of his son: *"So Abraham called that place The Lord Will Provide. And to this day it is said, 'On the mountain of the Lord it will be provided'"* (Genesis 22:14). The statement *"The Lord Will Provide"* is a compound name of the Lord, *Jehovah-Jireh,* which means "to see before." It means the Lord sees the need before we do, and the answer is already on the way!

The story of Abraham's split-second rescue of Isaac is very dramatic. Your situation may not be a pulse-pounding, but to you, it's just as serious. I can speak with confidence that as a Christian, I don't have to worry if God has my back. I stopped worrying about my "needs" a long time ago. I found out that spending more time trying to figure things out left me with less time to hear what God had to say about trusting Him to be my *Jehovah-Jireh.* The Lord's supply is unlimited and available to all who will trust Him (see Deuteronomy 29:5; Psalm 37:25; 81:10; Matthew 6:26; Philippians 4:19).

KEEP YOUR EYE ON THE FLAG

Moses built an altar and called it The Lord is my Banner.
He said, "Because hands were lifted up against the throne
of the Lord, the Lord will be at war against the Amalekites
from generation to generation" (Exodus 17:15-16).

T HE BATTLE WAS HOT, AND THE BODIES OF FALLEN SOLDIERS SCATTERED THE
field. On one side were the Israelites, and on the other side was her sworn
enemy, the Amalekites. Moses was leading the Jews to the Land of Promise, and
the Amalekites were determined to destroy them before they could ever realize
their God-given destiny.

Moses sent Joshua to lead the army on the field of battle, while he stayed on
top of the hill holding up the rod of God. Holding up the rod was a symbol of
God's presence and power. It signified their acknowledgment that if God didn't
lead them into battle, they were doomed to defeat. As long as Moses held up the
staff, the Israelites were winning, but when Moses grew tired, and his hands lowered, the enemy would start winning (Exodus 17:10-12). Aaron and Hur saw the
danger, so each man stood on either side of Moses and held up his hands.

Captain Joshua won the day, and Moses built an altar to memorialize the victory. He called the place *"The Lord is my Banner,"* or *Jehovah-Nissi,* which means
"our banner" or our "standard." You can just imagine how much strength and
courage was infused into the soldiers' will to fight when they looked up and saw
the banner of the Lord held high.

A flag was a symbol of the power and will of the invading force. For instance,
in the American Civil War, two things were true of a flag bearer. *First,* a regi-
mental flag bearer was a man of immense courage. The soldiers always wanted
to know the location of the flag, as it served as a rallying point on the battlefield
and a source of encouragement to the troops. *Second,* the flag bearer's life expec-
tancy was minutes, not days. The enemy knew if the flag fell, it was likely the
regiment would scatter.

My friend, the Lord was not only the Flag Bearer, *Jehovah-Nissi,* to the Israelites—we have His promise that He will cover us too and lead us too in our times
of battle against the evil one (see Isaiah 42:13; 45:1; 52:12; 59:19).

DOMESTIC DISTURBANCE

She gave this name to the Lord who spoke to her: "You
are the God who sees me," for she said, "I have now
seen the One who sees me" (Genesis 16:13).

ASK ANY POLICE OFFICER AND THEY WILL TELL YOU THAT TRYING TO BREAK up a domestic disturbance is one of the most dangerous parts of their job. There are even television shows that glorify fights between family members. These so-called entertainment shows will put family members right there in front of God and everybody and let them fight and curse each other just to entertain a sick audience.

Genesis 16 tells us that Abraham, Sarah, and Hagar are in the middle of a domestic disturbance. It all started when God said to Abraham that he and Sarah were going to have a son (see Genesis 15). Instead of waiting on God to bring the promise to life, they took matters into their own hands. Sarah said to her husband, *"Look I am too old to have a child. I want you to take my servant Hagar, and she will give us the promised son."* Instead of telling his wife it was not a good idea, Abraham obeyed. Hagar got pregnant, and suddenly the atmosphere at Abraham's house is as thick as molasses.

Running ahead of God eventually results in a major disaster. Hagar disrespects Sarah, and Sarah returns the favor by treating her servant harshly. Sarah told Abraham he must choose between the two. Hagar is kicked out of her home. She is alone, pregnant, without any hope for the future. But the Lord did not forget her in her time of trouble. The Lord saw what she was going through and gave her a promise (see Genesis 16:11-12). She was told to go home, be a faithful servant, and not worry about her future.

Hagar gave a name to the Lord that still speaks to our hearts today. She said, *"You are the God who sees me,"* or *El Roi* (Genesis 16:13). The Lord saw her distress and brought comfort, grace, and mercy just when she needed it. Do you understand that the Lord sees you this very hour? He knows what you are going through and has not turned His face from your distress. Psalm 121:3-4 says, *"He will not let your foot slip—he who watches over you will not slumber; indeed, he who watches over Israel will neither slumber nor sleep."*

READ THE RED

"I am the Alpha and the Omega," says the Lord God, "who is, and who was, and who is to come, the Almighty" (Revelation 1:8).

I REMEMBER THE FIRST TIME I PICKED UP A BIBLE AND SAW THE WORDS OF JESUS printed in red. I guess the publishers were keen on readers knowing those were the words of Jesus, and not someone else. Since then I don't know how many times I have said to someone if you want to know what Jesus thinks about something, just read the red.

Six times in Scripture Jesus Christ is called or referred to as the *"Alpha and Omega,"* the *"First and the Last,"* the *"Beginning and the End"* (Isaiah 44:6; 48:12; Revelation 1:8, 17-18; 21:6-7; 22:13). *Alpha* is the first letter of the Greek alphabet, and *Omega* is the last letter. Christ declared Himself to be the first and last of all things; therefore, He was applying the entire alphabet to Himself. If we use our English terminology, we would say that Christ is the complete alphabet from A to Z, and everything in between. Think about it this way, all of the literature sitting in libraries across the nation are comprised of words, using in a thousand different ways, the twenty-six letters of the alphabet.

The Lord Jesus, as the Alpha and Omega, is God's Word, or God's alphabet to humankind. John 1:1-2 tells us, *"In the beginning was the Word, and the Word was with God, and the Word was God. He was with God in the beginning."* He is talking about the Lord Jesus, *"The Word became flesh and made his dwelling among us…"* (John 1:14).

The spoken word is a means of *communication* and *revelation*. When you were a child and you wanted something from your mother but were afraid to ask, did she ever say, "Use your words, I'm not a mind reader"? Words are used to reveal our innermost thoughts, and if we never open our mouth to form words, our thoughts are forever locked away in our mind.

God had a small dilemma. What was the best way to communicate with His creation? He could send angels to write in bold letters across the sky, but He didn't. Instead, He chose to reveal Himself in human flesh in the form of a Man, and walk and talk among men (see Philippians 2:5-11). You don't have to wonder anymore what God thinks about your future. He opened His mouth and talked. It's all in the Bible. Pick it up and read the red!

WHAT'S HOLDING YOU BACK?

*Therefore we also, since we are surrounded by so great a
cloud of witnesses, let us lay aside every weight, and the sin
which so easily ensnares us, and let us run with endurance
the race that is set before us, looking unto Jesus, the author
and finisher of our faith...* (Hebrews 12:1-2 NKJV).

OUR CULTURE IS FILLED WITH PEOPLE ON THE MOVE, ALWAYS LOOKING FOR
the next level of success. Let me ask you: What is holding you back? The
word *"looking"* as used by the writer of Hebrews means to arrange things in their
proper perspective, or to look away from your present condition and get a different view of your circumstances.

We need to understand that if we are ever going to accomplish our goals and
reach our potential for that which we were created, we must view life from a
different perspective. The Christian life is a race to be run, not a game to be
played. It must be run by those who will endure with a patient persistence. It is
in the arena of life where our mettle is tested, to see if we will stick it out or walk
away. There are too many people sitting on the sidelines of life because they have
allowed some "weight" to hold them back.

Hebrews 12:1 tells us to *"lay aside every weight."* The weight he is referring to
does not necessarily mean sin. It is not always the bad things or the sinful things
that stop us dead in our tracks. It could be something that others might not consider "bad," but to us it is too heavy to carry. Can you imagine a runner wearing
heavy sweatpants and leg weights to run in a race? How far do you think the runner would get? Are you wearing the leg weights of an indifferent attitude toward
the things of God? Do you find when you try to worship, the heavy sweatpants
of spiritual fatigue keep you from enjoying the presence of God?

My friend, anything that saps your spiritual passion is a potential weight that
must be discarded. If you fix your gaze toward the finish line, you will see Jesus,
the *author and finisher of your faith.* He has already run ahead of you and will provide all the encouragement you need to cross the finish line with joy.

DON'T GET TRAPPED

Therefore we also, since we are surrounded by so great a
cloud of witnesses, let us lay aside every weight, and the sin
which so easily ensnares us, and let us run with endurance
the race that is set before us (Hebrews 12:1 NKJV).

To run the race with persistence, patience, and endurance, we are required to discard unnecessary hindrances. Carrying extra baggage—weight—is not the only thing that will keep a runner from staying in the race. The writer of Hebrews points to another area of our life that needs examination from a different perspective—*"the sin which so easily ensnares us."*

You will notice that no specific sin is named. I have heard all kinds of views on this verse. It becomes nothing more than speculation, since no particular sin is named. Some have suggested it is a sin of unbelief, while others say it is a sin of hanging out with the wrong crowd. Instead of spending time trying to figure out what the writer meant, let's just agree that *any and all* sin is missing the mark of God's standard.

The phrase *"and the sin which so easily ensnares us"* is from one word that depicts something that is comfortable or something that we are so used to that we don't realize the danger until it's too late. Getting comfortable with some things is not a bad, such as an old pair of bedroom slippers, but getting comfortable with sin is quite another. And where is the most relaxed place to get comfortable? You guessed it, with the negative atmosphere of our old life.

If we surround ourselves with people from the old life, how long will it take for their unbelief to rub off on us? I've heard all kinds of excuses as to why hanging around with the old crowd is necessary. Probably the most popular is the idea that hanging out with unbelieving friends is the best way to witness for Christ. Sure, sounds good. No doubt on occasion it might work, but most of the time the reverse happens. The quickest way to render our testimony powerless is to stay wrapped up with the attitudes and behaviors of the old life while trying to expound the virtues of the new. It doesn't add up.

Getting comfortable with our old lifestyle can happen so easily. Before we know it, the atmosphere of unbelief is clinging to us like an old smelly sweat suit that needs to be burned!

THE STARTING POINT

Then he went down to Nazareth with them and was
obedient to them. But his mother treasured all these things
in her heart. And Jesus grew in wisdom and stature,
and in favor with God and man (Luke 2:51-52).

THIS PASSAGE IN LUKE IS RECORDED SOON AFTER JESUS' RETURN FROM A TRIP to Jerusalem where it was noticed that He was missing. They found Him at the temple where He was listening to and asking questions of the religious leaders. We have only been given a few snapshots to put in our photo album of the early years of Jesus, this is one of them.

The Bible gives us only a brief glimpse of what was going on during those formative years. Jesus was growing, maturing, and learning the priorities of life. He is our pattern Man on how to put life together to reach our full potential. The starting point of a well-rounded life is to place wisdom at the top of the list: *"And Jesus grew in wisdom."* Without the proper foundation of wisdom, Jesus would not have been able to grow *"in favor with God and man."* Proverbs 4:7-8 tells us, *"The beginning of wisdom is this: Get wisdom. Though it cost all you have, get understanding. Cherish her, and she will exalt you; embrace her, and she will honor you."*

Wisdom is not just about having a truckload of knowledge or a brain filled with common sense. Wisdom and knowledge are not necessarily the same. Wisdom is the God-given insight into the truth of any circumstance. Wisdom enables us to perceive the difference between what is real and what is fake. Wisdom is the right use of knowledge, the search for her is to be pursued at all cost (see Proverbs 2:6-7).

The pursuit of wisdom is God-honoring and God-pleasing. He wants us to live our lives according to His wisdom, and not depend on our "street smarts" to get us to the next level. According to James 1:5, His wisdom is available to all who ask: *"If any of you lacks wisdom, you should ask God, who gives generously to all without finding fault, and it will be given to you."* So, what are you waiting for? Go ahead and ask, and watch what happens!

BECOME A CONDUIT
OF COMFORT

*Praise be to the God and Father of our Lord Jesus Christ, the Father
of compassion and the God of all comfort, who comforts us in all
our troubles, so that we can comfort those in any trouble with the
comfort we ourselves receive from God* (2 Corinthians 1:3-4).

WE ARE MORE VULNERABLE TO MAKE MISTAKES AND MISSTEPS WHEN TROU-
bles come than any other time. It is easy to become frustrated when we
don't have all the answers to whatever trial we are facing. Trying to focus on
someone else's trials when we are knee-deep in our own situation can be daunting.

A failure to understand that God has a divine purpose for our lives may put
us in danger of losing hope. Paul was not immune. He lamented, *"We were under
great pressure, far beyond our ability to endure, so that we despaired of life itself."* If
it can happen to Paul, it can happen to anyone. But, he didn't give up because he
knew that *"this happened that we might not rely on ourselves but on God, who raises
the dead"* (2 Corinthians 1:8-9).

When the pressure is on, the devil likes nothing more than to convince us
of two things: *First,* the enemy wants us to try to figure things out on our own
instead of going to God's Word for strength and comfort. *Second,* he will try to
convince us we are the only ones who have this kind of trouble. He whispers,
"Don't share anything with anyone because they can't possibly understand your
situation." Well, that's lie!

An often-overlooked reason for our trials is so we might become a source of
comfort and encouragement to others. As the Lord *"comforts us in all our troubles,"* we can in turn *"comfort those in any trouble with the comfort we ourselves
receive from God."* When it comes to trials, one size does not fit all. Our trials may look different from others, but that is not a reason to turn away and
withhold encouragement.

Consider the possibility that what we are going through is not punishment for
something we did wrong, but a time of preparation for future ministry to others
who need to hear a word of comfort and spiritual strength. Let's determine that
as the Father comforts us, we will be a conduit of the Father's love, and rivers of
comfort will flow out to our hurting brothers and sisters.

TRANSFORMING TRUTH

*Your word, Lord, is eternal; it stands firm
in the heavens* (Psalm 119:89).

We need to remember that God's Word is the unchanging truth, and it is the authority—not man. If God's truth changed in His Word, then we could not say that His Word is inerrant (i.e., free of errors), and therefore, we would not be able to trust it. Like Luther, let us shout to the world that the unchanging truth is in Scripture alone, and bring about a reformation back to the authority of the Word of God!

JEREMY HAM[66]

THE MIRACLE OF A MADEUP MIND

When she heard about Jesus, she came up behind him in the crowd and touched his cloak, because she thought, "If I just touch his clothes, I will be healed." Immediately her bleeding stopped and she felt in her body that she was freed from her suffering (Mark 5:27-29).

THE MIRACLE OF THE WOMAN WITH AN ISSUE OF BLOOD IS BY FAR ONE OF MY favorites. Even though her faith was weak, she received far more than she expected. She ignored her circumstances and got close enough to the garment of Jesus to receive her miracle.

On many levels, this poor soul took a high risk. According to Leviticus, her "blood issue" meant she was cut off from all of her relationships, including friends and family. She would not be allowed to worship traditionally. Just by interacting with the crowd she was breaking the law. So, her suffering was more than physical; it was an emotional and spiritual pain as well.

She didn't get her miracle because she deserved one or because Jesus felt sorry for her. No, it was, *"because she thought, 'If I just touch his clothes, I will be healed.'"* She made her up mind this was her last chance for help, and failure was not an option. What was it that drove her past the point of not caring what anybody thought? Maybe she was sick and tired of being sick and tired. Or perhaps she was fed up with the empty promises from doctors telling her if she only had enough money they could help her. She tried every approach to find a cure, and in the end, she was worse (see Mark 5:26).

Everybody has issues. Your issues may not be physical like this woman, but just as real all the same. It may be; a root of bitterness over a broken relationship; a financial disaster; or, past abuse by a family member. You can fill in the blank yourself. You may have tried to find help from other sources (like this woman) and found no relief. I challenge you to make up your mind that today is your day for a miracle.

Don't spend one more day in distress. You will be amazed what one touch from Jesus can do to change your circumstances. The Master is passing by—reach out and touch Him. You won't be disappointed!

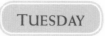
DON'T THROW AWAY YOUR FAITH

This is what the wicked are like— always free of care, they go on amassing wealth. Surely in vain I have kept my heart pure and have washed my hands in innocence. All day long I have been afflicted, and every morning brings new punishments (Psalm 73:12-14).

THE PSALMIST WAS DEALING WITH A GRAVE ISSUE. WHAT BOTHERED HIM IS not an uncommon challenge for those of us who live for the Lord. When he looked around and saw people who never cared about the things of God, it made him ask probing questions about his faith. He must have thought: *These people don't care anything about faith, or trusting in God, yet they never seem to have any of the problems I have.*

No doubt the psalmist looked to Heaven and said, "Lord, I have tried to live for You and all I get in return are troubles, sufferings, and sorrows." In so many words, he was musing if it was worth it to serve God. Maybe you have asked the same questions as the psalmist when probing your faith. Let's be honest, it can be alarming to look at others and wonder why they seem to prosper while those living for the Lord have nothing but challenges. It is in those moments of despair that we find out how stable our faith is. If serving the Lord is just about getting ahead of those we deem unworthy, then we are on the brink of ditching our faith.

As believers, we have been given many things the unbeliever does not have. When we came to the Lord, our sins were put under the blood of Christ. All of the guilt of past sin was removed from God's memory bank, never to be brought up again (see John 3:18). We can live every day with the assurance of God's wisdom, counsel, and guidance (see Psalm 73:23-28).

Our future has also been secured by Jesus Christ. Nobody knows what the future holds, but one thing is certain, we know the Lord holds our future in His hand. Don't throw away your faith just because it appears others are doing better than you are. Trust in the Lord; He will bring you through to the other side!

WHEN IS A CONVENIENT TIME?

Several days later Felix came with his wife Drusilla, who was Jewish. He sent for Paul and listened to him as he spoke about faith in Christ Jesus. As Paul talked about righteousness, self-control and the judgment to come, Felix was afraid and said, "That's enough for now! You may leave. When I find it convenient, I will send for you" (Acts 24:24-25).

PAUL NEVER WASTED AN OPPORTUNITY TO SPEAK OF HIS FAITH IN CHRIST. IT didn't matter to him whether it was the religious establishment or secular rulers, he was quick to say, "I'm not ashamed of the Gospel of Christ."

Governor Felix sent for Paul and gave him an opportunity to speak. If you were in Paul's situation, what would you do? Would you defend yourself and tell the governor there has been some mistake? Or would you accuse others of "setting you up" and the charges were a pack of lies? Not Paul. This veteran, who bore many scars of combat with the forces of hell, stood proudly and declared the good news of Christ.

We only have the general outline of his message. He spoke to Felix and his wife Drusilla about a righteousness they did not possess; a self-control they did not practice; and a judgment for which they were not prepared. You can be sure there was enough "meat on the bone" to point them to salvation, which they desperately needed.

When Paul concluded his brief message, I'm reasonably sure the room was deathly silent. The governor and his wife were now faced with a life-and-death decision. We can imagine Paul saying, "Felix, what do you have to say for yourself? I can see the message moved you to the point of fear and trembling." His answer? *"That's enough for now! You may leave. When I find it convenient, I will send for you."* Wow! That's it? Are you going to wait until there is a more convenient time to give your life to Christ? As far as we know, Felix and his wife never found a more convenient time, and they wasted the opportunity. Historians believe that Felix and his wife died in the eruption of Mount Vesuvius in A.D. 79.

We never know when we will face similar destiny moments. Just being moved by the message of salvation is not enough. When is the most convenient time to say yes to Christ? Now, because you have no guarantee there will be another.

DARE TO BE A DANIEL

But Daniel resolved not to defile himself with the royal food and wine, and he asked the chief official for permission not to defile himself this way. Now God had caused the official to show favor and compassion to Daniel (Daniel 1:8-9).

DANIEL WAS A TEENAGER WHEN TAKEN CAPTIVE BY THE BABYLONIANS. He, along with other young men of Israel, was taken to Babylon, the center of architecture, wealth, and knowledge. King Nebuchadnezzar had a grand plan for these young men. He wanted only the best and brightest men who could one day assist in leading his nation.

I have found the majority of teenager's want to blend in and go with the crowd. Among their peers, rocking the boat, or going against the grain is not in their playbook. It is a rare sight to see a young person not afraid to have the courage to be different.

Daniel had to make a decision. Should he go along to get along, or dare to take a stand? I'm sure he knew to make a decision based on his core values would place him in the "he's different" category! By different, I'm referring to having the courage to stand for what he believed, no matter how much pressure is receive from outside influences. Daniel could have used a variety of excuses; not the least of which was that he was far from home and nobody would ever find out if he bought into the Babylonian lifestyle.

A common trait of those who dare to shake nations is learning that self-discipline and uncommon courage are more important than gifting and talent. Just having a passion for something is not enough to get you to the finish line. Daniel knew that not following the king's diet was not the only test he would face. There would be more tests in his future, and each would require a new level of self-discipline.

By following Christ, you and I are already considered different. That is how we are described in First Peter 2:9: *"But you are a chosen people, a royal priesthood, a holy nation, God's special possession, that you may declare the praises of him who called you out of darkness into his wonderful light."* Daniel was tested for his faith, so will we; when the time comes, dare to be a Daniel.

THEY REFUSED TO BOW

But there are some Jews whom you have set over the affairs of the province of Babylon—Shadrach, Meshach and Abednego—who pay no attention to you, Your Majesty. They neither serve your gods nor worship the image of gold you have set up (Daniel 3:12).

KING NEBUCHADNEZZAR HAD AN IDEA. HE WOULD BUILD A GOLDEN IMAGE of himself to display before the people. A new law was passed that on a given day everyone would be required to worship before the image. Paying homage to the king was not optional. A refusal to bow was an invitation to be roasted in a fiery furnace (see Daniel 3:1-11). On the day of dedication, everyone complied; well, there were a few exceptions. As the spies looked over the crowd, they saw three teenagers standing. I can hear them shout, "Get the names of those cowards who refused to bow, and let's have a roast!"

If they had bowed down with the rest of the crowd, no one would have blamed them. They could have justified themselves, and said, "As long as we're standing up in our heart, that's all that counts." Refusing to go along with the crowd produced negative consequences, and now they had to answer before the king. The young men didn't need a second chance to obey. They said in no uncertain terms that the soldiers could do with them as they pleased, but the three would not sacrifice their values to please the king or the crowd (see Daniel 3:16).

Today our challenges are different from the ones faced by these young people. The last time I looked, there were no ninety-foot-tall golden images set up to worship. Today's culture is more sophisticated than to do something so obvious. We may argue that we would never worship a golden image, but it could be because our idols of gold are hidden in the recesses of our hearts. The best definition of an idol I have ever heard is, *"Anything you have to check with before you can obey God is your idol."*

There will always be times when we will be tested on our priorities. These young people passed the test. They would not sacrifice one minute of their worship that belonged to God to appease an ungodly king. They were wise enough to know one compromise always leads to another.

IF NOT...

*If we are thrown into the blazing furnace, the God we serve
is able to deliver us from it, and he will deliver us from Your
Majesty's hand. But even if he does not, we want you to know,
Your Majesty, that we will not serve your gods or worship
the image of gold you have set up* (Daniel 3:17-18).

SWIMMING UPSTREAM CAN PRODUCE NEGATIVE CONSEQUENCES. KING NEBU-chadnezzar was not about to let Shadrach, Meshack, and Abednego off the hook. These young guys are about to find out the seriousness of saying "no" to the most powerful ruler on earth. The punishment for refusing to worship the golden image was a date with a blazing hot furnace.

After the king gave them one more chance to obey and they still refused, he had no choice but to throw them in the fire. Their attitude was simple. They wanted this man to know they were not afraid of the fire. In essence they said, "God is able to deliver us from the fire, but if He decides not to save us, we will still not serve your gods or worship the golden image!" God did not save them from the fire. The Lord did one better; He walked with them *in the fire* (see Daniel 3:24-25) and they emerged unharmed.

The *"if nots"* are a sign of trust, not a lack of faith. The trio wanted the king to know the Lord is in control of the situation. Therefore, they had nothing to fear. Can anything good come out of a fiery furnace experience? What looked to be a death sentence for them was nothing more than a doorway to their promotion. All the fire did was burn away their bindings and set them free, and when they walked out, not even smelling of smoke. What next? *"Then the king promoted Shadrach, Meshach and Abednego in the province of Babylon"* (see Daniel 3:30).

At some point, all of us will face circumstances that feel like we've been thrown into the fire. The Word has given us many promises to claim. My personal favorite is Isaiah 43:2: *"When you pass through the waters, I will be with you; and when you pass through the rivers, they will not sweep over you. When you walk through the fire, you will not be burned; the flames will not set you ablaze."* If your situation is getting too hot to handle, go back and read this story again. You have many promises to stand on.

ARE YOU PUFFED UP?

*Now, brothers and sisters, I have applied these things to
myself and Apollos for your benefit, so that you may learn
from us the meaning of the saying, "Do not go beyond what is
written." Then you will not be puffed up in being a follower
of one of us over against the other* (1 Corinthians 4:6).

THREE TIMES IN FIRST CORINTHIANS 4 PAUL WARNS THESE *"PUFFED UP,"*
and *"arrogant"* believers that they have overestimated their importance (see
1 Corinthians 4:6,18,19). Here was a group of high-minded, boastful, and preoccupied people who were showing off all their spiritual gifts. The church was
divided into different camps based on their favorite preacher, and it was causing
confusion.

Paul used a very colorful term to describe the attitude of these Corinthians.
"Puffed up" means to "inflate by blowing; (figuratively) swelled up, like an egotis-
tical person spewing out arrogant ("puffed-up") thoughts."[67] They were boasting
of their spirituality like a balloon ready to pop! It is fairly obvious the main issue
causing so many problems in the church was their spiritual pride. If something
wasn't done, and quickly, God's blessings and favor would be withdrawn. The
Bible is not silent when it comes to pride. Whenever pride rears its ugly head, the
Lord will not allow it to stand. James 4:6 tells us, *"But he gives us more grace. That
is why Scripture says: "God opposes the proud but shows favor to the humble."*

If you want to see the result of taking glory that was due the Lord, read
Daniel 4. King Nebuchadnezzar learned the hard way what happens when a man
is filled with an inflated attitude of himself! None of us are immune to unbibli-
cal pride. The last thing we should want is to allow our pride to cause us to miss
out on what God wants for our lives (see Jeremiah 9:23; Proverbs 8:13; 11:2; 13:10;
16:18).

What should our attitude be? A good place to start is to let the air out of our
boasting and recognize that we have not arrived at spiritual maturity. An honest
view of ourselves is the one expressed in Philippians 3:12: *"Not that I have already
obtained all this, or have already arrived at my goal, but I press on to take hold of that
for which Christ Jesus took hold of me."*

DON'T FAINT BEFORE
REACHING THE FINISH LINE

*Therefore we do not lose heart. Though outwardly we are wasting
away, yet inwardly we are being renewed day by day. For our
light and momentary troubles are achieving for us an eternal
glory that far outweighs them all* (2 Corinthians 4:16-17).

I HAVE A FEELING THAT WHEN PAUL WROTE THAT WE SHOULD NOT *LOSE HEART,*
he had a mental picture of an athlete running a race. On more than one occasion, Paul used the analogy of a runner to encourage us not to faint before we
cross the finish line (see 1 Corinthians 9:24-27; 2 Timothy 2:5; Hebrews 12:1).

If anyone had a reason to give up the race it would have been Paul. I doubt
anyone would have blamed Paul if he had said things were too hard and he
couldn't complete his assignment. He refused to quit even though he suffered
physical, emotional, and spiritual conflict his entire ministry. He pressed on and
finished the race that was set before him. As he neared the end of his life, he
wrote to Timothy, *"I have fought the good fight, I have finished the race, I have kept
the faith"* (2 Timothy 4:7).

A great example of refusing to give up is a marathon runner named Chandler
Self. On Saturday, December 9, 2017, she was competing in the BMW Dallas
Marathon. As Self neared the finish line, some twenty meters away, she was about
to realize a life-long dream of winning a marathon. Suddenly, her dream turned
into a nightmare as she inexplicitly fell to the pavement. She tried to regain her
balance, but fell again, as her tired legs refused to hold her up. Close behind her
was a high school triathlete named Ariana Luterman who was competing in a
separate race. Instead of passing by the stricken runner, this teenage hero reached
out and picked her up, and held on to her arm to ensure Ms. Self crossed the finish line for the win.

As we daily walk with the Lord, our inner self is getting stronger as *"we are
being renewed."* If you feel like you can't go on, why not allow the Lord to take
your arm and give you the grace and strength you need to cross the finish line?
Don't give up so close to fulfilling your destiny!

How to Talk to a Brainless Moron

*Do not answer a fool according to his folly, or you yourself
will be just like him. Answer a fool according to his folly,
or he will be wise in his own eyes* (Proverbs 26:4-5).

I DON'T KNOW HOW MANY TIMES I HAVE SEARCHED THE BOOK OF PROVERBS when dealing with sensitive subjects, like how to talk to someone who speaks just to ignite verbal fireworks. You know the type, right? Their motto in life is, "If it pops into my brain, it's coming out of my mouth."

I don't recommend calling someone a brainless moron, although Solomon's words are straight to the point. If you combine the meaning of the word *"fool"* with both Old Testament and New Testament references, you can safely say these people are brainless morons who love to talk even if they don't have anything worthwhile to say.

So, how should we converse with such people?

First, never ever stoop to their level of foolishness. When we do that, it becomes very easy to cross the line, and before we know it their words have sparked a roaring forest fire of anger. Their goal is to get you upset, and responding to them in kind is what they want. I understand that when someone attacks us with absurd and unfounded accusations, our first response is a defensive position. It is a normal human characteristic that when we are attacked we load up our verbal cannon and fire a salvo of our own.

Second, there is a way to talk to foolish people without getting down into the conversational gutter with them. It looks like Solomon is a bit confused. On the one hand, he cautions, *"Do not answer a fool according to his folly,"* and then he says, *"Answer a fool according to his folly."*

So, which is it? Should I or shouldn't I speak to a brainless moron?

Here's the point. Don't engage in a war of words. If you do, you become just like them. If a neutral person overheard the conversation, they would surmise both of you are fools. But, you can answer with *truth,* without the verbal bombs. And where is that truth found? In the Bible. It is a safer and saner approach to let Scripture do your talking. Remember, you never have to apologize for something you thought, but never said!

PEACOCKS OR EAGLES

*Does the eagle soar at your command and build its nest
on high? It dwells on a cliff and stays there at night;
a rocky crag is its stronghold. From there it looks for
food; its eyes detect it from afar* (Job 39:27-29).

IT IS A BIBLICAL FACT THAT GOD'S DESIRE FOR HIS PEOPLE IS TO SOAR LIKE eagles. It is also true that many people who claim to have a relationship with the Lord are not eagles, but are instead satisfied to live in a bubble of predictable circumstances. I cannot find anywhere in Scripture where we are told to act like any bird other than an eagle. Sadly, when it comes to living for the Lord, some people behave more like a peacock.

When I think of a peacock, the first thing that comes to mind is when they fan their tail feathers and strut around in a colorful display. A peacock will give the appearance of being able to fly, but can only fly short distances when faced with danger. This large bird spends most of its time searching for food, or perched on the tallest spot they can find.

A peacock Christian gives off the appearance of being strong. But when the pressure of daily circumstances falls on their shoulders, they can only fly a short distance to avoid potential danger. Just as the peacock can fan its feathers and strut, so the peacock Christian wants everyone to know how gifted they are. If someone tries to move them off of their perch, they will leave to find others to impress with their enormous talent.

God created the eagle to not only fly above the storm clouds, but in fact fly so high that other birds cannot join it. He has no desire to join a flock and chirp like the rest of the birds. Except for when choosing his mate, the eagle is content to fly alone. While other birds are sitting on telephone lines, the eagle is high above using keen eyesight to search the earth below for the next meal.

Don't live like a peacock always fanning feathers of self-importance. Instead, live like an eagle Christian who is not afraid to soar high above the noise of busy activity to be still and hear the voice of God!

TWO SINNERS WENT TO CHURCH

*To some who were confident of their own righteousness
and looked down on everyone else, Jesus told this parable:
"Two men went up to the temple to pray, one a Pharisee
and the other a tax collector"* (Luke 18:9-10).

IN THIS STORY, JESUS IS PAINTING A PICTURE TO HIGHLIGHT THAT ALL THE externals of religion mean nothing if the person does not have a heart connection to the Lord. He chose two men to illustrate His point—one a Pharisee and the other a tax collector. I wonder if those listening to Jesus thought within themselves, *We know the outcome of this story. No doubt, the Pharisee is the hero.* Keep in mind there was one group who did everything in their power to stop Jesus, and eliminate His followers. The group? None other than the Pharisees. But the notion among the common folk of Jerusalem was if the Pharisees don't make it to Heaven, none of them would have a chance.

The Pharisee prayed something like, "Lord, my commitment to Your law is impeccable. I tithe, fast, and do everything I can to show everyone how religious I am. Lord, You ought to give me special treatment because I'm not like the low-life sinner standing over there in the corner" (see Luke 18:11-12).

The tax collector, or low-life sinner, would not look up. He just beat himself on the chest and said, *"God, have mercy on me, a sinner"* (Luke 18:13). His prayer was simple and to the point. Jesus said only one of these two went home in a right relationship with God. Of course it was the tax collector.

Time and again Jesus pointed out the danger of holding up the externals of religion to please God (see Matthew 23). The tax collector had the right view of himself. He confessed he was a sinner in need of salvation. He also understood that God was full of mercy and grace, and does not want *"anyone to perish, but everyone to come to repentance* (2 Peter 3:9).

The Lord received the prayer of one and rejected the prayer of the other. Never think that God is impressed with our "religious activity" to the exclusion of a heart-to-heart relationship with Him. *"For all those who exalt themselves will be humbled, and those who humble themselves will be exalted"* (Luke 18:14). Don't make the mistake of comparing yourself with others. If you want to compare with someone, try Jesus, and see how you stack up!

LESSONS FROM THE BACKSIDE OF NOWHERE

Moses answered, "What if they do not believe me or listen to me and say, 'The Lord did not appear to you'?" Then the Lord said to him, "What is that in your hand?" "A staff," he replied (Exodus 4:1-2).

AT FORTY YEARS OF AGE, MOSES WAS AT THE PINNACLE OF SUCCESS. BUT something was missing in his life—a nagging in his heart that there was more to his purpose than being a dominant political figure. According to the book of Hebrews, Moses made a conscious decision to turn his back on all that Egypt afforded. He walked away from social position, sinful pleasure, and staggering prosperity (see Hebrews 11:24-27).

One day Moses saw an Egyptian abusing a Hebrew slave, and he determined to start the liberation process of Hebrew slaves—one Egyptian at a time! Moses is now a hunted man. He escapes and eventually enrolls in the "Wilderness University," majoring in sheep-ology. Many people view the backside of the wilderness as a place of despair, and not a place to renew your calling (see Exodus 2:11-21).

But on the backside of nowhere is where we can learn:

- *God is still speaking.* There are times when we need to shut out all the noise and distractions swirling around us and open our spiritual ears to hear what God has to say. We might view the backside of the desert as a punishment, but it might be the only way God can get through to us (see Exodus 3:4).

- *God's calling has not been revoked.* Maybe Moses, like many of us, felt that he had one opportunity to obey his calling and he blew it. He thought his vision died along with the Egyptian he buried it in the sand. We all make mistakes and do things that we are not proud of, but rest assured God's call has never been removed. Moses will soon learn that God has not forgotten him (see Exodus 3:10; Romans 11:29).

- *Whatever is in your hand, turn it over to God.* Moses carried a shepherd's rod, an instrument needed to tend sheep. The rod is going to change hands, as it becomes a symbol of the Lord's power and protection (see Exodus 4:2-5; 14:13-16; 17:4-5, 8-9). Moses graduated from Wilderness University and became the spiritual force who liberated a nation. Not too bad for someone who thought his life was over!

WISDOM FROM A
FENCE STRADDLER

Therefore, in the present case I advise you: Leave these men alone!
Let them go! For if their purpose or activity is of human origin, it
will fail. But if it is from God, you will not be able to stop these men;
you will only find yourselves fighting against God (Acts 5:38-39).

IN THE FIFTH CHAPTER OF ACTS, PETER AND THE OTHER APOSTLES WERE accused of spreading the Gospel of Christ in direct violation of the religious authorities. The situation was about to go from bad to worse until Gamaliel stood up and imparted his wisdom. He was a highly respected doctor of the law who offered a solution that seemed logical and would undoubtedly avoid more conflict with these followers of *"the Way"* (see Acts 9:2). But there are times when human logic and worldly wisdom will lead to a serious compromise with eternal truth.

Gamaliel made a few mistakes:

1. *He compared Jesus to other leaders* (see Acts 5:36-37). There is a popular tendency to put Jesus in the same mold as ordinary men. In our day, we are told that Jesus, Mohammed, Buddha, and other religious leaders are all on par with each other. As far as I know, Jesus Christ is the only one who died and rose again. Friend, it does matter what you believe, because all roads do not lead to Heaven. Jesus says, *"I am the way and the truth and the life. No one comes to the Father except through me"* (John 14:6).

2. *He suggested a false criterion for success* (see Acts 5:38-39). He said we will measure these men and this movement by the success of it. He said if God is in it, then it will grow and be successful; and if not, it will die like all other movements. According to the viewpoint of his day, Jesus was a roaring failure. He lived in poverty, died in disgrace, and by the end of His ministry, only a handful of disciples were still around. But the fire of the Gospel could not be contained, and today there are several billion of us who name the name of Christ!

Dr. Gamaliel arrived false conclusions. He hopped up on the fence and said, "Let's not commit one way or the other." You cannot live with a hands-off approach when it comes to your eternal soul. The Gospel of Christ demands a decision. Make a decision and get off the fence (see Joshua 24:14-15).

LOST AND FOUND: ONE SHEEP

Then Jesus told them this parable: "Suppose one of you has a hundred sheep and loses one of them. Doesn't he leave the ninety-nine in the open country and go after the lost sheep until he finds it? And when he finds it, he joyfully puts it on his shoulders and goes home" (Luke 15:3-5).

IN THE FIRST TWO VERSES OF LUKE 15, THE PHARISEES ACCUSED JESUS OF spending too much time with tax collectors and sinners. They could not understand why He chose to waste His time on the dregs of society when He should be learning from the upper crust of the religious establishment. Jesus tried to tell them that *"the Son of Man came to seek and to save the lost,"* but they were too blind to see (Luke 19:10).

Jesus told three parables about things that were *lost and then found*. The first is about a lost sheep; second, is the story of a lost piece of silver; and third, the focus is on the lost son. In each of these stories Jesus highlights a different aspect of God's love and care for His own.

The parable of the lost sheep shows us the compassion of a loving shepherd who will go to any lengths to find one lost sheep. The "lost sheep" is a representation of unsaved humanity, and the shepherd is a picture of the Son of God who was willing to leave the ninety-nine to find the one that is lost.

When Jesus refers to us as sheep, it was not a compliment; rather He was showing the nature of humans apart from God. Isaiah 53:6 tells us, *"We all, like sheep, have gone astray, each of us has turned to our own way."* Sheep have no sense of direction, no defense against predators, and basically, they are some of the dumbest animals on God's earth. They need a shepherd who will lead, care for, and protect them. A sheep who gets separated from the flock and the protective eye of the shepherd is a dead sheep walking!

In John 10, Jesus portrays Himself as the *Good Shepherd who lays down His life for the sheep* (see John 10:7-18). Jesus has committed Himself to love, lead, and take responsibility for those who have given their heart to Him. He will lead you to green pastures if you are hungry; if you are thirsty, He will guide you beside still waters; and, if you are hurting, He will bind up your wounds. Jesus is your Shepherd—you have nothing to fear! (See Psalm 23.)

LOST AND FOUND: ONE PIECE OF SILVER

Or suppose a woman has ten silver coins and loses one. Doesn't she light a lamp, sweep the house and search carefully until she finds it? And when she finds it, she calls her friends and neighbors together and says, "Rejoice with me; I have found my lost coin" (Luke 15:8-9).

IF YOU HAVE EVER LOST ANYTHING OF VALUE, YOU CAN IDENTIFY WITH THIS poor soul who lost a silver coin. Don't think because she still had nine silver coins that it was not a big deal. Most Bible teachers agree that each coin represented a day's wage, so this was a lot of money. When she realized a coin was missing, she dropped everything and searched until she found it.

There is one phrase that sums up this parable for me: *the value of one.* The woman is a symbol of a loving God who would stop at nothing to find the most valuable thing in the world—you. God places the highest possible value on every single one of His creation. Even when we were in rebellion and lost, God did not give up His searching for us. He chose us from the foundation of the world (see John 15:6).

How does someone determine the value of an object? Television programs such as *Antique Road Show* or *American Pickers* are about determining the value of objects. People present items, and then experts give their best estimation as to how much they think the item is worth. What is amazing are the people's reactions. Because the item, usually an heirloom, is priceless to them, they assume it must be valuable. More often than not people walk away disappointed because they don't receive the value they were expecting. I submit the value of anything is determined by what someone is willing to pay for it.

How valuable are we to God? If the value is determined by the price someone is willing to pay, then the amount paid for our redemption was the highest in the universe—the life of God's Son! The apostle Peter tells us the price was *"the precious blood of Christ, a lamb without blemish or defect"* (see 1 Peter 1:18-19). Never devalue your worth, no matter what others say about you. God loved you so much He refused to stop searching for you until you were found!

LOST AND FOUND: ONE SON

Jesus continued: "There was a man who had two sons. The younger one said to his father, 'Father, give me my share of the estate.' So he divided his property between them" (Luke 15:11-12).

I'VE HEARD PEOPLE SAY THIS IS THE MOST SIGNIFICANT STORY EVER TOLD ABOUT the depth of God's love for humankind. The point of the story is not so much about a young man who left home and wasted his inheritance, but a loving father who refused to give up on his son.

The young man's attitude is best summed up when he said, *"Father, give me my share of the estate."* The phrase *"give me"* is the voice of rebellion, not the attitude of an obedient son. He would eventually pack up and move to the *"distant country,"* but the attitude of the *"distant country"* was already in his heart. The *"distant country"* is a symbol of anywhere we may go that removes us from a personal relationship with our heavenly Father (Luke 15:13).

The young man soon found out the place he moved to was not what it was advertised to be. It never is. Sin always looks good at the start, but when the devil presents his bill, we soon realize we can't cover the tab (see Luke 15:14-16). It was just his luck that at the same time he wasted all of his money, a severe famine swept the country. He had no money, no place to go, and no one to care. He ended up sloping pigs. It is amazing what fighting pigs for supper will do to your attitude. Thank God, he came to his senses and decided to go home (Luke 15:17-19).

The father never stopped praying or giving up hope that one day his wayward son would come home. Then it happened, *"But while he was still a long way off, his father saw him and was filled with compassion for him; he ran to his son, threw his arms around him and kissed him"* (Luke 15:20). The father didn't wait; he ran to meet his son. Later the father exclaimed, *"he was lost and is found"* (Luke 15:32).

What a description of a loving and compassionate heavenly Father who is waiting and watching for His wayward children to come home. Is your heart far from God? Have you spiritually moved to a *"distant country?"* The Lord wants you to know the light is always on, and the door is always open. *"The Lord is gracious and compassionate, slow to anger and rich in love"* (Psalm 145:8).

LET'S GET THE PARTY STARTED

I tell you that in the same way there will be more rejoicing
in heaven over one sinner who repents than over ninety-nine
righteous persons who do not need to repent (Luke 15:7).

JESUS TOLD THREE PARABLES IN LUKE 15, AND AT THE END OF EACH, HE SAID Heaven celebrates when *that which was lost is found*. No matter what we think we know, or don't, about Heaven, one fact is sure—it's going to be a place of celebration (see Luke 15:5-7,9-10; 22:24).

Do you think when we get to Heaven we are going to find the saints sitting on clouds playing harps? Or will Heaven look and sound like the average Sunday morning worship service. You know, where we sing, pray, and preach in hushed tones so as not too appear too happy or excited about God's presence. I submit there are going to be a lot of folks who are in for a rude awakening when they get there.

As you might expect, not everyone is thrilled about celebrating over a lost sinner or wayward son who comes home to Christ. The Pharisees were upset that the "wrong people" received the good news (see Luke 15:2) And the older brother was shocked that his father would throw a party for a son who lived in rebellion and wasted his inheritance (see Luke 15:1-2,28-31). Sadly, the attitude of the Pharisees and older brother is still with us. I tell folks that if being happy over one sinner rubs you the wrong way now, you are going to be as out of place in Heaven as a donkey running in the Kentucky Derby!

We must not focus our attention on the negative and spend all of our energy trying to please those who are blind to the truth. In each parable, our attention is drawn to the *one*, and it is the *one* who sets off a celebration. Heaven is full of rejoicing, with many sounds of worship over the *one* who is born again (see Revelation 5:11;7:9). You can imagine that with thousands around the world giving their hearts to Christ on a daily basis that Heaven is "party central" 24/7. May God help us to get as excited as the angels over one sinner who repents and gives his or her life to Christ.

A VOW IS SERIOUS BUSINESS

And she made a vow, saying, "Lord Almighty, if you will only look on your servant's misery and remember me, and not forget your servant but give her a son, then I will give him to the Lord for all the days of his life, and no razor will ever be used on his head" (1 Samuel 1:11).

HER NAME MEANS "GRACE" OR "FAVOR" IN THE HEBREW LANGUAGE; AND IF there was ever a woman in the Bible who needed the favor of the Lord, it was this woman named Hannah. Every year she was faithful to make her way to Shiloh (the place of worship) to beg God to give her a son. Her rivals mocked her (see 1 Samuel 1:7) and her spiritual leader accused her of being drunk (see 1 Samuel 1:12-13), but she would not stop asking for a miracle.

There came a day when everything changed, and her desperation paid dividends. She upped the ante and made a vow, which is a voluntary promise to God. She said, "Lord, if You will give me a son, I will give him back to serve You all the days of his life." Somebody forgot to tell Hannah that we can't bargain with God—God is not in the business of deal-making. Do you think God would ever answer a prayer like that? *"So in the course of time Hannah became pregnant and gave birth to a son. She named him Samuel, saying, 'Because I asked the Lord for him'"* (1 Samuel 1:20).

Her vow had two parts. God kept His part, and in turn, Hannah kept her part. She dedicated Samuel to serve God, and then the Lord blessed her with more children. *"And the Lord was gracious to Hannah; she gave birth to three sons and two daughters. Meanwhile, the boy Samuel grew up in the presence of the Lord"* (see 1 Samuel 2:21).

Hannah was not like a lot of people who make a vow to God in times of desperation, but after the storm passes suddenly get a case of spiritual amnesia. The fastest way to break trust with someone is to make a promise and then back out. The Bible is clear. Making a vow to God is serious business, and we should never make one if we don't intend to follow through. It breaks trust with God, and it makes us look foolish. Ecclesiastes 5:4 tells us, *"When you make a vow to God, do not delay to fulfill it. He has no pleasure in fools; fulfill your vow."*

WAKE UP—IT'S LATER THAN YOU THINK

And do this, understanding the present time: The hour has already come for you to wake up from your slumber, because our salvation is nearer now than when we first believed (Romans 13:11).

PAUL ISSUED A CLARION CALL TO THOSE IN ROME, AND TO US, THAT IN LIGHT of the closeness of the coming of the Lord we must *"wake up"* and take responsibility for our lives. The *"slumber"* Paul is referring to is not natural sleep, but a spiritual lethargy that can manifest itself by *apathy, dullness, or indifference to the things of God.*

There are many instances in the Bible where people went to sleep at the wrong time. My favorite is found in Matthew 26. We are told while Jesus was praying, the disciples were sleeping. These men, some of whom vowed to die with Him, could not stay awake and enter the arena of prayer for one hour. They fell asleep, not once, but twice, and almost missed out on the conversation between Jesus, Moses, and Elijah (see Matthew 26:40-43). Friend, falling asleep in church is one thing, but falling asleep next door to the world's greatest Bible conference is beyond words!

In the natural, if you want to put people to sleep, just feed them a big meal, stop any air from circulating, and turn up the heat. Whether it is in your living room or a church service, it won't be long before the atmosphere becomes stale, and heads start bobbing up and down.

In Paul's first letter to Timothy, he reminded him that the passion and zeal he demonstrated for the Lord was like a fire that must be maintained. If you have ever built a fire, you know it will soon die if you don't "fan the embers," and add fresh fuel, such as charcoal or wood. *"For this reason I remind you to fan into flame the gift of God, which is in you through the laying on of my hands"* (2 Timothy 1:6).

If we desire to stay awake and alert and avoid spiritual lethargy, we must fan our spiritual flame with the fresh wind of the Holy Spirit (see Ezekiel 37:1-10). And we must feed our spiritual self with the proper fuel such as prayer, worship, and Bible study. We are admonished in First Thessalonians 5:6 not to be like those who are asleep, but be awake and sober. Why? *It is later than you think!*

FRIDAY

LAST WORDS OF A POP STAR

*Show me, Lord, my life's end and the number of my days; let me
know how fleeting my life is. You have made my days a mere
handbreadth; the span of my years is as nothing before you. Everyone
is but a breath, even those who seem secure* (Psalm 39:4-5).

HE WAS PROBABLY NOT THE MOST FAMOUS POP STAR WHO EVER LIVED, BUT many considered David Cassidy somewhere near the top. On November 21, 2017, at the age of 67, the pop star died in a Florida hospital. He burst onto the scene starring in the hit television series, *The Partridge Family* that ran from 1970-74. Except for stints in rehab for drug and alcohol abuse, he continued to entertain audiences around the globe as a singer, songwriter, and actor.

A few days after his death, his daughter, Katie Cassidy, spoke of being by his bedside as he drew his last breath. She shared with the world on her Twitter feed what her father said as he stepped into eternity. Just four words that summed up his life: *"So much wasted time."* I don't think Cassidy was much different from many people who are fueled by the drive to be successful. But the tragedy is that many find out too late that the ladder they were climbing to reach the top was leaning against the wrong wall!

The psalmist declares, *"You have made my days a mere handbreadth; the span of my years is as nothing before you."* What the psalmist is saying is that compared to eternity, our lives are as brief as taking a breath. James 4:14 uses a similar analogy, *"Why, you do not even know what will happen tomorrow. What is your life? You are a mist that appears for a little while and then vanishes."*

When I was a young man, time didn't seem that important to me. But as I grew older I realized that to make an impact for Christ I must couple my time management with godly wisdom. Time is a universal commodity that is shared equally. No matter where we were born, our level of education, or our rank in society, we each have the same amount. How we manage it significantly determines our future. It would be a tragedy to waste one precious minute doing things that don't have eternal consequences.

ENDNOTES

1. The poem, *I am the New Year* cited by Heidi Busse, January 8, 2014; https://www.osv.com/Article/TabId/493/ArtMID/13569/ArticleID/15338/I-am
-the-New-Year.aspx (accessed January 3, 2017). Note: This poem has been quoted in various books, websites, and inspirational articles. No one has been given credit, and no one has claimed authorship.

2. James R. Sherman, PhD, *Rejection* (Bloomingdale, MI: Pathway Books, 1982); http://quoteinvestigator.com/2015/11/05/new-ending/ (accessed January 4, 2017). Note: Many variations of this quote exist but the earliest found in written form are from this author.

3. Merriam-Webster Online, s.v. "purpose," https://www.merriam-webster.com/dictionary/purpose (accessed January 4, 2017).

4. Myles Munroe, *Releasing Your Potential* (Shippensburg, PA: Destiny Image, 1999), 11.

5. Douglas Adams, *The Salmon of Doubt* (2002); https://en.wikiquote.org/wiki/Procrastination (accessed January 9, 2017).

6. Merriam-Webster Online, s.v. "procrastination"; https://www.merriam-webster.com/dictionary/procrastinate (accessed January 4, 2017).

7. Joseph Ferrari, PhD, cited by Hara Estroff Marano in *Why We Procrastinate,* published July 1, 2005; https://www.psychologytoday.com/articles/200507/why-we-procrastinate (accessed January 4, 2017).

8. Chris Widener, "The Seven Deadly Roadblocks to Success," *The Trio Times,* Volume 5, Issue 3, Winter 2009; https://www.mcc.edu/learning/pdf_learning/vol5_iss3_win09.pdf (accessed January 10, 2017).

9. Kent Crockett, *The 911 Handbook* (Peabody, MA: Hendrickson Publishers, 2003); http://kentcrockett.com/cgi-bin/illustrations/index.cgi?topic=Burn-Out (accessed January 13, 2017).

10. Kenneth S. Wuest, *Wuest's Word Studies, Volume Two—The Exegesis of II Timothy* (Grand Rapids, MI: Wm. B. Eerdmans, 1973), 129.

11. John A. Shedd, collection of sayings titled *Salt from My Attic* (Portland, ME: Mosher Press,1928); http://quoteinvestigator.com/2013/12/09/safe-harbor/ (accessed January 18, 2017).

12. Albert C. Fisher, *Baptist Hymnal: Love is the Theme* (Nashville, TN: Convention Press, 1975), 453.

13. Keith Krell, senior pastor, Fourth Memorial Church, Spokane, WA, "Love Knows No Limits"; https://bible.org/seriespage/28-love-knows-no-limits-1-corinthians-131-13 (accessed January 24, 2017).

14. Kenneth S. Wuest, *Wuest's Word Studies in the Greek New Testament Volume Three* (Grand Rapids, MI: Wm. B. Eerdmans Publishing Co, 1975), 111-113.

15. Rick Renner, *Sparking Gems from the Greek* (Tulsa OK: Teach All Nations Publishing, 2003), 671.

16. Greek definition of "kind" from online edition of Strong's Concordance & HELPS Word-studies, 1987, 2011; http://biblehub.com/greek/5544 .htm (accessed January 27, 2017).

17. Ibid.

18. Ibid.

19. Merriam-Webster Online, s.v. "tacky"; https://www.merriam-webster .com/dictionary/tacky (accessed January 31, 2017).

20. Charles R. Boyce, *The Spirit of Service, The Rotarian—the Magazine of Service.* Originally published July 1924; https://books.google.com/books?i d=Q0QEAAAAMBAJ&pg=PA5&dq=charles+r+boyce+the+spirit+of +service+the+rotarian&hl=en&sa=X&ved=0ahUKEwjm1rXVmfHYAhVS LKwKHaFgCncQ6AEIJzAA#v=onepage&q=charles%20r%20boyce %20the%20spirit%20of%20service%20the%20rotarian&f=false (accessed from online edition January 31, 2017).

21. Greek definition of "protects" from online edition of Strong's Concordance & HELPS Word-studies, 1987, 2011; http://biblehub.com/ greek/5544.htm (accessed February 5, 2017).

22. Baker's Evangelical Dictionary of Biblical Theology, "hope"; http://www .biblestudytools.com/dictionary/hope/ (accessed February 7, 2017).

23. Webster's Revised Unabridged Dictionary, "endure"; http://biblehub .com/topical/e/endure.htm#grk (accessed February 7, 2017).

24. Jonathan Edwards (1703-1758), *Christian Love and Its Fruits* (Mulberry, IN: Sovereign Grace Publishers, 2000), 22.

25. P. L. Travers, *In the World of the Hero* (1976); https://en.wikiquote.org/ wiki/Heroes (accessed February 15, 2017).

26. Merriam-Webster Online, s.v. "hero"; https://www.merriam-webster.com/ dictionary/hero (accessed February 15, 2017).

27. Alex Haley as quoted in *A Touch of Class* (2003) by Carol Vanderheyden, 60; https://en.wikiquote.org/wiki/Alex_Haley (accessed February 28, 2017).

28. "The Sinking of the USS Indianapolis, 1945," EyeWitness to History; http://www.eyewitnesstohistory.com/indianapolis.htm (2006) (accessed March 14, 2017).

29. Robert Lowry (1826-1899): *Baptist Hymnal: Low in the Grave He Lay* (Nashville, TN: Convention Press, 1975), 118.

30. Phillips Brooks (1835-1893) in *Holy-days and Holidays: A Treasury of Historical Material, Sermons in Full and in Brief, Suggestive Thoughts, and Poetry, Relating to Holy Days and Holidays* (1902), 150; https:// en.wikiquote.org (accessed April 3, 2017).

31. Isaac Watts (1674-1748): *Baptist Hymnal: At the Cross* (Nashville, TN: Convention Press, 1975), 157.

32. J. Wilbur Chapman, DD, *The Life & Work of Dwight Lyman Moody:* Chapter 27, The Funeral; https://www.biblebelievers.com/moody/27.html (accessed April 4, 2017).

33. Reported in Holmes Moss Alexander, *Aaron Burr: The Proud Pretender* (1937), 356. https://en.wikiquote.org/wiki/Aaron Burr (accessed February 23, 2018).

34. Russell Bradley Jones, *Gold from Golgotha* (Chicago, IL: Moody Press, 1945), 63.

35. The Greek-English lexicon by Moulton and Milligan: What does the Greek word *tetelestai* mean?; https://bible.org/question/what-does-greek -word-tetelestai-mean (accessed May 28, 2017).

36. Elvina M. Hall (1818-1899): *Baptist Hymnal: Jesus Paid It All* (Nashville, TN: Convention Press, 1975), 156.

37. Steve Green, *Broken and Spilled Out;* https://www.lyricsbox.com/steve -green-broken-and-spilled-out-lyrics-jn5dq2k.html (accessed June 13, 2017).

38. Easton's Bible Dictionary "Fallow-ground"; http://www.biblestudytools .com/dictionaries/eastons-bible-dictionary/fallow-ground.html (accessed June 8, 2017).

39. Japanese proverb, as quoted in *Civilization's Quotations: Life's Ideal* (2002) by Richard Alan Krieger, 280; https://en.wikiquote.org/wiki/Vision (accessed June 16, 2017).

40. Robert Lowry (1826-1899), *Baptist Hymnal: Nothing but the Blood* (Nashville, TN: Convention Press, 1975), 158.

41. Vance Havner, *Though I Walk Through the Valley* (Grand Rapids, MI: Fleming H. Revell Co., 1974).

42. Lance Wallnau, *The #1 Thing You Need to Know;* https://lancewallnau .com/2016/04/how-to-handle-the-strange-contradictions-of-life/ (accessed June 28, 2017).

43. Peter Whyte, *The King and His Kingdom* (Shippensburg, PA: Destiny Image, 1989), 1.

44. Myles Munroe, *Kingdom Principles* (Shippensburg, PA: Destiny Image, 2006), 31.

45. Greek definition "seek" from online edition of Strong's Concordance & HELPS Word-studies, 1987, 2011; http://biblehub.com/greek/5544.htm (accessed July 6, 2017).

46. Ibid.

47. Sammy Tippit, *The Prayer Factor* (Chicago, IL: Moody Press, 1988), 35.

48. Leonard Ravenhill, *A Treasury of Prayer: From the Writings of E.M. Bounds* (Zachary, LA: Ravenhill Books, 1973), 71.

49. Adrian Rogers, *Prayer and the Will of God*, Love Worth Finding; http://www.oneplace.com/ministries/love-worth-finding/read/articles/prayer-and-the-will-of-god-11630.html (accessed July 24, 2017).

50. Jack R. Taylor, *Prayer: Life's Limitless Reach* (Kent, England: Sovereign World, LTD, 2004), 35.

51. Dr. Joe Langley, *From Beyond Forgiveness: A Bigger Picture of Salvation* (Fort Myers, FL: Easter Press, 2016).

52. Merriam-Webster Online, s.v. "impossible"; https://www.merriam-webster.com/dictionary/impossible (accessed January 20, 2017).

53. *Foundations* magazine online, "Drop the Banana!"; http://www.foundationsmag.com/banana.html (accessed January 23, 2017).

54. Anna Warner (1827-1915): *Baptist Hymnal: Jesus Loves Me* (Nashville, TN: Convention Press, 1975), 336.

55. Crystal McDowell, *7 Of The Best Bible Verses About Miracles;* http://www.whatchristianswanttoknow.com/7-of-the-best-bible-verses-about-miracles/ (accessed August 16, 2017).

56. Kenneth S. Wuest, *Golden Nuggets from the Greek New Testament* (Grand Rapids, MI: Wm. B. Eerdmans Publishing, 1943), 65.

57. Charles Swindoll, *Grace Awakening* (Dallas, TX: Word Publishing, 1990), 4.

58. Philip P. Bliss, *Free from the Law, O Happy Condition;* http://www.hymnsite.com/baptist/tbh332-free-from-the-law-o-happy-condition.shtml (accessed September 27, 2017).

59. John Howard Payne, *Home Sweet Home* (1822), from the opera of "Clari, the Maid of Milan," reported in *Bartlett's Familiar Quotations*, 10th ed. (1919); https://en.wikiquote.org/wiki/John_Howard Payne (accessed October 10, 2017).

60. Merriam-Webster Online, s.v. "provoke"; https://www.merriam-webster.com/dictionary/impossible (accessed October 25, 2017).

61. Traditional Thanksgiving Hymn (translation by Theodore Baker: 1851-1934); https://www.thoughtco.com/thanksgiving-prayers-701483 (accessed November 1, 2017).

62. Abraham Lincoln issues Thanksgiving Proclamation (1863), Note: Only a portion of the Proclamation is quoted. To read the complete Proclamation visit: http://www.presidency.ucsb.edu/ws/?pid=69998 (accessed January 31, 2018).

63. Bryan Wilkerson, "Olympic Relay Runners Fail to Pass the Baton," *PreachingToday;* http://www.preachingtoday.com/illustrations/2007/february/5021907.html (accessed November 25, 2017).

64. John Mason Neale: (1818-1866), *O Come, O Come, Emmanuel;* https://hymnary.org/text/o_come_o_come_emmanuel_and_ransom (accessed November 27, 2017).

65. William Shakespeare's *Romeo and Juliet* (Act II, Scene II); http://www.bartleby.com/70/3822.html (accessed January 31, 2018).

66. Jeremy Ham, *Does Truth Change? Biblical Authority Devotional: Infallibility and Inerrancy of Scripture,* Part 11, July 22, 2010; https://answersingenesis.org/answers/biblical-authority-devotional/does-truth-change/ (accessed December 15, 2017).

67. Greek definition "puffed up" from online edition of Strong's Concordance & HELPS Word-studies, 1987, 2011; http://biblehub.com/greek/5448.htm (accessed December 12, 2017).

JOURNAL PAGES